The Great Redan
at Sebastopol

The Great Redan at Sebastopol

The Most Victoria Crosses Awarded for a Single Action

James W. Bancroft

AN IMPRINT OF PEN & SWORD BOOKS LTD
YORKSHIRE – PHILADELPHIA

First published in Great Britain in 2023 by
FRONTLINE BOOKS
an imprint of Pen & Sword Books Ltd
Yorkshire – Philadelphia

Copyright © James W. Bancroft, 2023

ISBN 978-1-39906-052-3

The right of James W. Bancroft to be identified as the author of this work has been asserted by him in accordance with the Copyright, Designs and Patents Act 1988.

A CIP catalogue record for this book is available from the British Library.

All rights reserved. No part of this book may be reproduced or transmitted in any form or by any means, electronic or mechanical including photocopying, recording or by any information storage and retrieval system, without permission from the Publisher in writing.

Printed and bound in England by CPI Group (UK) Ltd, Croydon CR0 4YY.

Printed on paper from a sustainable source by
CPI Group (UK) Ltd, Croydon, CR0 4YY

Pen & Sword Books Ltd incorporates the imprints of Aviation, Atlas, Family History, Fiction, Maritime, Military, Discovery, Politics, History, Archaeology, Select, Wharncliffe Local History, Wharncliffe True Crime, Military Classics, Wharncliffe Transport, Leo Cooper, The Praetorian Press, Remember When, White Owl, Seaforth Publishing and Frontline Books.

For a complete list of Pen & Sword titles please contact
PEN & SWORD BOOKS LTD
47 Church Street, Barnsley, South Yorkshire, S70 2AS, England
E-mail: enquiries@pen-and-sword.co.uk
Website: www.pen-and-sword.co.uk
or
PEN & SWORD BOOKS
1950 Lawrence Rd, Havertown, PA 19083, USA
E-mail: uspen-and-sword@casematepublishers.com
Website: www.penandswordbooks.com

Contents

List of Plates	vii
Introduction	1
The Crimean War	3
The Assault on the Great Redan	17
The Fall of Sebastopol	49
The Most Victoria Crosses	61
A Selection of Tributes and Commemorations	71
Appendix I: Crimean War VCs by Units	161
Appendix II: Redan 60th Anniversary Commemoration	169
Bibliography and Research Sources	173
Index	179

List of Plates

The Charge of the Light Brigade
Colonel John Campbell
Colonel Lacy Yea
Colonel Lacy Yea and Lieutenant James Hobson
Colonel William Eyre
Major General Harry Jones
Lieutenant Arthur Fisher
Lieutenant Gerald Graham VC
Lieutenant Bradford Hoskins
Lieutenant Francis Hurt
Lieutenant William Hope, VC action
Corporal Philip Smith, VC action
Punch cartoon
Captain John Croker
Camp of the 33rd (Duke of Wellington's) Regiment
Camp of the 34th (Cumberland) Regiment
Officers of the 57th (West Middlesex) Regiment
Captain Arthur Maxwell Earle
57th (West Middlesex) Regiment on parade
Interior of the Great Redan at Sebastopol
Graves on Cathcart's Hill
33rd (Duke of Wellington's) Regiment Graves
57th (West Middlesex) Regiment memorial at St Paul's Cathedral

The Great Redan at Sebastopol

34th (Cumberland) Regiment memorial at Carlisle Castle
33rd (Duke of Wellington's) Regiment memorial at York Minster
Colonel John Campbell memorial in Edinburgh
Colonel Lacy Yea memorial in Somerset
Captain Charles Agar memorial in the New Forest
Sergeant John Knox VC grave at Cheltenham
Redan memorial at Sebastopol

Introduction

On 18 June 1855 (6 June by the Russian calendar), which was the 40th anniversary of the Battle of Waterloo, and happened to be a Monday, British assault troops moved out of their trenches before Sebastopol in the Crimea and attacked the formidable Russian 3rd Bastion, known as the Great Redan to the British, while their French allies attacked an equally formidable bastion known as the Malakoff. They came under such a murderous fire from the Russian defenders that the attacks faltered and the Allies were eventually forced to fall back. The British left over a thousand comrades dead and dying out in the open and at the mercy of the enemy.

For over a hundred years it was stated in various publications that the most Victoria Crosses awarded for a single action was the eleven given for the defence of Rorke's Drift during the Zulu War in 1879. Many men who were awarded the Victoria Cross during the Crimean campaign received it for more than one action, and the assault on the Great Redan on 18 June 1855 was included in the citations for twenty of the men who received the coveted award, and therefore it was that action which produced the highest superlative.

The British force that assaulted the Great Redan included three soldiers who would be among the most famous in the history of the Victorian Army. Most of the officers were of aristocratic or distinguished military heritage. It was the first campaign when laborious and perilous trench warfare had to be endured, conditions that would be repeated during the American Civil War and the First World War, where men had to cope with dreadful deprivation.

Philip II of Macedon, the father of Alexander the Great, is quoted as saying, 'An army of deer led by a lion is more to be feared than an army of lions led by a deer'; although it is usually attributed to events which happened during the Second Boer War, soon after the assault on the Great Redan newspapers in Britain proclaimed:

> 'An Army of Lions led by Donkeys!' – such is the opinion entertained by the Russians of their English adversaries in the Crimea; such is the

opinion we ourselves long since expressed in regard to the constitution of the English army; and now – after our sad and disgraceful failure at the Redan – it will inevitably become the general opinion amongst all military nations.

However, even when enduring such terrible suffering, there are many stories of exceptional gallantry – among officers and men alike.

Most of the information for this project is taken from the JWB Historical Library, compiled over four decades, and I have cross-referenced my files with up-to-date official sources as far as possible. The narratives of the Victoria Cross actions are based on the recipient's own account if they left one, the citations in the *London Gazette*, and regimental archives and histories. The JWB files concerning biographical details are more comprehensive; however, I decided only to include information which I believe presents interesting anecdotes and informative stories to the general reader and historian about the men who did the fighting, as opposed to the politics of the war.

The Crimean War

By the middle of the nineteenth century the Turkish Ottoman Empire was falling apart, prompting Tsar Nicholas to refer to it as 'The sick man of Europe.' Britain and France were suspicious of Russia's expansionist intentions in the Balkans, and their suspicions hardened when the Tsar began to interfere in Turkish affairs, and the Sultan appealed to Britain and France for guidance. However, there was a lack of cooperation on both sides, and Turkey declared war on Russia on 5 October 1853. Russian forces destroyed a Turkish fleet at Sinope on 30 November, which caused a wave of international hostility.

The British and French Allied Fleet entered the Black Sea on 4 January 1854. A British peace deputation went to see the Tsar on 10 February, but diplomacy broke down and Britain drifted into war. 'The Long Peace' which had prevailed for Britain in Europe since the Battle of Waterloo in 1815 ended on 27 March 1854 when Queen Victoria issued a declaration of war against Russia. A British Expeditionary Force under General Lord Raglan had already set sail for the Balkans on 23 February, and British warships under Admiral Sir Charles Napier set sail from Spithead on 11 March heading for the Baltic Sea, the north-west frontier of the Russian Empire, from where they could threaten the Russian capital at St Petersburg.

The Russians could not have imagined the type of gallant and determined men who were coming to wage war against them. The Allied Expeditionary Force arrived at Varna in Bulgaria in the summer of 1854. As they waited for orders to proceed, their numbers were seriously depleted by the ravages of a cholera epidemic. On 14 August a massive fire burned down half the town, which would have been completely devastating had the wind not changed direction as Allied troops desperately tried to carry the ordnance to a place of relative safety.

The Crimea was invaded on 14 September 1854 at Calamity Bay near Eupatoria, and the Allied armies marched south down the coast, escorted by the ships of the Fleet out to sea, the objective being to attack the strategic Black Sea port of Sebastopol.

The British invasion force had the first skirmish with the Russians at the river Bulganek on 19 September 1854, and as they marched over the crest of a hill on the following day they came in sight of the river Alma and encountered Russian forces massed along a high causeway on top of rugged steep cliffs beyond the river. It was a formidable obstacle, and one of the Russian commanders stated that it was such a strong position that they could hold it for three weeks or more. However, one of their officers later stated: 'We did not think it possible for men to be found with such firmness of morale to be able to attack in this apparently weak formation our massive columns.' The British were victorious within three hours, and an officer later remarked: 'Effectual people are the English.'

The principal Russian position was an earthwork known as the Greater Redoubt, and in mid-afternoon Lord Raglan gave the order: 'The infantry will advance.' The 1st Battalion, Scots (Fusilier) Guards were among the units ordered to storm the redoubt with bayonets fixed and with colours flying. They came under heavy bombardment and rifle fire as they advanced over rugged ground, crossed the river, passed ruined buildings, burning huts and other obstacles, but they pressed on and up towards the redoubt. Sergeant John Simpson Knox was present at the battle, and wrote in his diary:

> We Guards immediately formed line and advanced, meeting a warm reception as we closed in, in the form of shot, shell and bullets. The force opposed to us was five-to-one, so the bayonet was levelled and on we rushed, but no stand was made by the enemy. At them we went, loading and firing as quickly as possible, and the foe were in such numbers that one could not miss very easily. The scene that met my gaze was the most awful description; it made me shudder. The bodies of our opponents were so thick on the ground that for some distance I had to go on tiptoe to pass without touching the bodies.

Private John Park, 77th (East Middlesex) Regiment, was noted for conspicuous bravery during the fighting at the Alma.

The Times newspaper correspondent William Howard Russell described the actions of Colonel Lacy Yea of the 7th Royal Fusiliers:

> At the Alma he never went back a step, and there were tears in his eyes on that eventful afternoon as he exclaimed to me, when the men had formed on the slope of the hill after the retreat of the enemy, 'There! look there! That's all that remains of my poor Fusiliers! A colour's missing, but,

thank God, no Russians have it. At Inkerman his gallantry was conspicuous.

The Allied armies were totally victorious, but their casualties were such that it took two days for them to tend to their wounded and bury their dead.

One of the wreaths sent to the funeral of Field Marshal Frederick Paul Haines of the 21st Regiment at Brompton Cemetery in 1909 bore a message that read: 'From the bugler at Alma who gave you a drink of water on the battlefield, and whom you remembered many years afterwards, when he was overtaken by misfortune.' This was sent by 2299 Bugler J. McLaughlin of the 21st Regiment. He stated that he had given Captain Haines a drink of water on the Alma battlefield and 'Many years after, when I was in trouble, I found that he had neither forgotten the help I was able to render him nor allowed his gratitude to lessen.'

The following is an extract from a letter written by an officer in the 2nd Division of the army under General de Lacy Evans. It is dated 'Hospital, Scutari. Sept. 25th 1854':

> Owing to the fortunes of war I have returned here sooner than I expected, as I was fortunate enough to be hit three times and yet to be alive. On the 19th started at six am on the march, and a magnificent sight it was. The Light Division on the left, then the First and Second; then the reserve. Men very much done up on the march, no water, lots of poor fellows obliged to fall to the rear. In the evening got under fire, the men plucked up and wanted to be at it. We were ordered up and placed in line; several of the 11th Hussars and 13th Light Dragoons and their horses shot. The Artillery pitched into the enemy pretty sharp, and the third shot (a shell) fell among them, and made them retire to a better position. A great number of Cossacks killed – these were the Russian outposts in front of the river and heights of Alma. Got something to eat and slept with the men who were ordered to be ready at any moment.
>
> 20th. Under arms about six am. Took up a good position near the sea; took off our packs and waited for orders. After a little time ordered to move towards the river Alma; formed again, and lay down. From what I could make out from the smoke of the village (Burliuk), which the Russians had set on fire, I saw below me in a valley from half a mile to a mile in width, and beyond mountains of great height, extending for miles down to the sea. About one o'clock the Russians opened their fire upon us, their shot and rockets whistling over our heads. We did not long remain idle, having been told off to attack the centre of the enemy.

Formed line and lay down for a few minutes, while the Artillery peppered them pretty well; we then formed column and advanced to the village, where we formed line behind a wall, about 18 inches high. The shot began to fall around us like hail. Sir de Lacey Evans rode up to us and said: 'Now's your time, boys, over you go,' and away we went.

We had to cross the plain, exposed to a most terrific fire, without being able to fire a shot in return. I advanced about twenty paces, when a round shot struck my neck and tore off the button and face of my coatee; about thirty more, when another shot struck my ankle, and was turned by my thick boot, only bruising me. Another spell, and I was knocked down by a 24-pound ball against my left side and arm. I thought it was all up with me; men were lying dead and dying all around me.

The regiment then crossed the river which was up to their waists, under a most gallant fire, and lots of poor fellows fell. After crossing, they had to climb a very steep bank. It was here that Woolcombe had his leg smashed. The men now advanced up the hill, and drove the Russians out of the batteries and forts and took up a good position. The Russians were lying six and seven deep, when fellows had time to look about them, all killed, few wounded, while our men were nearly all wounded in the leg. I remained on the spot where I fell till some men carried me down to the river, where I found Woolcombe and others wounded, waiting for doctors. After being bandaged, we were carried off to the hospital Cottage on stretchers, near eight o'clock pm. I found a delicious bed of straw and a couple of blankets ready for me.

21st. They commenced moving us on board ship. General Adams and others came to see us; in fact, we are quite lions – carried down to the beach on a stretcher by sailors, and hoisted on board the *Andes*, which had her sail up for Scutari. The people here are very kind, and send us grapes. There are twenty other wounded officers in the same room with me. The smell of wounds is fearful. Four poor fellows died of their wounds on the passage, and were thrown overboard.

At dawn on Wednesday, 25 October 1854 the Russians made a threatening advance across a wide valley towards the harbour at Balaclava, to the south-east of Sebastopol. A causeway ran across the valley where six redoubts had been constructed, and British naval guns manned by Turkish troops had been positioned. After an hour Turkish troops had fled from their posts leaving guns behind, and the Russians occupied the three most easterly. A large force of Russian cavalry then came over the causeway and entered the south valley and four squadrons broke off, making directly for Balaclava. Suddenly, a 'Thin Red Line' of 93rd (Sutherland) Highlanders, led by the dominant figure of General Colin Campbell, appeared from behind a hill and blocked their way. Volley fire from the Highlanders checked the Russian advance and unnerved them, and they were soon put in reverse.

The Heavy Brigade of British cavalry, totalling only 300 men, had been ordered to support the Highlanders, and they made a courageous charge against this superior number of Russian cavalry. Against all odds the Russian nerve broke and they began to fall back and retreat from the battlefield in hopeless disorder.

After a lull in the action, Lord Raglan had his attention brought to the distant high ground to the east where there seemed to be movement in the captured redoubts, and it was suggested that the Russians were limbering up the British naval guns to take them away. This was the equivalent of an infantry regiment losing its colours and Lord Raglan was alarmed. He told his aide Richard Airey to write a hasty note, which was given to Captain Lewis Edward Nolan of the 15th (King's) Hussars to take to Lord Lucan, the cavalry commander. The note read:

> Lord Raglan wishes the cavalry to advance rapidly to the front, follow the enemy & try to prevent the enemy carrying away the guns. Troop Horse Artillery may accompany. French cavalry is on your left. Immediate. R. Airey.

Nolan was a cavalry fanatic, who was agitated by the inaction of the Light Brigade, but he was a good horseman and he arrived safely with the message. However, Nolan disliked both Lord Cardigan and Lord Lucan, or 'Look-on' as he called him. The message is known to have been misinterpreted – if it was ever passed on?

A version of the conversation between Captain Nolan, Lord Lucan and Lord Cardigan was written in a letter by Colonel Somerset Calthorpe, a staff officer who was up on the ridge with Lord Raglan and was also known to dislike Lord Cardigan, which he reproduced in his 1857 book *Letters from Headquarters*. Most subsequent narratives are based on this letter, although Lord Cardigan 'declared it to be totally without foundation', and in 1863 brought a libel action against Calthorpe, which contained several contradictory remarks.

A different version of the conversation, which was not mentioned during the libel action, was recorded by Bugler McLaughlin, who had helped Major

Haines at the battle of the Alma. It is the only unbiased account, and does not include Lord Lucan:

> I had received permission to retire for a few minutes, and was about 200 yards from our men, when I saw Captain Nolan leave the group round Lord Raglan, and dash full gallop towards our cavalry. Lord Cardigan saw him coming, and rode full tilt to meet him. They met quite close to me, and I could hear all that passed.
>
> 'What are the orders, Captain Nolan?' says Lord Cardigan.
>
> 'The orders are, sir,' said Captain Nolan, 'that the guns that have been taken you are to take back again.'
>
> 'But there have been no guns taken,' Lord Cardigan replied; 'there's none to take back.'
>
> Just then an officer of the French cavalry rode up to Lord Cardigan and asked what the orders were.
>
> Lord Cardigan told him there was some misunderstanding, and repeated what Captain Nolan had told him.
>
> 'What are you going to do?' the French officer asked him, and Lord Cardigan looks at him, and he says, 'I am going to take the battery.'
>
> The officer turned away with a laugh, as if at the conceit of our cavalry leader, and Lord Cardigan galloped right to the front of our line, and then wheeled to the right-about.
>
> 'The cavalry will prepare for action,' he shouted to the line, and in a second the men had mounted, and were waiting orders.

Indeed, Private (later Lieutenant) James Wightman, who rode with the 17th Lancers in the front line of the Brigade, and later became secretary of the Balaclava Commemoration Society, stated in his account in the *Nineteenth Century Magazine* of June 1892:

> I cannot call to mind seeing Lord Lucan come to the front of the Light Brigade and speak with Lord Cardigan, although I know now that he did so. But I distinctly remember that Nolan returned to the Brigade and his having a mere momentary talk with Cardigan ...

The original note has been preserved in the National Army Museum, but was it retrieved from Lord Lucan – or from the body of Captain Nolan?

About 700 cavalrymen took part in the Charge of the Light Brigade and during the action Captain Nolan was killed. Although the Brigade reached the Russian guns, under murderous fire from three sides of the valley, and captured some of them, they could not hold on to them and had to retreat back up the valley towards the British lines. About 200 men were killed, but it was the loss of over 400 horses which put the Brigade out of action.

The Light Brigade action at Balaclava was doomed before it began, and had little effect on the outcome of the battle. However, contrary to popular belief, the men who took part were proud of what they had achieved, and several said that they would have done it again had they been ordered to do so. Certainly it had a devastating effect on the enemy cavalry, who were reluctant to face the British for the rest of the campaign, and it is still considered by many to be, as Lord Raglan was to state later, 'The finest thing ever done.'

Midshipman Edmund St John Daniel of HMS *Diamond* was among the sailors who formed a Naval Brigade of over a thousand men under Captain Stephen Lushington from HMS *Albion*, which came ashore to help with the siege. Daniel wrote home to his family on 16 October 1854:

> We are encamped with a thousand of our blue jackets and we have twenty of our guns ashore. We have had a good many shots fired at us, but none of our men have been wounded. I am the Captain's aide-de-camp. I have been obliged to provide myself with a horse as we are six miles from Admiral Lyons and very often I have to go to him twice a-day, and after that to go in the trenches all night with the Captain. Thank God, our battery will be completed by daylight tomorrow. I am very much obliged to you for the pistols.

The captain he spoke of was William Peel, a son of the former Prime Minister, who suggested to his two teenage ADCs that they should 'disregard fire in the battery, by always walking with head up and shoulders back and without undue haste'. Midshipman Wood remembered that: 'He himself was a splendid example. I know that he felt acutely every shot which passed over him, but the only visible effect was to make him throw up his head and square his shoulders.'

On 18 October Captain Peel was with several men working at one of the Naval Brigade cannon. As several men were passing cases of gunpowder into the magazine, a 42-pounder Russian shell smashed through the parapet. Its fuse still burning, it rolled into the middle of one gun's crew, who immediately threw themselves to the ground – but they were still in great peril. Seeing the danger, Peel sprang into action. At the greatest possible risk to himself, he stooped down and picked up the heavy shell and clasped it to his chest as he carried it back to the parapet. He heaved it over the edge and it had barely rolled down the outside when it exploded. He thus saved the magazine and the lives of all the men around it.

On the same day Midshipman Daniel watched a team of horses bringing supplies of ammunition to a battery come under heavy fire, and after some poor animals had been disabled the others became spooked and refused to move. The wagon was in an exposed position, but Daniel and Midshipman Wood took it upon themselves to try to empty it. A destructive fire sent bullets whizzing over their heads, or smashing dangerously into the boxes and ricocheting in all directions, but they took the advice of Captain Peel and disregarded the fire, and when they scrambled over the parapet for the last time with their arms full of the last of the ammunition, they were met by cheers from their comrades.

Another man who showed great gallantry in the trenches was Sergeant William McWheeney of the 44th (East Essex) Regiment, who had volunteered as a sharpshooter at the start of the siege. On 20 October 1854 Private John Keane of his regiment was outside the front of an advance trench when he came under fire and was dangerously wounded. Sergeant McWheeney got together a party of volunteers and led them out to where their comrade was lying. They came under the same heavy enemy rifle fire, and, with no time to lose, Sergeant McWheeney lifted Keane onto his back and carried him for a long distance until he could place him in safety.

On 5 December a corporal of the 44th Regiment named William Courteney was shot in the head and severely wounded, and was lying in the open in front of the trenches. On being informed of the situation, Sergeant McWheeney again ran out of the trenches to the assistance of a comrade. They came under such fire that it was too dangerous to move, so the gallant sergeant dug a dirt cover with his bayonet, where they both sheltered, and when darkness fell they made their escape.

On 4 November 1854 Florence Nightingale and her team of thirty-eight nurses arrived at the hospital in Scutari, and when they eventually got past most of the red tape and petty jealousy, they began to make life better for the soldiers. The timing could not have been better, for on the very next day one of the bloodiest battles in British military history was fought. The Russians tried to relieve the pressure on Sebastopol by launching an attack on British positions at Inkerman, with 40,000 men advancing from three directions, supported by 135 guns. Their main objective was the Inkerman Ridge, held by just under 3,000 men of the 2nd Division and twelve field guns. The mighty force intended to drive the Allies into the sea. The morning of 5 November was cold and wet, and the fierce combat was fought to gain features such as Shell Hill, Home Ridge and the Inkerman Caves, across large areas of mist-shrouded rough terrain. Units did not know how other units were doing, and it was more like several separate battles than just one. Because of this it came to be known as the Soldiers' Battle.

During the early stages of the fighting British forces of the 2nd Division captured the Sandbag Battery, and by eight o'clock they found themselves defending it against heavy odds. Eventually they were overwhelmed by superior numbers and forced out of the position, and the enemy entrenched themselves within. They manned the embrasures and parapets of the battery, from where they kept up a most severe fire of musketry.

The Grenadier Guards were among the units which advanced to try to regain the Sandbag Battery. Captain Peel had joined the officers of the Grenadiers, with ever-faithful Midshipman Daniel remaining alongside him. Peel led seven charges, and helped to save the colours of the battalion from capture.

It was the first time the 57th and 77th (Middlesex) Regiments had fought together. They were ordered to recapture the Home Ridge, which had already changed hands three times with furious fighting, and the unit was out of ammunition. Nevertheless, they moved up to the position and lay down along the ridge with their bayonets at the ready. The Russians were already in possession of part of the ridge, but when the artillery came forward through the lines of the 77th, the 77th also advanced, and faced with this combined force the Russians retreated. Private John Park, 77th (East Middlesex) Regiment, was again noted for conspicuous bravery.

Lieutenant Graham, Royal Engineers, wrote to his sister two days after the battle making a reference to Guy Fawkes Night: 'We need no longer to be told to remember the 5th November, for it is a day to be marked red in our annals.'

It was stated that the enemy left a greater number of killed and wounded on the field of battle than the entire force of British and French soldiers engaged, and they made no more large-scale attempts to defeat the Allies on the battlefield.

The Crimean winter of 1854/55 was the most severe for many years, and prompted Tsar Nicholas to remark that the weather produced his three most effective generals: January, February and March.

A disaster occurred on 14 November 1854 when a hurricane devastated the Crimea. Sergeant Major George Smith of the 11th Hussars was sitting in his tent waiting for the coffee, or 'warm, dirty water and sugar' as he described it, 'when all of a sudden, without any warning, came a mighty rush of wind accompanied by driving rain', which increased to a hurricane and blew everything away. Twenty-one British ships were smashed to pieces, many against the rocks in the harbour at Balaclava, and *The Prince* went down with all hands on board, along with warm clothing, footwear, blankets and medical supplies. Sergeant Major Smith lamented: 'This was a wretched night for tens of thousands.'

The *Dublin Evening Mail* of 8 January 1855 published an 'Extract of a letter from a son of George W. Boileau of the old and respected firm of Boileau Brothers':

HMS *Queen*, Belcos Bay, December 14 1854

My Dearest Father – We arrived here on the 5th inst, all safe, and are now making good our damages, which we received in action, and also in the late gale. I have been under orders, with 230 men, for this last week, to hold ourselves in readiness for Sebastopol, to the trenches. My mind is made up to go anywhere the service requires me, and must trust to God for the rest.

Should the papers at home say anything about our boats going to the rescue, on the night of the eventful storm in the Black Sea, you may say I was the lieutenant left in charge of the boats, and thanked publicly before all hands on our quarterdeck by Captain Mitchell. I volunteered and went in charge of three boats, and managed with difficulty to take 46 men and officers from the three transports *Rodsley*, *Pyrenees* and *Ganges*. Our ship's boats were the only boats that ventured to perform this humane act. I made two trips from my ship to the *Rodsley*, took off ten men the first trip, and 14 the second. Whilst going off on the latter, through the surf, my boat nearly had her back broken and swamped, being the last boat, and the poor fellows crowded into her, which brought the boat too deep. Two of the ships, *Pyrenees* and *Ganges*, belong to Messers Dunbar and Sons of London. The captains have promised to bring my name forward, through their owners.

We were under fire from Cossacks on the cliff, and had one man shot through the head; poor fellow only lived six hours. The Cossack that shot him, when he saw what he had done, stood up and waved his hat, and in the act of doing so he was shot by the chief officer of the *Pyrenees*. They are a most barbarous set, so I hope I shall not fall into their hands.

There was a significant lull in hostilities during Christmas and the early months of 1855, when just surviving the cold weather and hunger became more important than fighting the enemy. The terrible conditions the troops were suffering was brought to the attention of the British people, and following a public outcry Lord Aberdeen's government fell. The new government under Lord Palmerston sent out fresh supplies of warm clothing, which began to reach the army in January. The soldiers were obviously grateful, but this was tempered with regret by the fact that they 'didn't come before so many fellows were in their graves'.

Some officers were growing concerned about the lack of discipline which was beginning to show among the rank-and-file, and not surprisingly there was increased misconduct among some of the units. The 18th (Royal Irish) Regiment had only recently returned from India when they received orders for active service in the Crimea, arriving in the war zone in January 1855. On taking over command of the 18th Regiment in March 1855, even a stern disciplinarian such as Lieutenant Colonel Clement Edwards was anxious:

> I am much afraid that it will be a long time before I can see the results for my improvement of the regiment; the malady was too deep and of too long a standing to hope for any great sign of amendment, or any substantial change for the better, till the whole system is restored.

Perhaps more importantly, at least he could be confident that his Irishmen were tough soldiers who knew how to fight a campaign. Lieutenant Gordon stated:

> They [the Royal Irish] were a favourite regiment with the Royal Engineers for work, both in the trenches and in the destruction of the docks, from the energy and pluck of the officers and men, and it was then that I formed my opinion of Irishmen being of a different nature than other Britishers inasmuch as they required a certain management and consideration, which if given them would enable you, so to speak, to hold their lives in your hand. The officers liked the men and the men liked the officers; they were a jovial lot altogether, but they would do anything if you spoke and treated them as if you liked them, which I certainly did. You know what great hardships they went through in the docks in working at the shafts which, 30ft deep, were full of water if left un-pumped out for twelve hours. Poor devils! Wet, bedraggled, in their low ammunition boots, I used to feel much for them, for the Generals used to be down on them because they were troublesome, which they were when people did not know how to manage them.

Once again speaking highly of Colonel Yea, William Russell recorded:

> Throughout the winter his attention to his regiment was exemplary. They were the first who had hospital huts. When other regiments were

in need of every comfort, and almost of every necessary, the Fusiliers, by the care of the colonel, had everything that could be procured by exertion and foresight. He never missed a turn of duty in the trenches, except for a short time, when his medical attendant had to use every effort to induce him to go on board ship to save his life.

Plays and musicals were among the recreations pursued by the troops to break the boredom, and they even built a theatre on Cathcart's Hill. A programme of events still survives, which advertises performances of 'Little Toddlekins', which was a popular comic drama first performed in London in 1852, and 'Going to the Derby', a comic song which was still being performed by people like Stanley Holloway a hundred years later.

With the coming of spring the situation for the Allies improved. Reinforcements of experienced troops arrived from Britain and the colonies, and their weaponry improved. The British Army was in the midst of a significant weapons transformation from smooth-bore muskets to the Enfield P53 Minie rifles, which were more accurate at a much longer range.

The re-commencement of serious hostilities began on the night of 22 March 1855, when the Russians, pretending to be French soldiers, used the advantage of the darkness, 'as black as a wolf's mouth', to make a powerful sortie in vast numbers to try to capture some of the French positions along the Dock Ravine at the foot of the Mamelon, and the British forward trenches to the right of Frenchman's Hill. The battle was fought in atrocious weather conditions, as sleet and rain obliged the men to advance ankle-deep in mud.

The Russians had hidden in hollows in the ground until nearly midnight, when they launched an attack with 'diabolical yells' and were among the British working parties before the latter could reach their weapons and fight back, and being taken by surprise they were in danger of being driven out of their positions. For an hour or more both sides were forced to grope at each other in the darkness, firing at the gun-flashes facing them, thrusting with butt and bayonet, and kicking and punching as they scrambled over dead bodies, comrade and foe, all the time being encouraged by the shouts of their officers. Eventually the British gained the advantage in the desperate struggle, but several men were taken prisoner.

At first light many men discovered that the fighting had been so fierce that their bayonets were twisted and bent. Sergeant Major Timothy Gowing of the 7th Royal Fusiliers was of the opinion that the actual hand-to-hand fighting was worse than Inkerman. He wondered by what name this great battle would go down in history. Men considered the battle to be equal in significance to anything that had been fought previously and thought 'The Battle of the Quarries' would become just as well-known. Some men referred to the assault on the Redan on 18 June as being 'a second great attack'.

Detachments of both the 57th (West Middlesex) and 77th (East Middlesex) Regiments acquitted themselves nobly during this engagement. Sergeant George Gardiner of the 57th Regiment kept his head and helped to rally the men, and 'with his fine example they regained the position'.

A third bombardment began on 7 June and on the following night the British attacked the Quarries. At five o'clock the whole of the Light Division was ordered to parade with arms and accoutrements, and an hour later they occupied the forward trenches preparing to attack. When the signal came that the French had taken the Mamelon, the British launched an attack made mainly by the 7th and 88th Regiments, which took the Russians by surprise and British bayonets and bullets drove them back yet again. The firing was fierce, and amongst the confusion, uproar and smoke some men in the rear noticed that their comrades had started to pelt the enemy with stones because they were running out of ammunition.

The deadly fighting lasted all night, and there was terrible slaughter as the British were driven back three times before they finally took control of the Quarries and were able to hold on; with picks and shovels they made parapets and embrasures which faced the enemy on the other side and protected them from bombardment by grape and shell. The Russians tried no fewer than fourteen times during the night to try to win back the position, but the British had established themselves and by morning they were under good cover. One of the engineers who helped them to dig-in was Captain Wolseley, who later became Viscount Wolseley and led the British Army on numerous expeditions in defence of the British Empire. Lord Raglan visited the trenches and thanked them for their conduct, and the Quarries became known as the Shambles.

Gunner Thomas Arthur of the Royal Artillery was suddenly taken ill while his battery was in action, so he left it without leave, returning to find that the guns were gone. Noticing that the 7th Regiment was running short of ammunition, he ran to a magazine and collected a barrel of ammunition; carrying the barrel on his head, he brought it to them under a tremendous fire, and throwing it at their feet he exclaimed, 'Here you are, my lads, fire away!' He then ran back and brought another, continuing to bring as many cartridges as he could to the front. Eventually Gunner Arthur was marched away under custody for having been absent from his gun, and there was talk of a court-martial, but Colonel Yea of the 7th Fusiliers had been watching his gallant actions through his field-glasses, and intervened in time for his dereliction to be turned into an act of heroism.

The diminutive Private Matthew Hughes of the 7th Royal Fusiliers, 'smoking his clay pipe all the time', twice went for ammunition across open ground. He continually encouraged the men, shouting 'Keep it up, lads,' and even told a young officer to 'Lend a hand, sir, to distribute these pills.' Later he saw Private John Hampton of his regiment lying wounded so he ran out and brought him in from the front, during which time he was hit in the knee by a shell. His brave actions were noted by Colin Campbell of the 90th Light Infantry.

The Assault on the Great Redan

The Allies had been encouraged by the success of the attack on the Quarries, and on 10 June Lord Raglan and Marshal Pelissier held a meeting, during which it was decided that another assault should be made on the morning of 18 June 1855. The French would try to take control of the Malakoff Tower and the British would battle for the Great Redan. The date was of great significance in that it was the 40th anniversary of the British victory over the French at the battle of Waterloo. It was considered to be a good omen for the British – but not so much for the French.

The Great Redan had been constructed by throwing up thick walls of earth stretching 70ft in length and about 15ft high on each side of a middle section that jutted out like the front of a ship; this was known as the salient, and it was slightly higher than the rest. It was protected by an enormous ditch approximately 11ft deep and 15ft wide, and beyond that was a rampart of brush and bushes that had been tied together and placed with their branches facing outward as a kind of defensive entanglement (or *abattis*) as an obstacle to impede the advance of attacking troops. It was very high and many feet deep. Fougasses (rudimentary landmines) were buried all around. The fortification bristled with guns, some in two tiers, which could enfilade all the approaches. The cannon were placed behind embrasures protected by rope mantlets to shield the gunners from musket fire. Looking out from the British trenches, the men saw that they had to advance across a large expanse of rising open ground and negotiate a steep slope, or glacis, before they even got to the Great Redan's defences. The Great Redan was virtually impregnable to attacking infantry.

The bombardment on 8 June had been instrumental in the success of the attack on the Quarries, so it was decided that a similar bombardment would take place throughout 17 June and for a few hours before the attack on the following morning; this would demoralise the enemy by destroying the defences they had struggled to repair overnight, put most of their guns out of action, and force a gap through the *abattis* by blasting it away or setting it on fire.

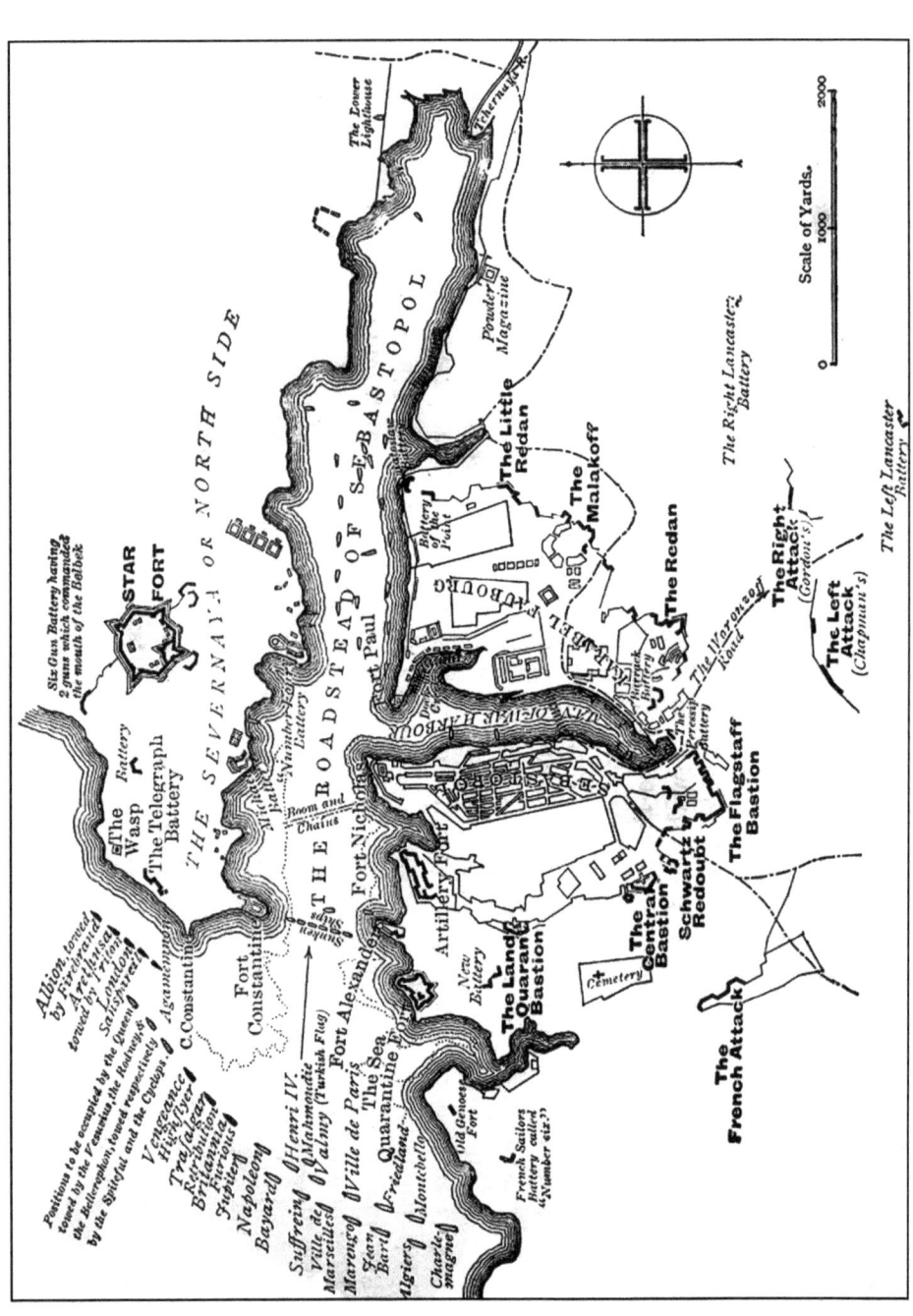

A sketch map of Sebastopol showing the major positions along the Russian defence line.

The Assault on the Great Redan

The columns from the Light and 4th Divisions were to be formed up in the Quarry outwork ready to simultaneously attack the two flanks of the Redan, the trenches leading towards the Redan and also the Russian trenches. The column of the 4th Division assembled on the left of the Quarry work, and that of the Light Division formed up on the opposite side, that being on the right as it faced the Redan. The First Brigade furnished the assaulting columns, support and working parties, and the Second Brigade formed the reserve.

The storming column of the Light Division was under the immediate command of Lieutenant Colonel Daniel Lysons, 23rd (Welsh) Fusiliers, with Colonel Lacy Yea, 7th (Royal) Fusiliers, acting as brigadier general. It originally consisted of 200 men of the 23rd (Welsh) Regiment and 200 men of the 33rd (Duke of Wellington's) Regiment. These were supported by the 34th (Cumberland) Regiment and elements of the 7th Fusiliers and the 23rd Fusiliers. However, this line-up was eventually changed so that the storming column consisted entirely of 400 men of the 34th Regiment. This also necessitated other changes in the composition of the supports and working parties.

The column which would assault the left of the Redan as they looked at it consisted wholly of men of the 57th Regiment, under the command of Lieutenant Colonel Thomas Shadforth of that regiment. Captain William Peel was placed in command of the Naval Brigade. On 7 June 1855 Colonel John Campbell of the 38th (1st Staffordshire) Regiment was superseded by General Henry Bentinck of the Coldstream Guards, who, on hearing of the plans to assault the Great Redan, volunteered to lead the left column.

The columns would each be preceded by a covering party of 100 riflemen skirmishers, who were to go forward and use rapid fire to try to pin down the enemy at the walls. Royal Engineer officers would lead units of sappers and miners carrying woolsacks and a body of sailors carrying scaling-ladders to fill in and bridge the ditches, ready for the storming parties to follow, and the first men over were to use the same ladders to scale the walls. Spiking parties were to disable the enemy guns. When these were carried and a lodgement effected, the column of the 2nd Division was to attack the salient angle and to make a road there for the entrance of the working parties. If a retrenchment were to be found within the work, it was to be converted into part of the cover; if there were none, the working parties would at once establish the necessary protection.

A Brigade of the 3rd Division, under Colonel William Eyre, was tasked to make an attack upon the Cemetery and Garden Battery on the far left, and on the outer harbour. A Brigade consisted of the 18th (Royal Irish),

28th (1st Stafford) and 44th (East Essex) Regiments. The 10th Hussars had received orders to hold themselves in readiness for special service, and fifty troopers from each regiment of the cavalry division were ordered to move to the front at daybreak.

On the morning of the attack Lord Raglan was in the trench in rear of the Quarries, and Marshal Pelissier was in a battery to the rear of the Mamelon; thus they were a considerable distance apart. The British troops had already moved down to the forward trenches to prepare for the attack when Pelissier made the extraordinary decision to cancel the preliminary bombardment and to bring forward the French attack to first light. Perhaps he thought his men would get forward quickly in a surprise attack and take the Malakoff by storm, and any bombardment could have put them in danger. He announced his new intentions to the English Engineer-in-Chief who, after some delay, relayed the message to Lord Raglan.

The troops included many teenagers and it is hard to imagine how such young men must have felt when they realised the task set before them. Four of them would be rewarded with the Victoria Cross. An assistant-surgeon had to accompany each regiment and the medical men drew lots to see who would have to go. One of those chosen commented that 'I did not esteem the privilege very highly.' What they did not know was that the Russians had worked strenuously to rebuild the defences, and they too had realised the significance of the date. They were anticipating an assault, and when they saw the British moving down to their forward trenches they were ready.

The signal to commence the assault on the Mamelon was the firing of three 'Whistling Dicks' (rocket mortars), which cascaded up in what was described as 'a spectacular sight'. The French advanced, only to be met by bullets and grape-shot, which smashed into them and broke their nerve, and their attack quickly faltered. Lord Raglan was able to witness the French failure. He was in the habit of referring to the French as 'the enemy' – as he had done at Waterloo, and a captain of the 38th (1st Staffordshire) Regiment said: 'Lord Raglan, they say, cannot make up his mind to do anything, and is undecided in everything.'

Instead of delaying the British assault, or even cancelling it completely, he thought that his army would come under criticism for not supporting the French, and that British pride was at stake. Times differ on exactly when the attack began, but the flag to commence the assault was hoisted, the order was given, 'and away we went'.

The Russians allowed the front ranks of the Right Attack to get well out into the open, where there was no cover, before they opened up a thunderous fire with rifles and grapeshot, and other iron missiles of all descriptions ploughed up the ground. The assault columns went forward and they bent down as they rushed into the storm in a futile attempt to make a more difficult target, but it was impossible for them to make much progress under such a horrific barrage. The burden of the heavy ladders slowed down the seamen and Rifles.

Lord Raglan stated later: 'I have never before witnessed such a continued and heavy fire of grape combined with musketry from the enemy's works, which appeared to be fully manned.'

Lieutenant Arthur Fisher RE strode on at an unhurried pace, with his sappers at his side, suffering under a shower of grape and musketry. On reaching the first main obstacle at the abattis, they halted and waited for the ladder party, stormers and supports. They were left waiting longer than they expected, still being swept by grape from the Redan. Looking back with some anxiety, they watched through the dim grey light to see the progress of the seamen and Rifles, but not a single ladder appeared. Captain William Jesse RE had also reached the abattis, and he and Lieutenant Fisher were discussing what to do next when Captain Jesse was shot through the head. Lieutenant Thomas Molyneux Graves had got within the abattis, and close to the ditch beyond it, when he was hit by three missiles and fell.

The Royal Engineers' history described the action:

> Emboldened by the apparent hesitation which had held back the column, the enemy sprang upon their parapets and fired upon the little force which had the temerity to reach the barricade. Crouched as the men were under the boughs of the abattis and doubled up in shell-holes, they were somewhat saved from its fierceness, but every moment augmented the chances of their not returning. Cool and lion-hearted, Lieutenant Fisher was everywhere among his parties commending their bravery and endurance; and Sergeant Landrey, nobly assisting his officer, encouraged by his conspicuous example and his cheers the dislocated files of the forlorn hope. Still the ladders were unseen; the stormers were yet in rear, and, at length, as no means for scaling the ramparts were with the advance and its numbers were reduced to a handful, Lieutenant Fisher, seeing no officer present senior to himself, reluctantly, but wisely, retreated with his men to the trenches.

Colonel Lacy Yea was shot through the head as he led the men on, and the men of the 34th Regiment storming party were taking heavy casualties. Captains John Robinson and John Shiffner were killed by grapeshot, while

Lieutenants Henry Alt and Francis Hurt were also killed. Ensign Robert Browne-Clayton fell mortally wounded.

Captain Thomas Basil Fanshawe of the 33rd Regiment stated:

> We had to cross, on leaving the trenches, 150 yards of open ground, exposed to a very heavy fire of grape-shot from the enemy . . . Our loss, I regret to say, was very considerable, having had 50 men killed and wounded. Lt-Colonel Johnstone has lost his left arm, Mundy is hit in the leg with a bullet; Bennett, I am sorry to say, is killed; Quayle shot in the elbow and arm. Wickham is so hit in the foot that he is likely to be disabled for some time to come; Collings was stunned by a blow for a moment. I have had a bruise in the shoulder from a stone or spent ball which has made it stiff. The rest of our fellows have escaped unhurt.

Colonel Mundy had actually been wounded in the shoulder in an earlier engagement, but had discharged himself from the sick list to take part in the assault. Officially he was hit in the hip by grapeshot, but Quayle's memorial states that he was shot through the body.

Many men repeatedly went out across the open ground in front of the advance trenches under a very heavy fire of musketry and grape to assist in rescuing wounded comrades from exposed situations, at great personal risk to themselves. Those most noted for this were Corporal Philip Smith of the 17th (Leicestershire) Regiment, Private John Sims of the 34th (Cumberland) Regiment and Private John Alexander of the 90th (Perthshire) Light Infantry.

Lieutenant William Hope of the 7th (Royal) Fusiliers was informed by Sergeant Major William Bacon, who had a gunshot wound to his left shoulder, that his fellow officer Lieutenant James Hobson was lying severely wounded outside the trenches. He went to search for him and found him lying in an agricultural ditch leading towards the left flank of the Redan. Seeing that he could not be moved without a stretcher, he went back to Egerton's Pit to collect a stretcher and returned to Hobson with four other men, including Private Hughes, and this time succeeded in bringing the officer to shelter. All the time they were under continuous fire, and Private Hughes was severely wounded. Unfortunately, Lieutenant Hobson later died of his wounds, and it seems the three other men in the stretcher party were killed.

The men of the Left Attack scrambled out of their trenches and advanced towards the Redan. Gunner Thomas Arthur RA, who had already shown his desire to act without orders for the chance to go into action, ran out of his battery and formed up with one of the spiking party. However, no sooner had they shown themselves than they were hit by a murderous fire of grape and musketry, and all in the advance were either killed or wounded. Many senior officers clambered onto the parapets and waved their swords in the air, shouting words of encouragement. Captain Peel used unit rivalry to spur his men on, calling out: 'Come on sailors, don't let the soldiers beat you.'

For a third time Captain Peel displayed his bravery by volunteering to lead the first ladder party. He was about half-way up the glacis when he came under a hail of withering rifle bullets which tore up his tunic and sliced open the pistol case he had recently received from home. One shot went right through his left arm. As usual, Midshipman Daniel was close by and immediately came to his aid. In full view of the enemy, he tied a tourniquet around Peel's arm to try to stop the bleeding. During the action Danicl's pistol case was twice shot through and his clothes were cut to pieces, but he managed to get his leader to a place of comparative safety without himself being wounded.

The skirmishers went boldly forward, followed by Lieutenant James Murray of the Engineers, leading the sappers and carpenters with destroying tools and powder-bags. They edged to the left, taking a sort of cart-track winding along the broken crest of the Woronzoff Ravine. Close upon them were the ladders under Lieutenant Gerald Graham, who had in his party two able leaders, Corporal Paul and Private John Perie. The sappers with this column were less familiar with the characteristics of the ground than were those on the right.

'Who of the Sappers here know anything of the ground?' asked Lieutenant Graham.

'I do, sir,' cried Perie, with an impatience that evidenced his desire for selection. 'I know every inch of it', and he was accordingly appointed to head the sailors with the ladders.

Lieutenant Graham's unit had advanced about 50 yards and reached the hindmost spur of the hill when they came under intense enemy fire from all directions. Many of them were hit and the skirmish faltered. Lieutenant Murray was hit and fell mortally wounded. Sergeant Coppin and Private Mole bound up his shattered arm as best they could; despite the agonising pain, Murray declined to be carried away by his men, and so alone and unaided he walked in a sinking state to the trench and soon after expired. The men were ordered to lie down for a few minutes, ready to spring onwards when the fire should lessen.

Lieutenant Graham took Murray's place. Tall, commanding and collected, vigorous in purpose and brave in danger, he took the direction of the contingents. It was observed that, despite his vast stature, which made him strangely conspicuous in the field, Lieutenant Graham seemed to lead a charmed life and was not hit as he directed his men.

At this point Colonel Richard Tylden RE rushed to the front waving his sword above his head, and shouted for his men to go on. Lieutenant Graham pointed out that it was better to assault the salient instead of the right flank, and the colonel agreed:. 'Anywhere, as long as you get on!' Barely had he approved of Lieutenant Graham's suggestion than a grape-shot passed through his thighs. Lieutenant Graham raised him from the ground, and Sergeant Coppin and Private Ewen of the 8th Company, both of whom more than once had proved their devotion to their officers, carried the colonel to a sheltered spot under a ledge of rock at the side of the Woronzoff Ravine and there laid him down. Faint as he was from the loss of blood, he would not retain the sergeant and so dismissed him to his party. Ewen remained to soothe the colonel by his attentions, and later in the day assisted four or five sappers in bearing him from the nook to the camp.

With cool courage Lieutenant Graham returned to collect his sword and rejoined his men, where he directed the woolpack and ladder parties towards the salient. All around them men were being hit by all kinds of metal and falling or being blasted out of existence.

To their horror and disappointment the defences were still very strong. The Russians had been employed during the night of the 17th in repairing the abattis where it was destroyed by cannon ordnance. The ditch beyond the abattis was still intact, and the bottom was filled with bayonets fixed firmly in the earth. The cheval-de-frise had been repaired, and the enemy had made every effort up to the moment before the assault to render the defences formidable obstacles to the advance.

Some men got beyond the abbatis and reached the ditch. Lieutenant Graham halted them there and waited for the riflemen to cover them before he gave the order to advance further. However, most of the attacking force seemed to be moving westward, under the command of Colonel Lord West of the 21st Regiment, where he had decided to lead another storming party made up of men from the Reserves. Many of the soldiers in the ladder parties had been cut down by the furious fire, but the sailors were eager for another try. Lieutenant Graham could only muster four men for each ladder instead of six, but at Lord West's request he moved his gallant party of men out under a murderous fire. They got as far as some open ground, where they lay down on the grass and waited for the skirmishers to arrive. However, when no skirmishers or stormers appeared, Lieutenant Graham had no option but to order his surviving men to fall back and try to return to the British lines.

Colour Sergeant Leitch immediately began to tear down the gabions from the parapet. Hastily refilling them, he threw some down into the ditch and placed others across the gap to form a ramp, and built up a caponier to try to provide some protection for the stormers. However, as he did so he was disabled by enemy fire. As Sapper Perie was attempting the same difficult work, he was wounded in his side, but still found the strength to rescue an injured man.

Colonel John Campbell displayed 'a courage amounting to rashness, when he rushed out of the trenches and was shot through the head in the act of cheering his men on'.

Command of the Left column fell to Colonel Shadforth, as his men of the 57th Regiment storming party raced forward into the storm of missiles. However, Shadforth had barely had time to reorganise, shouting 'Colonel Warre, you mind the right, I will take the left, and Major Inglis the centre', when he was shot in the head and fell dead. Lieutenant James Ashwin fell from a round shot which struck him on the breast, and Lieutenant George Norman was mortally wounded in the head by a musket ball, while gallantly leading his company.

Colour Sergeant Gardiner showed unflinching and devoted courage as he encouraged his comrades to find shelter in the craters made by the explosion of the shells; by making parapets of the dead bodies of their comrades, they kept up a continuous fire and managed to keep the enemy back from the parapet of the Redan until their ammunition was exhausted. This was done under a fire in which nearly half the officers and a third of the rank-and-file were killed or wounded. Gardiner's actions were noted and remarked for determined resolution.

Soon after Lieutenant Knox left the trench, he came upon Captain Edward Blackett of his battalion, dragging himself back to the British lines dangerously wounded, and the command thus fell upon Knox. On seeing many men carrying the ladders being shot down, he realised that there was no point in reaching the parapet if they could not scale it, so he left the skirmishers of the Rifle Brigade and volunteered to assist the ladder party. He and Captain Edward Forman reached the abattis, where they took the chance to fire some rounds in the direction of the enemy positions, and discussed what they should do next. Lieutenant Knox had his rifle trained on a Russian when he was shot in the left arm. Captain Foreman remarked, 'You are wounded.' To which Lieutenant Knox replied: 'I fancy I am.' The captain was in the process of binding up the wound with a handkerchief when he was struck by grapeshot and fell dead at his injured comrade's feet. Lieutenant Knox decided he could do no more and made his way back. As he did so, a grape shot struck him in his already injured arm and lodged there. He remained on his feet until he got into the British trenches, where he collapsed from loss of blood and shock. Four soldiers of the 23rd Fusiliers put him on a stretcher, and as they rushed him to the nearest casualty station Lord Raglan enquired about him. Lieutenant Knox was twice offered some brandy but refused.

The three sappers already mentioned showed devoted heroism in sallying out of the trenches on numerous occasions and bringing in wounded officers and men. Sapper Perie did so despite his own wound. That night another Engineer, Captain Howard Elphinstone, requested permission to command a party of volunteers who proceeded to search for and bring back the scaling ladders left behind after the repulse; and while successfully performing this task, and rescuing trophies from the Russians, Captain Elphinstone conducted a long search for wounded men who had fallen close to the enemy, twenty of whom he rescued and brought back to the trenches.

Lieutenant Henry Raby of HMS *Wasp*, Naval Brigade, acted as second-in-command to Lieutenant Edward D'Aeth of the 4th ladder party. This ladder party did not actually take part in the assault on the Redan fortifications, but later that day a soldier of the 57th Regiment, who had been wounded in both legs, was observed sitting up and calling for help. Climbing over the breastwork of the advance sap, Lieutenants Raby and D'Aeth, and two sailors of the Naval Brigade named Henry Curtis of HMS *Rodney*, and John Taylor of HMS *London*, at once left the shelter of their battery works and, as hundreds of men were running away from the Redan, at the imminent risk of their own lives they ran through heavy gunfire across the open ground towards the danger for a distance of 70 yards as far as the salient angle of the Redan. The heavy gunfire persisted throughout the rescue attempt, and they were continuously dodging bullets, but they succeeded in carrying the wounded man to safety.

After bringing the remains of his party safely into the trenches, Lieutenant Thomas Kidd RN again returned to the open to recover some wounded men, and in this gallant act of devotion to his duty he was shot through the chest by a rifle ball and died shortly after reaching the camp.

The column under General William Eyre was directed to attack the far left of the defences, about three-quarters of a mile west of the Redan, and push down the picket-house ravine past the cemetery into the rear of the barrack battery, and there cooperate with General Barnard in its capture. The column moved forward into the grounds near the graveyard, but became pinned down among some houses of the suburb, beyond which it would have been more than madness to proceed. They held the position until evening under a harassing fire, and retreated with the loss of no fewer than thirty-one officers killed and wounded. Colonel William Eyre was seriously wounded in the face, and Captains Bowes Fenwick, Charles Agar, William Caulfeild and Henry Mansfield of the 44th Regiment were mortally wounded.

The men of the 44th Regiment included Sergeant William McWheeney, and Captain Thomas Esmonde of the 18th (Royal Irish) Regiment was with them. General Eyre's section of the line of attack was comparatively successful, and captured a number of positions. Sergeant McWheeney volunteered for the advance guard of his regiment during this assault.

When engaged in administering to the wants of a dying brother officer in the heat of action, a shot from the enemy guns pierced the body of Lieutenant Smith, 9th Regiment, from which he suffered manfully and then died.

William Howard Russell reported:

> The brigade under Major-General Eyre, which was destined to occupy the Cemetery and to carry the Barrack Batteries, consisted of the 9th Regiment, 18th Regiment, 28th Regiment, 38th Regiment and 44th Regiment. Four volunteers from each company were selected to form an advanced party, under Major Fielden of the 44th Regiment, to feel the way and cover the advance. The 18th Royal Irish followed as the storming regiment. The brigade was turned out at twelve o'clock and proceeded to march down the road on the left of the Green Hill Battery to the Cemetery, and halted under cover while the necessary dispositions were being made for the attack.
>
> General Eyre, addressing the 18th, said, 'I hope, my men, that this morning you will do something that will make every cabin in Ireland ring again!' The reply was a loud cheer, which instantly drew on the men a shower of grape. The skirmishers advanced just as the general attack began, and, with some French on their left, rushed at the Cemetery, which was very feebly defended. They got possession of the place after a slight resistance, with small loss, and took some prisoners, but the moment the enemy retreated their batteries opened a heavy fire on the place from the left of the Redan and from the Barrack Battery.
>
> Four companies of the 18th at once rushed on out of the Cemetery towards the town, and actually succeeded in getting possession of the suburb. Captain Hayman was gallantly leading on his company when he was shot through the knee. Captain Esmonde followed, and the men, once established, prepared to defend the houses they occupied. As they

drove the Russians out, they were pelted with large stones by the latter on their way up to the battery, which quite overhangs the suburb. The Russians could not depress their guns sufficiently to fire down on our men, but they directed a severe flanking fire on them from an angle of the Redan works.

There was nothing for it but to keep up a vigorous fire from the houses, and to delude the enemy into the belief that the occupiers were more numerous than they were. Meantime the Russians did their utmost to blow down the houses with shell and shot, and fired grape incessantly, but the soldiers kept close, though they lost men occasionally, and they were most materially aided by the fire of the regiments in the Cemetery behind them, which was directed at the Russian embrasures; so that the enemy could not get out to fire down on the houses below.

Some of the houses were comfortably furnished. One of them was as well fitted up as most English mansions, the rooms full of fine furniture, a piano in the drawing-room, and articles of luxury and taste not deficient. Our men unfortunately found that the cellars were not empty, and that there was abundance of fine Muscat wine from the south coast of the Crimea, and of the stronger wines, perfumed with roses and mixed with fruits, which are grown in the interior, in the better sort of houses. Some of the officers, when they went away, carried off articles of clothing and papers, as proof of their entrance into the place, and some others took away pigeons and guinea pigs which went tame in the houses.

The troops entered the place about four o'clock in the morning, and could not leave it till nine in the evening. The Russians blew up many of the houses and set fire to others, and when our men retired the flames were spreading along the street.

The 18th Regiment lost 250 men. In the middle of the day, Captain Esmonde wrote to General Eyre to say that he required support, that the men were short of ammunition, and that the rifles were clogged. The rifles, which were of the Enfield pattern, had been only served to the regiment the day before, and again it was found that these admirable weapons are open to the grave defect which has been so frequently mentioned, and that they are liable to become useless after firing 20 rounds. A sergeant volunteered to creep back with this letter, but when he reached the place where the general ought to have been, he found that the latter had been obliged to withdraw owing to his wound, and he therefore delivered the document to Colonel Edwards. As there was no possibility of getting support down to the troops, Colonel Edwards crept down along with the sergeant and into the houses to see how matters were going on. The officer in command, on learning the state of the case, ordered the men to keep up the hottest fire they could; and meantime they picked up the rifles and ammunition of the killed and wounded, and were by that means enabled to continue their fusilade.

The 9th Regiment succeeded in effecting a lodgement in the houses in two or three different places, and held their position, as well as the 18th. A sergeant and a handful of men actually got possession of the little Wasp Battery, in which there were only twelve or fourteen Russian artillerymen. They fled at the approach of our men, but when the latter turned round they discovered they were quite unsupported; and the Russians, seeing that the poor fellows were left alone, came down on them and drove them out of the battery. An officer and half-a-dozen men of the same regiment got up close to a part of the Flagstaff Battery, and were advancing into it when they, too, saw that they were by themselves, and, as it was futile to attempt holding their ground, they retreated. About fifteen French soldiers on their left aided them, but as they were likewise unsupported they had to retire. Another officer with only twelve men took one of the Russian rifle pits, bayoneted those they found in it, and held possession of it throughout the day.

Meanwhile, while these portions of the 9th and 18th and parties of the 44th and 28th were in the houses, the detachment of the same regiments and of the 38th kept up a hot fire from the Cemetery on the Russians in the battery and on the sharpshooters, all the time being exposed to a tremendous shower of bullets, grape, round shot, and shell. The loss of the brigade under such circumstances could not but be extremely severe. One part of it separated from the other, was exposed to a destructive fire in houses, the upper portion of which crumbled into pieces or fell in under fire, and it was only by keeping in the lower storey, which was vaulted and well built, that they were enabled to hold their own. The other parts of it, far advanced from our batteries, were almost unprotected, and were under a constant *mitraille* and bombardment from guns which our batteries had failed to touch.

Captain Smith, of the 9th, was struck by a grapeshot in the back as he was in the act of getting Captain Armstrong of the 18th into a litter, with the assistance of Captain Gaynor. The shot broke his spine, and drove his ribs into his lungs. He died yesterday. Lieutenant Douglas and Lieutenant McQueen were also wounded. Of this regiment six men were killed and 53 wounded.

On the 18th, Lieutenant Meurant was killed, and the wounded were Major Kennedy, Captain Hayman (slightly), Captain Cormack (severely), Captain Armstrong (slightly), Captain Wilkinson (slightly), Ensign Fearnley and Ensign Hotham (severely). 34 men killed and 116 wounded.

In the 38th, Lieut. Davies, a brave and esteemed young officer, was killed, and five were wounded more or less severely, among who were the gallant Lieut-Col. Lowth and Lieut French; the latter has a fractured thigh.

In the 44th Regiment no less than seven officers were wounded, of whom three, namely Captain Bowes Fenwick, Captain the Hon. Herbert Agar, and Captain F. Caulfeild, are reported to have died of their wounds. Captain Mansfield's thigh fractured; 17 men were killed, 108 wounded. The 88th Regiment was in the trenches and had a few men wounded.

The total number of killed and wounded in the Brigade was, up to the last returns I could see, 107 killed, 552 wounded. Total 659. Some of the officers got away in the great storm which arose about eleven o'clock, and blew with great violence for several hours.

General Eyre has issued the following order – Second Brigade Orders, Third Division, June 30 – The Major-General commanding the brigade requests that the officers, non-commissioned officers and men will accept his thanks for their conduct yesterday. He cannot sufficiently express his admiration of their coolness, gallantry and discipline during a most trying day. He must tender his thanks to the medical department for their judicious arrangements to provide for the wounded, which arrangements were most successful. To assistant-surgeon Gibbons, 44th Regiment, and Geeves, 38th Regiment, especially, much praise is due for their zealous and humane exertions in the field, while exposed to a galling fire from the enemy.

Sergeant Timothy Gowing wrote to his parents:

How to express my feelings to the God of all mercies I do not know. I drop a line as quickly as possible, in order to catch the mail, to let you know that I am still safe and sound, as I know that long before this can reach home you will have heard of the slaughter we have sustained. Slaughter is hardly a name for it – massacre. We have been cut to pieces in an attempt upon the town. I have not time to say much, and am too low-spirited. About two o'clock this morning we attacked the Redan, the

7th Fusiliers leading the stormers. Our dear old Colonel was killed. He was one of the bravest of the brave, for where all were brave he would lead the way. Almost every officer of ours has been either killed or wounded. I am the only sergeant of my company returned to camp without being wounded. Oh, what a morning! But through the mercy of God I have been spared, although my poor comrades fell in heaps all around me, one on the top of the other. But truth will go the farthest; the enemy has beaten both French and English this morning. Our poor fellows could not get at them, but were mowed down with grape, canister, and musketry, and broadside after broadside from their shipping. The sights all around are horrible, men continually being brought into camp with every description of wound. I heard one of our old hands say, a short time ago, although wounded and limping to hospital: 'This is only lent; we'll pay them off for it yet, and that before long.' The sole cry in the camp is – 'Let's go at them again.' I hope you will excuse this short letter, as I must be off. I am for the trenches to-night.

PS – I was robbed of all I had in this world while out fighting (except the small *bible* you gave me – they would not have that).

In a letter from the photographer Roger Fenton to his wife Grace, written on the night of 18 June 1855, he described how:

slightly wounded men came up, supported by the other soldiers, and the tale they told confirmed all our fears. Our men had attacked twice, and been driven back each time by a frightful fire of grape. Next an officer was borne up on a litter. They had spread green boughs over his face to keep the sun from him; he was a Captain Lea, I think of the 57th. Soon the wounded came up in numbers. After waiting an hour, and there being no signs of an immediate renewal of the attack, I accepted an invitation to breakfast from Gough, lieutenant of the Naval Brigade. On the way an ambulance came up and in it [was] a naval officer named Cave shot through the thigh. He said to Gough, 'It has been a disgraceful attack, no management, no orders.' We saw him to his tent, and sat down to breakfast. Litter after litter came pouring in, bringing wounded men to the Hospital; one poor fellow, a seaman, was brought in dead. Gough spoke of him as one of his best men, so I went to look at him. One could scarcely believe he was dead; he seemed just to be resting a little, [and] beside him lay sewn up in a blanket a sailor killed yesterday in my sight by a fragment of a shell. I went into the hospital. It was an awful sight, but I will not shock you with the description. Returning to breakfast, for it is an odd thing that in the midst of all these horrors no one loses his appetite.

News kept dropping in, first of one officer then of another of the Naval Brigade being wounded. We had scarcely heard of the escape of one of them named Kidd when he was brought in mortally wounded by a shot through the chest. He had got through the fight and was quite happy and elated at his escape, when he saw some of our men lying outside the trench, and in the attempt to drag them in got his death wound. We went into the Hospital where he lay; poor fellow, he turned his glazing eyes upon us, then closed them, panting vainly for breath. He died in a few minutes. Out of 60 of the Naval Brigade only 12 came out intact. News kept coming of well-known names that were henceforth to be only memories. Col Yea was killed by the same shot which took off poor Sir John Campbell's head. Col Tylden was shot through both thighs and several regiments suffered terribly in their officers.

William Howard Russell described the armistice of 19 June:

The sad history of the 19th, which I was obliged to interrupt on the departure of the mail, is soon finished. The bodies of many a brave officer whom I knew in old times – old times of the war, for men's lives are short here, and the events of a life are compressed into a few hours – were borne past us in silence, and now and then, wonderful to relate, men with severe wounds were found still living and able to give expression to their sufferings by moans and sighs of pain. The spirit of some of these noble fellows triumphed over all their bodily agonies.

'General!' exclaimed a sergeant of the 18th Royal Irish to Brigadier Eyre, as he came near the place in the cemetery where the poor fellow lay with both his legs broken by a round shot, 'thank God, we did our work, anyway. Had I another pair of legs, the country and you would be welcome to them.'

Many men in hospital, after losing leg or arm, said they would not have cared if they had only beaten the Russians. The torments endured by the wounded were very great; they lay in holes made by shells, and were frequently fired at by the Russian riflemen when they rolled about in their misery. Some of our men, however, report that the enemy treated them kindly, and even brought them water out of the embrasures. They pulled all the bodies of our officers which lay within reach up to the abattis, and took off their epaulettes, when they had any, and their boots, and did not strip them.

The Assault on the Great Redan

A line of sentries was formed by the Russians as our burying parties came out, and they advanced so far in front of the abattis that General Airey was obliged to remonstrate with an aide-de-camp of General Osten-Sacken, who ordered them to retire nearer to the abattoirs. It was observed that these men were remarkably fine, tall, muscular, and soldier-like fellows, and one could not but contrast them with some of the poor weakly-looking boys who were acting as privates in our regiments, or with the small under-grown men of the French line. They were unusually well-dressed, in clean new uniforms, and were no doubt picked out to impose upon us. Many of them wore medals, and seemed veteran soldiers. Their officers had also turned out with unusual care, and wore white kid gloves, patent leather boots, and white linen.

The mass of the Russians were gathered on the towering parapets of the Redan and Malakoff, and were not permitted to come to the front. Their working parties brought out all our dead, and laid them in front of their line of sentries, whence our people carried them away. The precautions which had been taken to prevent officers and men getting through the lines sufficed to keep any great crowd away, but the officers on duty and the lucky men, and some amateurs, who managed to get through the lines, formed groups in front of the Redan, and entered into conversation with a few of the Russian officers. There was, however, more reserve and gravity in the interview than has been the case on former occasions of the kind.

One stout elderly Russian of rank asked one of our officers 'How are you off for food?' 'Oh! We get everything we want; our fleet secures that.' 'Yes,' remarked the Russian, with a knowing wink, 'Yes; but there's one thing you're not so well off for, and your fleet can't supply you, and that's sleep.' 'We're at least as well off for that as you are' was the rejoinder. Another officer, in the course of conversation, asked if we really thought, after our experience of the defence they could make, that we could take Sebastopol. 'We must; France and England are determined to take it.' 'Ah! well,' said the other, 'Russia is determined France and England shall not have it, and we'll see who has the strongest will, and can lose most men.'

In the midst of these brief interviews, beginning and ending with bows and salutes, and inaugurated by the concession of favours relating to cigars and lights, the soldiers bore dead bodies by consigning the privates to the burial-grounds near the trenches, and carrying off the wounded and the bodies of the officers to the camp.

Poor Forman's body was one of the first found. It was far in advance of where he came out of the trench with his company of the Rifle Brigade, and it was terribly torn with shot.

It was generally observed by some of the surgeons, that the wounds were cleaner than they have been in previous engagements. This is somewhat remarkable, for the Russians fired all kinds of missiles, bags of nails and fragments of bullets, shells, and balls, as well as grape and canister. They were seen as we advanced 'shovelling' the shot into the muzzles of the guns. No one can deny many of their officers the praise of extreme bravery and devotion. In the midst of our fire they got upon the top, and on the outside of the parapets, and directed the fire of their men upon us. Several of them were knocked over by round shot, shell, and rifle balls, while exposing themselves in this manner; but it scarcely speaks well for their soldiers that they felt it necessary to set them such examples.

Colonel Dickson succeeded in obtaining Lord Raglan's permission to open on the Russians from the 21-gun battery, and swept them away in numbers as they crowded out to fire on our broken columns, and on our wounded men and fugitives. The armistice lasted for upwards of two hours, and when it was over we retired from the spot soon moistened with our blood.

All the advantage we gained by the assault was the capture of the Cemetery, and even that we had nearly abandoned, owing to the timidity of one of our generals. As you have already learnt, the men in the Cemetery and houses suffered severely during the 18th from the enemy's fire, and the soldiers in the latter were not able to withdraw till nightfall. It was left to one of the Generals of Division to say what should be done with the Cemetery, and he gave orders to abandon it.

On the following morning an officer of Engineers, Lieutenant Donnelly, heard to his extreme surprise that the position for which we had paid so dearly was not in our possession. He appreciated its value – he saw that the Russians had not yet advanced to re-occupy it. With the utmost zeal and energy he set to work among the officers in the trenches, and begged and borrowed some 30 men, with whom he crept down into the Cemetery, just before the flag of truce was hoisted. As soon as the armistice began the Russians flocked down to the Cemetery, which they supposed to be undefended, but to their great surprise they found our 30 men posted there as sentries, who warned them back, and in the evening the party was strengthened, and we are now constructing most

The Assault on the Great Redan

valuable works and batteries there, in spite of a heavy fire, which occasions us considerable loss.

Such is the story that is going the round of the camp. Raglan is said to have found fault with General Eyre for losing so many men, but the latter observed that he had done what he was ordered, and that he had taken the Cemetery. There can be no doubt but that our troops could have got into the town in the rear of the Redan from the houses on the 18th, had they been strong enough to advance from the Cemetery. Whether they could have maintained themselves there under the fire of forts, ships, and batteries is another question.

It is now shrewdly suspected that inside the Redan, behind those outward and visible walls of earth, there is another very strong work – a kind of star fort of earth with sunken batteries – and it is certain that inside the Malakhoff works there are several lines of battery which have never been unmasked. The enemy have probably constructed large funnel shaped pits behind these works, into which shells roll and burst, as such a 'dodge' was found in the Mamelon.

Inside the latter work were splendid bomb-proofs for the men to retire into when our fire became hot. They were large pits with 10 feet of earth, and beams of wood across them, and were capable of holding a strong body of men. In one some new sacks marked with the broad arrow were found, in which were packets of cartridges ready for use. Where did these sacks come from? It is almost as strange as the English bread found at Tchorgoun. There is talk of a spy being taken, or rather discovered, in a sub-interpreter to the Commissariat, who confesses he has been in communication with the Russians, and revealed our attack to them. He will be shot if this be true.

Exactly three months after the assault, many British newspapers published the following Russian account of the attack on the Malakoff and Redan:

We have just received the following detailed report from Aide-de-Camp General Prince Gortschakoff of the assault of the French on the 6th [18th] June on bastions 1, 2, 3, and Kornileff, of the line of defence of Sebastopol, and of their repulse by our troops.

The enemy having resolved to make a decisive attack upon our left flank, opened on the 5th (17th) of June, at 3.30am, a 'fire of hell' against the fortifications of the Karabelnaia Faubourg (sections 3 and 4). For two consecutive hours all their batteries fired almost uninterrupted broadsides. On our sides we kept up a quick fire in return. At two in the afternoon at a given signal, the besiegers opened a heavy fire against our right flank; the fire, which opened along the whole line of our defences, lasted till an advanced hour of the evening. At dusk, and throughout the night, the enemy threw shells and rockets into the town, into the roadstead, and the north side. A steam frigate, which had left the Allied fleet at the same time, fired broadsides into this roadstead and against the town. The greatest portion of its projectiles fell into the sea without striking our ships. This terrible cannonade and increased bombardment did not prevent the brave defenders of Sebastopol from actively repairing the damage done to the works; despite a terrible front and flank fire, the works were successfully completed, the guns which had been dismantled replaced by new ones on every point, and on the morning of the 6th (18th) of June we were perfectly prepared to receive and drive back the enemy. On the night between 5th and 6th (17th and 18th) June, to be prepared for an assault, our troops were disposed as follows on the left flank of our line of defence.

Bastion number 3 and the neighbouring batteries were defended by the second brigade of the 11th division of infantry, a regiment of the Briansk Chasseurs, and a battalion of reserve, consisting of men of the Minsk and Yedimar regiments. In the Kornileff Bastion and in the Gervais Battery there was the first brigade of the 8th infantry division and the Sevesk Regiment of infantry. In Bastion Number 2, the Vladimir Regiment of Infantry and the 1st battalion of the Sevesk Regiment; another battalion of the same regiment was drawn up along the curtain between Bastion Kornileff and Bastion number 2. Bastion number 1 was occupied by the Chasseur regiments Krementbourg and Prince of Warsaw. The general reserve of troops who defended the works of the Karabelnaia Faubourg consisted of the 1st brigade of the 11th division of infantry, with 18 pieces of field artillery of the 17th brigade.

On the 6th (18th) of June, at daybreak, the enemy in a dense chain, supported by strong reserves, attacked simultaneously Bastion number 1, the fortified barracks between Bastion 1 and 2, Bastion number 2; the Kornileff Bastion number 3, and the so-called Gribok work, situated on the right of the Peressyp; the enemy entertained the hope of forcing a passage somewhere along this long line of defence. The number of troops brought to the assault was 35,000 men, without counting their distant reserves. The French advanced on the right flank and centre, the English on the left flank. The besiegers, provided with ladders, fascines, and sappers' tools, advanced rapidly to the attack. Despite the heavy fire of grape and musketry we poured into them, their columns advanced, reached our ditches and commenced scaling our parapets. But the line of intrepid defenders of Sebastopol never swerved. They received the daring assailants with the points of their bayonets, and threw them back into the ditches. The enemy's columns then threw themselves on the Gervais Battery, entered it, drove out the battalion of infantry in charge of it, and following in pursuit, occupied the houses nearest the Karabelnaia Faubough from the Malakhoff Mamelon to the bay of the docks.

The success of our adversaries was not of long duration. Lieutenant-General Chrouleff, the vigilant chief of the line of defence of the Karabelnaia Faubough, ordered up a reserve of 600 riflemen to the curtain between Bastion 2 and Kornileff. When the enemy had passed through our line near the Gervais Battery, Lieutenant-General Chrouleff, placing himself at the head of a company of the Sevesk Regiment of Infantry, which was returning from a corvee, and taking with him a battalion of the Poltawa Regiment, led them to a charge. These troops reinforced in good time by five companies of the Ylakoutsk Regiment, and later by a battalion of the Yelets Regiment, routed the French, and having driven them out of the Gervais battery pursued them into their own trenches, putting the stragglers in the rear to the bayonet. The company of the Sevak Regiment distinguished itself by its intrepidity during the combat.

On all the other points of the line of defence the troops, animated by their commanders, Rear-Admiral Panfiloff and Major General Prince Ouronssoff, fought with exemplary courage, and drove back the assailants. Our batteries on the north side, and our steamers, which swept the enemy's columns at every point upon which they could bring their guns to bear, contributed considerably to the success of this brilliant affair; the steamer *Vladimir* in particular, commanded by Captain Boutakoff, approached repeatedly the entrance of Careening Bay, from which point it swept the enemy's reserves.

The heroism and disregard of danger of the garrison of Sebastopol, in which all from the General to the private, fought with most extraordinary daring and intrepidity, are above all praise. Amongst those who most distinguished themselves, in addition to the commander of the garrison, Aide-de-Camp Count Osten-Sacken, and his colleague Admiral Nachimoff (who so valiantly directs the whole defence of Sebastopol), I must mention Lieutenant-General Chrouleff, to whom the chief honour of the day is due, as commanding the whole of the line attacked;

Rear Admiral Panfiloff, who drove back the assault on Bastion number 3; Major-General Prince Ouronssoff, who defeated the assailants between Bastion 1 and 2; the chiefs of sections and naval captains De Kern and Perelischive; Major-General Youferoff; Colonel Goleff; Lieutenant-Colonel Malofsky and Captain Boutakoff.

Our losses during the bombardment of the 5th and 6th (17th and 18th) of June, and during the assault, consist of 1 superior officer, 4 subalterns, and 530 men killed; 5 superior officers, 42 subalterns, and about 3,378 men wounded.

Amongst the brave defenders of Sebastopol we have unhappily to deplore the loss of some distinguished officers. Thus, the brave Captain Boudistcheff of the navy was killed. Among the wounded are Major-General Zamarine; the gallant Captain Yourkovsky, of the navy, commander of the fourth section (seriously); [and] the captain of naval artillery, Stanislavsky, commander of the artillery of the Kornileff Bastion.

The loss of the enemy, whose columns were exposed to a most terrible fire of grape and musketry, is very considerable; the removal of the dead, which took place on the following day, at the request of the Commander-in-Chief of the Allies, at 6 in the evening, is a proof of it. The number of corpses was so considerable that the French had not sufficient stretchers to carry them off, and the officer entrusted with the duty requested us to bury those they could not remove.

Such is the recital of this unexampled exploit of the garrison of Sebastopol, which after nine months of siege and three terrible bombardments, repulsed the desperate assault of the enemy, occasioned them an immense loss, and with heroic devotion is still ready to meet any attempt on their part.

The British casualty list totalled over 1,500 men. Lieutenant Graham wrote to his father on the day after the battle, saying: 'Sad work we have had today. The attack on the Redan failed . . . I was through it all, but not hurt, only very exhausted and depressed by our failure.'

Lord West wrote: 'I wish I could do justice to the daring and intrepid conduct of the sailors. Lieutenant Graham of the Engineers evinced coolness and a readiness to expose himself to any personal risk, which does him the greatest credit.'

The day's events had such a bad effect on the men that one soldier remarked to some of them as they returned: 'All you fellows who have been in action today look about ten years older.'

The Assault on the Great Redan

Two days later Captain Esmonde was in command of a working party when an enemy fire-ball fell close by, intended to light up the area, and exposed the position of the party of men. He called out to his men to take cover, then with the most prompt and daring gallantry he rushed out to the spot where the fire-ball had lodged; as he had anticipated, a hail of fire was directed at him, but he effectively extinguished the fire-ball before it had betrayed the position of the working party under his protection – thus saving it from a murderous fire of shell and grape.

Lieutenant Knox's arm had to be amputated from the socket during an operation performed without chloroform, and according to Knox himself he felt no pain. Apparently, only a week later this intrepid man was back on his feet, a 'none the worse man … although only one arm left'.

Lord Raglan sent a Despatch concerning the action of 18 June 1855. It is dated 'Before Sebastopol, June 19, 1855', and reads as follows:

My Lord – I informed your Lordship on the 16th that new batteries had been completed, and that, in consequence, the allies would be enabled to resume the offensive against Sebastopol with the utmost vigour.

Accordingly, on the 17th, at daylight, a very heavy fire was opened from all the batteries in the English and French trenches and maintained throughout the day; and the effect produced appeared so satisfactory that it was determined that the French should attack the Malakhoff works the next morning, and that the English should assail the Redan as soon after as I might consider it desirable.

It was at first proposed that the artillery fire should be resumed on the morning of the 18th, and should be kept up for about two hours, for the purpose of destroying any works the enemy might have thrown up during the night, and of opening passages through the abattis that covered the Redan; but on the evening of the 17th, it was intimated to me by General Pellissier that he had determined, upon further consideration, that the attack by his troops should take place at three the following morning.

The French, therefore, commenced their operations as day broke, and, as their several columns came within range of the enemy's fire, they encountered the most serious opposition, both from musketry and guns in the works, which had been silenced the previous evening, and observing this, I was induced at once to order our columns to move out of the trenches upon the Redan.

It had been arranged that detachments from the Light, 2nd, and 4th divisions, which I placed for the occasion under the command of Lieutenant-General Sir G. Brown, should be formed up into three columns and that the right one should attack the left face of the Redan between the flanking batteries and that the centre should advance upon the salient angle, and that the left should move upon the re-entering angle, formed by the right face and flank of the work; the first and last preceding the centre column.

The flank columns at once obeyed the signal to advance, preceded by covering parties of the Rifle Brigade, and by sailors carrying ladders, and soldiers carrying wool bags; but they had no sooner shown themselves beyond the trenches than they were assailed by a most murderous fire of grape and musketry. Those in advance were either killed or wounded; and the remainder found it impossible to proceed. I never before witnessed such a continued and heavy fire of grape, combined with musketry, from the enemy's works, which appeared to be fully manned, and the long list of killed and wounded in the Light and 4th divisions, and the seamen of the Naval Brigade, under Captain Peel, who was unfortunately wounded, though not severely, will show that a very large proportion of those that went forward fell. Major-General Sir John Campbell, who led the left attack, and Colonel Shadforth of the 57th, who commanded the storming party under his direction, were both killed, as was also Colonel Yea of the Royal Fusiliers, who led the right column.

I cannot say too much in praise of these officers. Major-General Sir J. Campbell had commanded the 4th division from the period of the battle of Inkerman till the arrival very recently of Lieutenant-General Bentinck. He had devoted himself to his duty without any intermission, and had acquired the confidence and respect of all. I most deeply lament his loss.

Colonel Shadforth had maintained the efficiency of his regiment by constant attention to all the details of his command; and Colonel Yea was not only distinguished for his gallantry, but had exercised his control of the Royal Fusiliers in such a manner as to win the affections of the soldiers under his orders, and to secure to them every comfort and accommodation which his personal exertion could procure for them.

I shall not be able to send your Lordship correct lists of the killed and wounded by this opportunity, but I will forward them by telegraph as soon as they are made out.

The Assault on the Great Redan

I have not any definite information upon the movements of the French columns, and the atmosphere became so obscured by the smoke from the guns and musketry that it was not possible by personal observation to ascertain their progress, though I was particularly well situated for the purpose; but I understand that their last column, under General d'Autemarrie, passed the advanced works of the enemy, and threatened the gorge of the Malakhoff Tower, and that the two other columns under Generals Meyren and Brunet, who both I regret to say, were killed, met with obstacles equal to those we encountered, and were obliged in consequence, to abandon the attack.

The superiority of our fire on the day we opened led both General Pelissier and myself, and the officers of the artillery and engineers of the two services, and the armies in general, to conclude that the Russian artillery fire was, in a great measure, subdued, and that the operation we projected could be undertaken with every prospect of success. The result has shown that the resources of the enemy were not exhausted, and that they had still the power, either from their ships or from their batteries, to bring an overwhelming fire upon their assailants.

Whilst the direct attack upon the Redan was proceeding, Lieutenant-General Sir R. England was directed to send one of the brigades of the 3rd division under the command of Major General Barnard, down the Woronzov Ravine, with a view to give support to the attacking columns on his right; and the other brigade, under Major-General Eyre, still further to the left, to threaten the works at the head of the Dockyard Creek.

I have not yet received their reports, and I shall not be able to send them to your Lordship today, but General Eyre was very seriously engaged, and he himself wounded, though I am happy to say not seriously, and he possessed himself of a church-yard, which the enemy had hitherto carefully watched, and some houses within the place; but as the town front was not attacked, it became necessary to withdraw his brigade at night. I shall make a special report upon this by the next mail, and I shall avail myself of the same opportunity to name to you the officers who have been particularly mentioned to me.

I am concerned to have to inform you that Lieutenant-Colonel Tylden, of the Royal Engineers, whose services I have had the greatest pleasure in bringing so frequently before your Lordship's notice, is very seriously wounded – The account I received of him this morning is upon the whole satisfactory, and I entertain strong hopes that his valuable life will be preserved.

I feel greatly indebted to Sir George Brown for the manner in which he conducted the duties I entrusted to him, and my warmest acknowledgments are due to Major-General Harry Jones, not only for his valuable assistance on the present occasion, but for the able, zealous, and energetic manner in which he has conducted the siege operations since he assumed the command of the Royal Engineers. He received a wound from a grape shot in the forehead yesterday, which I trust will not prove serious.

I brought up the first division from the vicinity of Balaclava as a reserve, and I shall retain them on these heights.

The Sardinian troops under General La Mamora, and the Turkish troops under Omar Pasha, crossed the Tchernaya on the 17th instant and occupied positions in front of Tehorgoum. They have not come in contact with any large body of the enemy.

William Howard Russell recorded in *The Times*:

Colonel Yea's body was found near the abattis on the night of the Redan; his boots and epaulettes were gone, but otherwise his clothing was untouched. His head was greatly swollen, and his features, and a fine manly face it had been, were nearly indistinguishable.

Colonel Shadforth's remains were discovered in a similar state. The shattered frame of Sir John Campbell lay close up to the abattis. His sword and boots were taken, but the former is said to be in the Light Division camp. It is likely he was carried away from the spot where he fell up to the ditch of the abattis for the facility of searching the body. Already, his remains were decomposing fast, and his face was much disfigured. Captain Hume, his attached aide-de-camp, had the body removed, and this evening it was interred on Cathcart's Hill, his favourite resort, where everyone was sure of a kind word and a cheerful saying from the gallant brigadier.

It was but the very evening before his death that I saw him standing within a few feet of his own grave. He had come to the ground in order to attend the funeral of Captain Vaughan, an officer in his own regiment (the 38th), who died of wounds received two days previously in the trenches, and he laughingly invited one who was talking to him to come and lunch with him next day at the Clubhouse of Sebastopol.

The Assault on the Great Redan

I saw in one place two of our men, apart from the rest, with melancholy faces. 'What are you waiting here for?' said I. ' To go out for the colonel, sir,' was the reply. 'What colonel?' 'Why, Colonel Yea, to be sure, sir,' said the good fellow, who was evidently surprised at my thinking there could be any other colonel in the world, and indeed the Light Division will feel his loss. Under occasional brusqueness of manner he concealed a most kind heart, and a more thorough soldier – one more devoted to his men, to the service, and to his country, never fell in battle than Lacy Yea. I have reason to know that he felt his great services and his arduous exertions had not been rewarded as he had a right to expect.

In the 34th, Captain Shiffner and Captain Robinson were killed close by their leader, and in a few moments Captain Gwilt, Captain Jordan, Captain Warre, Captain Peel, Lieutenant Alt, Lieutenant Clayton, and Lieutenant Harman, of the same regiment, fell more or less wounded to the ground.

A gallant and fine young soldier, poor Hobson, the Adjutant of the 7th, fell along with his chief mortally wounded, and is since dead, after amputation of his right thigh. The 7th Fusiliers has now only three or four officers left for duty. Major Pack, Lord Richard Browne, Lieutenant (Inkerman) Jones, Ensign Malan, Ensign Wright, Lieutenant Robinson, Captain Appleyard, and the Honourable E. Fitzclarence were wounded. The latter has had his left thigh amputated.

In the 33rd Colonel Johnstone had his left hand shot away, since amputated; Lt-Colonel Mundy was slightly wounded; Captain Quayle was shot through the body (doing well); Captain Wickham wounded; Lieutenant Bennett and Lieutenant Heyland were killed.

In the 23rd Regiment, which was favourably placed, the only officer injured was Lt-Colonel Lysons, who received a severe contusion.

In the 88th Regiment Captain Browne had his right arm carried clean away by a round shot.

In the Rifle Brigade Captain Blackett and Lieutenants Knox and Freemantle were wounded. The division has lost upwards of 320 men killed and wounded, and it suffered severely as it retired from the futile attack.

Captain Smith, of the 9th Regiment, was struck by grapeshot in the back as he was in the act of getting Captain Armstrong, of the 18th, into a litter, with the assistance of Captain Gaynor. The shot broke his spine and drove his ribs into his lungs. He died yesterday. Lieutenant Douglas and Lieutenant McQueen were also wounded. Of this regiment six men were killed and 53 wounded.

In the 18th Regiment, Lieutenant Meurant was killed, Major Kennedy, Captain Hayman (slightly), Captain Cormick (severely), Captain Armstrong (slightly), Captain Wilkinson (slightly), Ensign Fearnley and Ensign Hotham (severely) wounded; 34 men were killed, 216 wounded.

In the 38th Regiment, Lieutenant Davies, a brave and esteemed young officer, was killed, and five were wounded more or less severely, among who was the gallant Lieutenant-Colonel Lowth and Lieutenant French; the latter has a fractured thigh.

In the 44th Regiment no less than seven officers were wounded, of who three – namely, Captain Bowes Fenwick, Captain the Hon. Herbert Agar, and Captain Caulfeild, are reported to have died of their wounds. Captain Mansfield's thigh is fractured; 17 men were killed, 108 wounded. The 89th Regiment was in the trenches, and had a few men wounded.

* * *

The following list of officers killed and wounded on 18 June 1855 is compiled from official casualty returns, statements made by eyewitnesses and participants, letters home and information taken from memorials.

Royal Navy (Naval Brigade)

Captain William Peel, HMS *Leander* (seriously)
Lieutenant Osborne William Dalyell, HMS *Leander* (severely)
Lieutenant John Halliday Cave, HMS *Diamond*
Lieutenant Thomas Osborne Kidd, HMS *Albion* (killed)
Lieutenant William Brabazon Urmston, HMS *Queen*

Royal Regiment of Artillery

Captain W.J. Williams (slightly)

Corps of Royal Engineers

Major General Sir Harry David Jones (slightly wounded in the forehead by a spent grapeshot)
Colonel Richard Tylden (mortally, shot through both thighs by grapeshot; died in Malta on 2 August 1855)
Brevet Major and Brigade Major Eustace Fane Bourchier (slightly)
Captain William Howard Jesse (killed, shot through the head)
Lieutenant Thomas Molyneux Graves (killed within the abattis, and close to the ditch of that work, fell, pierced with three balls)
Lieutenant James Murray (killed)

The Assault on the Great Redan

4th (King's Own) Regiment
Colonel Henry Clermont Cobbe (mortally; died 6 August 1855)

7th Royal Fusiliers
Colonel Lacy Walter James Yea (killed, shot through the head)
Major Arthur John Reynell Pack (severely)
Captain Frederick Ernest Appleyard (contusion)
Lieutenant and Adjutant James St Clare Hobson (mortally; died 18 June 1855, after having his right thigh amputated)
Lieutenant Hon. Edward Fitzclarence (mortally, left leg and right hand amputated; died at the English Hospital in Constantinople, 23 July 1855)
Lieutenant Lewis John Fillis 'Inkerman' Jones (seriously)
Lieutenant Charles Hamilton Malan (severely, wounded four times)
Lieutenant George Henry Waller (slightly)
Lieutenant William L.L.G. Wright (slightly; killed on 8 September 1855)
Lieutenant Napier Douglas Robinson (missing)
Lieutenant Lord Richard Brown (slightly)

9th (East Norfolk) Regiment
Captain Frederick Smith (mortally, struck by grapeshot in the back, which broke his spine and drove his ribs into his lungs; died 20 June 1855)
Lieutenant and Adjutant John McQueen (severely)
Lieutenant A.G. Douglas (slightly)

17th (Leicestershire) Regiment
Captain John Lacy Croker (killed)

18th (Royal Irish) Regiment
Major John Clarke Kennedy (slightly, in the neck)
Captain A. Armstrong (slightly)
Captain John Cormick (dangerously)
Captain M.J. Hayman (dangerously)
Captain J.G. Wilkinson (slightly)
Lieutenant J.W. Meurant (killed)
Lieutenant W. O'Bryen Taylor (slightly)
Lieutenant W. Kemp (severely)
Lieutenant Fairfax Fearnley (severely)
Lieutenant Charles Hotham (slightly)

20th (East Devonshire) Regiment
Lieutenant Colonel F.C. Eveleigh (slightly)
Lieutenant J.J.S. O'Neill (slightly)
Ensign F.G. Holmes (slightly)

21st (Royal North British) Fusiliers
Lieutenant John G. Image (slightly)

23rd (Welsh) Fusiliers
Lieutenant Colonel Daniel Lysons (seriously, severe contusion)

28th (North Gloucestershire) Regiment
Captain J.G.R. Aplin (slightly)
Captain H.R.C. Godley (severely)
Captain J.D. Melcolm (severely)
Lieutenant Francis Brodigan (severely)
Lieutenant C.E.B. Lennard (severely)

33rd (Duke of Wellington's) Regiment
Lieutenant Colonel George Valentine Edward Mundy (slightly)
Lieutenant Colonel John Douglas Johnstone (severely, left hand shot away)
Captain John Edward Taubman Quayle (severely, received six wounds, including being shot in the elbow and arm)
Captain T. Wickham (severely, hit in the foot)
Captain Thomas Basil Fanshawe (slightly, hit in the shoulder by a spent ball)
Lieutenant Valentine Bennett (killed)
Lieutenant Langford Rowley Heyland (killed, pierced by six wounds)
Lieutenant J.T. Rogers (slightly)

34th (Cumberland) Regiment
Captain John Robinson (killed, grapeshot passed through the middle of his body)
Captain John Shiffner (killed by grapeshot)
Captain John G. Gwilt (slightly)
Captain Joseph Jordan (severely)
Captain William Warry (slightly)
Lieutenant Henry D. Alt (killed by grapeshot)
Lieutenant Francis Richard Hurt (killed; body not recovered)

Lieutenant G.B. Harman (severely)
Lieutenant Francis Peel (slightly)
Ensign Robert John Browne-Clayton (mortally; died in camp, 12 July 1855)

38th (1st Staffordshire) Regiment

Major General Sir John Campbell (killed, shot through the head)
Colonel John Jackson Lowth (mortally, struck down by a stone in the head, and wounded severely in the right leg above the knee by the bursting of a shell; died in Portsmouth on 28 July 1855)
Captain Archibald C. Snodgrass of the 4th Division Staff (severely)
Captain the Hon. Charles John Addington (severely)
Captain Ludford H. Daniel (dangerously)
Lieutenant Owen Gwyn Saunders Davies (killed by the same bursting shell which wounded Colonel Lowth)
Lieutenant J.B. French (severely, fractured thigh)
Lieutenant H.B. Fielden (severely)

41st (Welch) Regiment

Lieutenant Colonel Julius Edmund Goodwyn (wounded in the forehead)

44th (East Essex) Regiment

Captain Bowes Fenwick (mortally; died on the following day, 19 June 1855)
Captain the Hon. Charles Welbore Herbert Agar (mortally, both his legs carried off by a round shot; died that evening, 18 June 1855)
Captain Francis William Thomas Caulfeild (mortally; died on the following day, 19 June 1855)
Captain William Henry Mansfield (mortally, fractured thigh; died 28 June 1855)
Captain the Hon. Augustus Almeric Spencer (slightly)
Lieutenant Bradford Smith Hoskins (severely)
Lieutenant T. Orton Howarth (severely)
Lieutenant Joseph Logan (severely)

57th (West Middlesex) Regiment

Lieutenant Colonel Thomas Shadforth, in command (killed, shot in the head)
Brevet Major Arthur Maxwell Earle (severely)
Captain George Herman Norman (mortally, hit in the head by a musket ball; died 30 June 1855)
Captain F.P. Lea (severely)

Captain Charles William St Clair (severely)
Lieutenant James Collins Ashwin (killed, struck in the breast by a round shot)
Lieutenant C. Venables (severely)
Lieutenant Alfred Frederick Adolphus Slade (severely)

73rd (Perthshire) Regiment
Colonel William Eyre (seriously, wounded in the face)

88th Regiment (Connaught Rangers)
Captain George Richard Browne (dangerously, right arm carried clean away)

1st Rifle Brigade (Prince Consort's Own)
Lieutenant C.A.P. Boylan (severely)

2nd Rifle Brigade (Prince Consort's Own)
Captain the Hon. J. Stuart (severely)
Captain Edward William Blackett (seriously, lost a leg)
Captain Edward Rowland Forman (killed, struck by grapeshot)
Lieutenant Charles Augustus Penrhyn Boileau (mortally; died 3 August 1855 in Malta)
Lieutenant Fitzroy William Freemantle (severely)
Lieutenant John Simpson Knox (severely, shot in left arm, later amputated)

The Fall of Sebastopol

On 16 August the Russians launched an attack from the Mackenzie Heights to the north-east, across the Tchernaya river, against French and Sardinian troops on the Fediukhine Heights. Even the Russian commander, Prince Gorchakov, had little faith in the likely success of the attack, and his forces were defeated suffering heavy casualties within hours. Russian morale began to waver, and a pontoon bridge linking the south and north sides of Sebastopol was completed on 26 August, in preparation for an emergency evacuation of the city.

The Allied command made plans for what they believed would be the final assault on Sebastopol, and gave orders to recommence a massive bombardment of the city by over a thousand field pieces on 5 September. It lasted for three days. The assault was to commence at about midday on 8 September. The French would assault the Malakoff Tower, and if (or when) they were successful they were to raise the tricolour on the bastion, which was the signal for the British to attack the Redan.

The morning of 8 September 1855 broke cold and wintry. The troops of the 2nd and Light Divisions fell in at nine o'clock, with two days' rations in their packs, and each man was issued with a dram of rum. There were a lot of very young men in the ranks, who had not much idea of the terrible struggle they were about to endure, and others who knew all too well how difficult and dangerous their task would be. From about half-past-nine they waited under arms for the outcome of the French attack on the Malakoff, and for the order to advance.

The wait was long and the trenches were soon congested and units became mixed up, but one lesson learned from the assault on 18 June was that no British attack was to begin unless the French were successful. The tricolour to signify a French victory was raised at about midday and the order to advance was given.

Men will go into situations with great vigour when they have not yet realised what they are letting themselves in for, as they did during the First World War, but for many of the men who were ordered to assault the Great

Redan for a second time, it was a case of once bitten, twice shy. Some men were of the opinion that if the Malakoff was taken, the Allies would already command Sebastopol, and therefore the British attack would be a waste of lives – which indeed it was.

The pattern of events was similar to the first assault. Men were cut down by showers of grape and canister as they ran across the open ground. This time many got over the defences, planted the ladders and scaled the parapet of the Redan, but there were always signs that most of them had not much stomach for the fight. In defiance of their officers' exertions to get them to advance, they held back, preferring to retain some cover, and they would not charge forward and take the Redan. At first, the Russians faltered and fell back from the parapet, but when they saw that the British were reluctant to advance, they rallied and, with reinforcements arriving, they ran forward and with bayonets, bullets and even stones, they beat the British back down into the ditch and forced them to retire to the advance trenches. Even so, there were some men who performed gallant deeds against all the odds that day.

Captain Gronow Davis of the Royal Regiment of Artillery showed great coolness and gallantry while in command of a spiking party. Lieutenant Gilbert Howard Saunders of the 30th Regiment had received several severe wounds, the worst of which was a broken leg, which prevented him from getting back to the British lines. On seeing Lieutenant Saunders in distress, Captain Davis leaped over the parapet of a sap and twice proceeding some distance across the open under a murderous fire, assisted in rescuing the officer and placing him under cover. He repeated the act in the conveyance of other wounded soldiers from the same exposed position.

Bombardier Daniel Cambridge of the Royal Regiment of Artillery was severely wounded in the leg early in the day, and was asked to leave the assaulting party to get his wound attended to. However, he volunteered for the spiking party to go out of the advance trenches in front of the Quarries. Later he went out to bring in a wounded man, and during the rescue attempt he was shot for a second time. However, finding that he still had the strength to stand up, he went forward again with the 3rd (East Kent) Regiment ('The Buffs'), and it was only when he received a bullet in his jaw that he was finally put out of action.

Lieutenant Colonel Frederick Maude of the 3rd Buffs showed conspicuous and most devoted gallantry when in command of the ladder and covering party of the 2nd Division, and gallantly led his men to the Redan. Having entered the Redan with only nine or ten men, they held a position between traverses, and only retired when all hope of support was given up. Maude was dangerously wounded.

Private John Connors of the 3rd Buffs distinguished himself most conspicuously in personal combat with the Russians; he rescued an officer of the 30th Regiment who was surrounded by Russians, by shooting one and bayoneting another, and was observed in personal combat with the Russians inside the Redan for some time.

Captain Henry Jones was hit by a piece of shrapnel during the assault on the 5th Parallel and fell to the ground dangerously wounded. Assistant-Surgeon Thomas Hale of the 7th (Royal) Fusiliers remained with the officer when everyone but he and Lieutenant Hope had retreated. Later that day, after the regiment had retired to the trenches, he and Sergeant Charles Fisher of his regiment cleared the most advanced sap of the wounded and then carried into the sap, under heavy fire, several wounded men from the open ground.

Assistant-Surgeon William Sylvester and Corporal Robert Shields of the 23rd (Royal Welsh) Fusiliers went out under a heavy fire in front of the 5th Parallel, Right Attack, to a spot near the Redan where Lieutenant and Adjutant Douglas Dyneley, 23rd Fusiliers, was lying mortally wounded in a dangerous and exposed position. Under withering fire they dressed his wounds.

Sergeant Luke O'Connor, 23rd Fusiliers, who had already distinguished himself at the Alma, was shot through both thighs as he behaved with great gallantry during this part of the attack.

Sergeant Andrew Moynihan of the 90th (Perthshire) Light Infantry was one of the men who got into the Redan, where he personally encountered and killed five Russians, and rescued Lieutenant Swift and Ensign Maude from certain death. He received twelve wounds during this gallant action.

Captain Charles Lumley of the 97th (Earl of Ulster's) Regiment had been selected to lead a storming party, and he distinguished himself highly by his bravery, being among the first inside the work, where he fought fiercely. He was immediately engaged with three Russian gunners reloading a field piece, who attacked him. He shot two of them with his revolver, when he was knocked down by a stone, which stunned him for the moment, but, on recovery, he drew his sword, and was in the act of cheering his men on when he received a ball in his mouth, and he was brought back to the British lines wounded severely and in a bad state.

The British assault had failed. In a desperate attempt to save face, Colonel Simpson ordered that another assault was to be undertaken on the following morning. However, it never took place because the capture of the Malakoff prompted the Russians to form the opinion that further defence was futile and they decided to evacuate the south of Sebastopol.

For six hours, beginning at about six o'clock on the night of 8 September 1855, a constant stream of people with their wagons, carts and livestock swarmed across the pontoon bridge, covered by some riflemen and gun crews. As they retreated, they spiked their guns, blew up their ammunition magazines, booby-trapped the outer bastions and destroyed anything they thought would have been of use to the Allies. When everyone was across the bridge, they blew it up.

In what seems to have been the last act of bravery which would be rewarded with the Victoria Cross during operations around Sebastopol, Corporal John Ross, the engineer who had already performed two deeds worthy of the award, showed intrepid and devoted conduct in creeping to the Redan, where he witnessed the evacuation of Sebastopol. On his return he came upon a wounded man and brought him back to the British lines, and reported what he had seen.

Critical questions were asked in the House of Commons on 14 March 1856:

> Colonel French rose to ask the First Lord of the Treasury whether any inquiry had taken place, or was to take place, as to the causes which led to the failure of the attack on the Great Redan, at Sebastopol, by Her Majesty's troops, on the 8th of September last – a failure which had somewhat detracted, unjustly as far as the soldiers and regimental officers were concerned, from the glory acquired by the English army at the Alma, Balaklava, and Inkerman. His object in bringing the notice of the House was that the blame of that failure should rest on those to whom [it was] justly attributable.
>
> The arrangements preliminary to the assault on the Redan were notoriously and inexcusably defective; the trenches were not pushed on towards it, as they should have been, nor was there a place d'armes prepared where a force sufficient to have secured the success of the attack could have been stationed. It was not thus Marshal Pelissier acted in preparing for his assault on the Malakoff: his trenches were carried up to the walls of Sebastopol; he had a place d'armes sufficient to hold and which did hold 30,000 men. Had the same precaution been taken by the English commander-in-chief that was taken by the French, the result would have been the same – success in both cases. Nor was there any

reason why this should not have been done; there was sufficient time, and the difficulties of ground were not greater in one case than in the other. The dip between the Quarries and the Redan was not greater than that between the Mamelon and the Malakoff, and the ground was as easily worked.

In addition to our arrangements having been so defective, the attack was made by an insufficient force. Out of the large force under his command, General Simpson ordered but 5,000 men for this purpose. Every competent military authority, both English and French, declare that the supporting columns should have been at least 10,000 strong. Small as the force was, it was not used; one half of them never left the trenches. The troops who so gallantly made good their entrance into the Redan were left unsupported for upwards of an hour and a half to struggle as they best could against fearful odds and an overwhelming force. Nobly and gallantly did they do so; shamefully and disgracefully were they sacrificed. The General in Chief was three-quarters of a mile distant, separated by a deep ravine from the trenches, with which it was not possible for him to communicate, were he desirous of doing so. He left two officers in command, without any definite orders, to exercise their own discretion. The result, as was to be expected in every divided command, was that nothing was done, or attempted to be done.

The management of the whole affair was well described in a paper he held in his hand – it was the testimony of an eye-witness, who viewed the attack from Stony Hill – Here I found a French soldier seated on the ground, behind a heap of stones; he made room for me, and I sat down beside him. He told me that he had seen our gallant fellows get into the Redan, but said he had only seen one attacking party enter, and that they had suffered most severely in the approach. 'Are you sure they are inside?' I asked. 'Certain,' he replied, 'at the first pause of the wind you will see the musketry fire in the Redan.' When, after a few minutes, I caught sight of the Redan, I distinctly observed that there were two fires opposed to each other inside the works, ours the most stoutly maintained; at the same time, though the corpses lay thickly about the abattis and ditch, I could occasionally distinguish some of our men on the parapet, or in small and straggling numbers in the open. The space between the abattis and the Redan was perfectly bare of moving masses, and the Frenchman got into a violent passion. 'My God!' he said, 'where are your supports? Where are your reserves? Do they expect that handful of men I saw enter to maintain that place? It is impossible for them to do so. Depend on it you will lose the day unless reserves are sent up, and that quickly.'

Alas! They never came. Nearly an hour did that Frenchman and I sit there, and during the intervals we were able to distinguish objects, no one large body of men advanced to the support, though the fire was continued with great obstinacy. Had our attacking party been supported as they should have been in the Redan, it would have been held, and the escape of the remnant of the Russian army prevented; not a man of them could have crossed the bridge – they must have surrendered themselves prisoners of war.

What had been the conduct of Her Majesty's Government? They promoted and rewarded the General-in-Chief, made him a full General, gave him a regiment and a Grand Cross, and at the same time refused all recognition of the services of the regimental officers engaged because the attack was a failure, a decision which combined undue favouritism with glaring injustice, which declared that zeal and valour were to be disregarded, whilst neglect and incapacity were to be promoted and honoured.

He (Colonel French) should have preferred the inquiry should have been demanded by an officer of the line, but as it had not been, he felt it his duty to ask for it. Having lost a gallant and near relative who was killed at the head of his regiment in the Redan, having led them to the attack through that sea of fire, in a manner worthy of a British soldier – Colonel Hand-cock of the 97th – he trusted the House would excuse his asking for an inquiry, essential for the honour and reputation of the English army and for the satisfaction of the English people.

Viscount Palmerston said that on first receiving the account of the attack, his noble friend, Lord Panmure, wrote for further details. Those details were quite satisfactory, and entirely exonerated from blame all the persons who were concerned in the attack. He quite concurred with his honourable friend that so far from this day casting any slur upon British arms, it was honourable to the valour of both the officers and soldiers. He would only remind the House that the attack on the Redan was the result of a joint arrangement between the French and British officers, and that if the British troops did not succeed in that undertaking, so also the French troops failed in three other attacks on the same day. The difficulties in the way were very great. All the operations were intended to contribute to the taking of the principal point – the Malakoff; and, although one might lament the misfortunes which had occurred at other points, very probably the assault in this quarter might not have succeeded had not those attacks been made. So far from thinking that 8 September was any reproach to British arms, he thought that both that day and 18 June might be mentioned as days which shed lustre on the British army.

Charles Dickens was present at Portsmouth Docks when a ship brought in soldiers who had been wounded in the Crimea. Under the title 'Back from the Crimea', he recorded what he witnessed in his weekly journal *Household Words* for the last week in September 1855:

> Yesterday was a great day for the seaport where I live – the day of the landing of the convalescent sick and wounded from the trenches of the battlefields of the Crimea – a long, long line of wan pale warriors tottering to their resting place, the hospital; and those who could not walk borne after them on litters. This was not the first sight of this kind we have witnessed here, and it will not be the last by many. The deepest feelings of gratitude and commiseration are weakened not one wit within us; but the enthusiasm that requires novelty to awaken it has almost died out. No shouting crowds now follow these poor soldiers to the hospital gates – no flags wave from the windows – no cannon roar. We have found out other ways of welcome – there is a subscription list lying open at the Town Hall, where-to you may add your help in supplying books and papers to the invalids; and volunteers who understand the art and mystery of letter writing are plentiful by the sick beds to send for their disabled occupants a word of comfort homeward. Today a still more solemn scene took place, – the sick and wounded that were too ill yesterday – no convalescents, but men well nigh death's door – were brought back to their fatherland to die.
>
> The great three-decker lies in the offing that conveyed them from Scutari, watched by us these three days with dim eyes, a vast death ship and floating hospital between decks, and gay with flags and full of life above.
>
> There has been sad work at these dread landings of the wounded; but today at least were all things fitting and in readiness. The Royal Hampshire sent its hundred men or so to the Dockyard Pier with litters, and almost all its officers were in attendance. A score of hardy seamen too were there, contrasting strangely with the slight slim figures of the young militiamen, official people, with the fear of the *Times* before their eyes, surgeons and dockyard dignitaries. It is cold enough waiting upon

harbour piers for steam tugs, with the wind and tide against them, and a little leap-frog does not seem out of place among the gallant Hampshire men, but directly the first puff of smoke is seen above the Bastion, the order is given to 'fall in', – all eyes are directed to the approaching vessel, all hearts beat quickly, all faces lose their smiles.

First the dark dismal hull, and then the decks spread thick with dim white tarpaulins, whose shapes as they drew nearer, are as of sheets above the dead, and there the dying, perhaps dead men are, – the worst cases that would not bear moving underneath, but lie with heaps of blankets over them, and perhaps only a prominence observable at heads and feet. The vessel is brought alongside, and four tars descend the narrow plank to bear the sick men, feet foremost. The litters cannot here be used, so bad are all these cases, but through the thick canvas of these cots great poles are inserted, and shouldering these with difficulty, and keeping in step for the sufferer's sake, which is hard work also, the sailors land their burden. Sometimes from under the great piles of clothes an ashy white thin face just shows itself, or rather is shown by chance, for the eyes are lustreless, and expresses no gleam of interest. The heavy moustache and the military cap, still worn as bed gear, contrast most painfully with the dependent prostrate condition of their wearers. What expression yet remains to some is still a thoughtful cast – they have seen and suffered much these last six months, and want and danger are such teachers as the most careless may not disregard. The bearers are warned of all impediments; and tenderly and skilfully do they lift their heavy burden, and the 'wheelers' start with the left foot, and the 'leaders' with the right, and so slow-march to the hospital. Now, too, must the less dangerous cases be brought from between decks, and transferred from their cots to litters. Each man is dressed in his great coat, and his knapsack lies beside him, as though he should presently rise and walk; but it is easy to see there is no walking for him these many weeks, though his eyes are bright with happiness, and he will answer softly if you address his ear; and these, too, are carried to the sick wards, to join their less fortunate brethren.

These wards are warm and comfortable, with a fire at each end of them. 'We have not seen a fire since we left old England,' say many of the sufferers; and medicines are in plenty and attendance good, though medical help is still greatly needed; but things were not so at first, by any means. Ragged and swarming with vermin (as we are credibly informed) did our poor fellows lie for days; for there was signing and countersigning to be effected, and the proper channel to be quite decided upon before the official mind could rightly understand the matter, and provide clean linen. Let however, bygones be bygones. Now, we repeat, were there a larger medical stuff (especially in the matter of dressers), all would be well.

Accompany us, then, with some of the officers from the Royal Hampshire, and bring pen, ink, and paper, and a little writing-case; seat yourself down on one of the deal stools that stand beside each bed, and hear a story of the war, quite un-pictorial, and without rose-colour, flame-colour, drum accompaniment, or any such thing – and let the look of each sad reciter be before you when men prate of glory for glory's sake; and believe him, as he gasps upon his scanty pallet in the bare white-washed room, without one friend about him, and (but for you) unable to appraise one of his fate, when he affirms that this is Eden, Paradise, Heaven, to what he has endured these six months. Be sure this is the reality of the whole matter – war stripped of its pomp and circumstance.

First is a foot-soldier, wounded by a shell in the knee, who thinks he would like to write to his first-cousin. The first-cousin is his only relative, and does not know even of his having volunteered for foreign service. He is not sure about the direction but knows that it is somewhere in the county Clare. In the next bed a woe-begone sad creature answers your question in a hollow, despairing voice: 'I have no friends,' he says, and 'Let me alone.' The brain of this poor fellow is affected, and we can be of no service to him at present, so pass on. There is a boy of only seventeen wounded at the battle of the Alma. His face is quite beautiful, round, and healthy-looking. He seems quite happy and contented, and answers cheerfully enough that he would wish to write to father or mother, and tell them that he had lost his leg; such a letter he dictates as would shame a whole army of philosophers – when he gets used to 'those', he says, pointing to the crutches by his bed's head, he will do well enough.

The next case is one of dysentery. A giant of a hussar – the skeleton of one at least – all shaggy hair and eyes, with cough accompanied by moaning, would like to let his wife and children know about him; they have not heard since he went out five months ago; they will not see him again in this world, he feels sure; and truly his state is very sad; his attenuated legs find even the weight of bedclothes insupportable; he can only fetch his breath to speak at intervals; has been deadly ill these six weeks, as far as he could take note of lagging time; would have sent home money long ago, but that they robbed him in Scutari hospital of all he had – which they cut from around his naked neck, where he wore it in a bag. There was some more due to him if he had his rights, and they should have it all; they must have wanted it, he knew, through this sad winter. Yes, he was in the great horse-charge that was so famous – borne up by the men around him through the rain of bullets – borne and back again – to the Russian guns and back again – he means, without much thought of danger; there was no time. He does not wish that to be set down in the letter; said it to inform us only. We have written all he wishes; and so, with a 'Thank ye, thank ye,' he sinks back in his bed and groans. The fifth place has no tenant; its latest occupant was borne out yesterday to a still narrower resting place.

The sixth is a maimed man; his right arm was shot off at Inkerman. He was in all the previous battles. This man talks freely of the war and without pain in utterance, which most can do (and let it be kept in remembrance by all those making themselves useful to the sick, not to allow their compassion to be sacrificed to curiosity). The fearfullest thing of a battlefield is the treading upon the bodies of the fallen. The thunder of the guns and the flashes, the trembling of the ground under the horses, seemed as though heaven and earth were coming together; but the stepping on a wounded man – that was the worst; before the fighting it was not unpleasant, perhaps, and after, it was a dreadful time – but the fighting itself was enough to flush a man a great while of excitement and madness; often and often he used to think of it as he lay in bed and on board ship.

The seventh bed is occupied by a living being at present, and that is all we can call the shadowy form; the eyes are sunken into the head, and all the features have the sharpness of death. He has ceased to disturb the ward (as he did at first) with coughs and groans, and in a few hours will rid them of his presence. We must here mention that the want of a smaller apartment for the reception of those who cannot cease from coughing and expressions of pain is much felt in all our hospitals here.

In striking contrast to this dying man is his neighbour, the eighth and last-patient of the line; he has lost three fingers of his left hand by a cannon-ball, and has received a fracture of the leg, but is getting on capitally, and is in the highest spirits. He has no occasion to tell us he is an Irish man, for he has an accent as broad as from here to Cork; indeed it is with the greatest difficulty we can understand what he wishes us to write; it takes us five minutes to unravel 'respects to enquiring friends' (always 'respects', however near the relationships) from the mass of r's which he is pleased to insert amongst that sentence. Russia, as far as he knows of, is absolutely good for nothing: except, indeed, he must say, for grapes and lice. Amidst a heap of extraneous matter of this kind, he writes to his mother in Tipperary, 'Don't let our Patrick, mother, go for a soldier; not that I mind for myself,' he says, pointing to his shattered hand, 'but one's enough.'

The Most Victoria Crosses

The Distinguished Conduct Medal was instituted on 4 December 1854 for gallantry in the field performed by Other Ranks of the British Army, and the Conspicuous Gallantry Medal was established on 13 August 1855 as the naval equivalent of the DCM, but there was no universal medal that could be awarded for all ranks of the British armed forces. However, stories of the gallantry being performed by her soldiers in the Crimea, set against reports from the first war correspondents of their neglect and suffering, which caused no little discontent among the British public, prompted Queen Victoria to try to do something within her power to give them due recognition. Consequently, the Victoria Cross was instituted by her royal warrant on 29 January 1856, and 111 men who fought in the Crimean campaign became the first recipients for 'Conspicuous bravery and devotion to country in the presence of the enemy.' Rank, long service or wound was to have no special influence on who qualified for the award – only death!

Queen Victoria took a great interest in the establishment of the award and in the design of the medal. Prince Albert suggested that it should be named after her, and the original motto was to have been *For the Brave*, but Victoria was quite rightly of the opinion that this would lead to the inference that only those who have been awarded the cross are considered to be brave, and decided that *For Valour* would be more suitable. The design was not to be particularly ornate and not of high metallic value. All the medals have been cast from the bronze cascabels believed to be from two guns, said to be of Chinese origin, which the British had captured from the Russians at Sebastopol. The original ribbons for the medal were blue for the navy and crimson for the army. Queen Victoria thought that 'the person decorated with the Victoria Cross might properly be allowed to bear some distinctive mark after their name'. She pointed out that at that time 'VC' meant Vice Chancellor, and she suggested either 'DVC' (Decorated with the Victoria Cross) or 'BVC' (Bearer of the Victoria Cross). However, in the end 'VC' was finally agreed on. On its institution, it carried an annuity of £10. Many rank-and-file soldiers who gained the Victoria Cross are known to have felt great satisfaction from the fact that military regulations state that all officers must salute a man of any rank who passes by them wearing the Victoria Cross on his breast.

The first man to perform a deed which would be rewarded with the Victoria Cross was Mate Charles Davis Lucas on 21 June 1854, whilst serving aboard HMS *Hecla* during the bombardment of Bomarsund in the Baltic Sea. The first eighty-five recipient announcements were published in a supplement to the *London Gazette* for 24 February 1857, most of them extremely understated. The first named was Lieutenant William Buckley of HMS *Miranda*, Royal Navy. The first investiture took place at Hyde Park in London on 26 June 1857, when sixty-two Crimean veterans received the medal from the Queen herself, in a ceremony which is said to have taken only about ten minutes. She performed the deed in the rather awkward position of sidesaddle on a horse, presumably because most of the men were tall and it would be easier for her to reach them, and she actually pinned the medal to the skin of Commander Raby, who was first in the queue and therefore became the first man ever to wear the Victoria Cross – literally! It seems she didn't get much better with practice, as she did it again to Lieutenant Graham, who was twenty-fourth in line. Some men were dressed in plain clothes, another as a gatekeeper and Constable George Walters was wearing his police uniform. The Queen recorded in her diary: 'It was indeed a most proud, gratifying day.' However, even after seeing men in the line with limbs and eyes missing, and other disfigurements, it is unlikely that she or any British civilians really understood what horrors they had witnessed and experienced to gain the award.

Numerous sources have stated that the most Victoria Crosses awarded for a single action were gained for the defence of Rorke's Drift on 22/23 January 1879, during the Zulu War. However, while the total of eleven Victoria Crosses for that battle has never been equalled since (and it did produce the record of seven Victoria Crosses awarded to one regiment for a single action, they being the 24th Foot, now amalgamated into the Royal Welsh), my original research from 1992 to 1994 for compiling *The Chronological Roll of the Victoria Cross* first brought to light that there were three prior superlatives.

At that time I carried out a comprehensive study of all the citations for the Victoria Cross which were announced in the *London Gazette* from 24 February 1857 to date, and my findings were published in my 1994 book *Deeds of Valour*, announcing that the superlative award of the Victoria Cross for a single action is the twenty for the first attack on the Great Redan at Sebastopol on 18 June 1855, during the Crimean War. This is followed by the seventeen awarded for the assault on the Sikandar Bagh at Lucknow on 16 November 1857, and the twelve (probably thirteen) for the second attack on the Redan on 8 September 1855.

Some military enthusiasts I have consulted still want to believe that the eleven Victoria Crosses awarded to the defenders of Rorke's Drift should be recognised as the highest, based on the fact that it was an individual fight, while the assault on the Sikandar Bagh was part of a continuing battle (the twenty-four Victoria Crosses gained at Lucknow on 16/17 November 1857 was the most for a single 24-hour period), and the men who were awarded the Victoria Cross for both attacks on the Redan performed other acts of gallantry which were recorded. My theory is that if an action is mentioned in a Victoria Cross citation, then it should be included in the total number for that particular action, and should not be devalued because other deeds are quoted in the same citation.

* * *

The following are the citations published in the *London Gazette* on 24 February, 5 May and 25 September 1857 and 2 June 1858, which make reference to the assault on the Great Redan at Sebastopol on 18 June 1855:

1. Captain William Peel, Naval Brigade

- 'For having, on 18 October 1854, at the greatest possible risk, taken up a live shell, the fuse still burning, from among several powder cases, outside the magazine, and thrown it over the parapet (the shell bursting as it left his hands), thereby saving the magazine, and the lives of those immediately around it.'
- 'On 5 November 1854, at the battle of Inkerman, for joining the officers of the Grenadier Guards and assisting in defending the colours of that regiment when hard pressed at the Sandbag Battery.'
- *'On 18 June 1855, for volunteering to lead the ladder party at the assault on the Redan, and carrying the first ladder until wounded.'*

2. Midshipman Edward St John Daniel, Naval Brigade

- 'For answering a call for volunteers to bring in powder for the Battery, from a wagon in a very exposed position under a destructive fire, a shot having disabled the horses.'
- 'For accompanying Captain Peel at the battle of Inkerman as aide-de-camp.'
- *'For devotion to his leader, Captain Peel, on 18 June 1855, in tying a tourniquet on his arm on the glacis of the Redan, whilst exposed to a very heavy fire.'*

3. Commander Henry Raby, 4. Captain of the Forecastle John Taylor, and 5. Botswain's Mate Henry Curtis, all Naval Brigade

- 'On 18 June 1855, immediately after the assault on Sebastopol, a soldier of the 57th Regiment, who had been shot through both legs, was observed sitting up and calling for assistance. Climbing over the breastwork of the advanced sap, Commander Raby and the two seamen proceeded upwards of seventy yards across the open space towards *the salient angle of the Redan*, and in spite of the heavy fire which was still continuing, succeeded in carrying the wounded soldier to a place of safety, at the immediate risk of their own lives.'

6. Gunner and Driver Thomas Arthur, Royal Artillery

- 'When in charge of the magazine in one of the left advanced batteries of the Right Attack on 7 June 1855, when the Quarries were taken, he, of his own accord, carried barrels of infantry ammunition for the 7th Fusiliers several time during the evening across the open.
- '*He volunteered for and formed one of the spiking-party of Artillery at the assault on the Redan, 18 June 1855.*'

7. Captain Howard Elphinstone, Royal Engineers

- 'For fearless conduct, in having, on the night after the unsuccessful *attack on the Redan, 18 June 1855*, volunteered to command a party of volunteers, who proceeded to search for and bring back the scaling ladders left behind after the repulse; and while successfully performing the task of rescuing trophies from the Russians, Captain Elphinstone conducted a persevering search, close to the enemy, for wounded men, twenty of whom he rescued and brought back to the trenches.'

8. Lieutenant Gerald Graham, Royal Engineers

- 'Determined gallantry at the head of a ladder party *at the assault on the Redan, 18 June 1855.*'
- 'Devoted heroism in sallying out of the trenches on numerous occasions and bringing in wounded officers and men.'

9. Colour Sergeant Peter Leitch, Royal Engineers

- 'For conspicuous gallantry *in the assault on the Redan, 18 June 1855*, when, after approaching it with the leading ladders, he formed a caponniere across the ditch, as well as a ramp, by fearlessly tearing down gabions from the parapet, and placing and filling them until he was disabled from wounds.'

10. Sapper John Perie, Royal Engineers
- 'Conspicuous valour in leading the sailors with the ladders to *the storming of the Redan, 18 June 1855*. He was invaluable on that day.'
- 'Devoted conduct in rescuing a wounded man from the open, although he himself had just previously been wounded by a bullet in the side.'

11. Lieutenant William Hope, 7th (Royal) Fusiliers
- 'After the troops had retreated on the morning of *18 June 1855*, Lieutenant W. Hope being informed by the late Sergeant-Major William Bacon, who was himself wounded, that Lieutenant and Adjutant Hobson was lying outside the trenches badly wounded, went out to look for him, and found him lying in an old agricultural ditch running towards *the left flank of the Redan*. He then returned and got four men to bring him in. Finding, however, that Lieutenant Hobson could not be removed without a stretcher, he then ran back across the open to Egerton's Pit, where he procured one, and carried it to where Lieutenant Hobson was lying. All this was done under a very heavy fire from the Russian batteries.'

12. Private Matthew Hughes, 7th (Royal) Fusiliers
- 'on 7 June 1855, at the storming of the Quarries, for twice going for ammunition, under a heavy fire, across the open ground; he also went to the front and brought in Private John Hampton, who was lying severely wounded; and *on 18 June 1855, he volunteered to bring in Lieutenant Hobson, 7th Royal Fusiliers*, who was lying severely wounded, and, in the act of doing so, was severely wounded himself.'

13. Corporal Philip Smith, 17th (Leicestershire) Regiment
- 'For repeatedly going out in front of the advance trenches *against the Great Redan, on 18 June 1855*, under a very heavy fire, after the column had retired from the assault, and bringing in wounded comrades.'

14. Captain Thomas Esmonde, 18th (Royal Irish) Regiment
- 'For having, *after being engaged in the attack on the Redan, on 18 June 1855*, repeatedly assisted at great personal risk under a heavy fire of shell and grape, in rescuing wounded men from exposed situations. And also, while in command of a covering party, two days after, for having rushed with the most prompt and daring gallantry to a spot where a fire-ball from the enemy had just been lodged, which he effectually extinguished, before it had betrayed the position of the working party under his protection, thus saving it from a murderous fire of shell and grape, which was immediately opened upon the spot where the fire-ball had fallen.'

15. Private John Joseph Sims, 34th (Cumberland) Regiment
- 'For having, *on 18 June 1855*, after the regiment had retired into the trenches from *the assault on the Redan*, gone out into the open ground, under a heavy fire, in broad daylight, and brought in wounded soldiers outside the trenches.'

16. Sergeant William McWheeney, 44th (East Essex) Regiment
- 'Volunteered as sharpshooter at the commencement of the siege, and was in charge of the party of the 44th Regiment; was always vigilant and active, and signalised himself on 20 October 1854, when one of his party, Private John Kenne, 44th Regiment, was dangerously wounded in the Worontsoff Road; at the time the sharpshooters were repulsed from the Quarries by overwhelming numbers, Sergeant McWheeney, on his return, took the wounded man on his back, and brought him to a place of safety. This was under a very heavy fire.'
- 'He was also the means of saving the life of Corporal Courtney. This man was one of the sharpshooters, and was severely wounded in the head, 5 December 1854. Sergeant McWheeney brought him from under fire, and dug up a slight cover with his bayonet, where the two remained until dark, when they retired.'
- 'Sergeant McWheeney volunteered for the advance guard of General Eyre's Brigade *in the Cemetery, Redan, on 18 June 1855*, and was never absent from duty during the war.'

17. Colour Sergeant George Gardiner, 57th (West Middlesex) Regiment
- 'For distinguished coolness and gallantry upon the occasion of a sortie by the enemy on 22 March 1855, and when he was acting as Orderly-Sergeant of the Field Officers of the trenches – Left Attack upon Sebastopol – in having rallied the covering parties which had been driven in by the Russians, thus regaining and keeping possession of the trenches.
- Also, for unflinching and devoted courage in the *attack on the Redan on the 18 June 1855*, in having remained, and encouraged others to remain, in the holes made by the explosions of shells, from whence, by making parapets of the dead bodies of their comrades, they kept up a continuous fire until their ammunition was exhausted, thus clearing the enemy from the parapet of the Redan. This was done under a fire in which nearly half the officers and a third of the rank and file of the party of the regiment were placed *hors de combat*.'

18. Sergeant John Park, 77th (East Middlesex) Regiment
- 'For conspicuous bravery at the battles of Alma and Inkerman.'
- 'Highly distinguished at the taking of the Russian rifle pits, on the night of 19 April 1855. His valour during that attack called forth the approbation of the late Colonel Egerton. He was severely wounded.'
- 'Remarked for determined resolution on *both attacks on the Redan.*'

19. Private John Alexander, 90th Light Infantry
- '*After the attack on the Redan, on 18 June 1855*, he went out of the trenches under very heavy fire, and brought in several wounded men.'
- Also, when with a working party in the most advanced trench, on 6 September 1855, went out in front of the trenches, under a very heavy fire, and assisted in bringing in Captain Buckley, Scots Fusilier Guards, lying dangerously wounded.'

20. Lieutenant John Simpson Knox, Rifle Brigade
- 'When serving as a sergeant in the Scots Fusilier Guards, Lieutenant Knox was conspicuous in his exertions in reforming the ranks of the Guards at the battle of the Alma.'
- 'Subsequently, when in the Rifle Brigade, he volunteered for the ladder party in *the attack on the Redan, 18 June 1855*, and (in the words of Captain Blackett, under whose command he was) behaved admirably, remaining on the field until twice wounded.'

Inkerman VCs

The total of twenty Victoria Crosses had been equalled by those gained during the Battle of Inkerman on 5 November 1854. However, the battle was fought over an extensive area of mist-shrouded rough terrain and the regiments were so far apart that the troops did not know how other units were doing, and it was more like several separate battles than just one. For instance, the Victoria Cross actions fought at Home Ridge, the Sandbag Battery and the Lancaster Battery/Inkerman Caves were a long way from each other, and must arguably be considered to have been stand-alone actions.

If all the Inkerman actions are to be added together, then it is my conclusion that the actions such as those fought at the Sikandar Bagh (17 VCs) and the Shah Najeff (5 VCs) at Lucknow on 16 November 1857, and the actions at Isandlwana (3 VCs) and Rorke's Drift (11 VCs), fought during the Zulu War on 22 January 1879, should be considered in the same light.

The Sandbag Battery – First Attack (5)
Lieutenant Mark Walker, 30th (Cambridgeshire) Regiment
- 'On 5 November 1854, at Inkerman, Lieutenant Walker jumped over a wall in the face of two battalions of Russian infantry which were marching towards it. This act was to encourage the men, by example, to advance against such odds – which they did and succeeded in driving back both battalions.'

Captain Hugh Rowlands, 41st (Welch) Regiment and Private John McDermond, 47th (Lancashire) Regiment
- 'On 5 November 1854, at Inkerman, Captain Rowlands and Private John McDermond rescued Colonel William O'Grady Haly of the 47th Regiment who had been wounded and surrounded by Russian soldiers.'

Sergeant George Walters, 49th (Hertfordshire) Regiment
- 'Sergeant George Walters highly distinguished himself at the Sandbag Battery, battle of Inkerman, in having rescued Brigadier-General Adams, CB, when surrounded by Russians, one of whom he bayoneted.'

Private Thomas Beach, 55th (Westmoreland) Regiment
- 'On 5 November 1854, at the battle of Inkerman, when on piquet duty, Private Beach attacked several Russians who were plundering Lt-Colonel Carpenter, 41st Regiment, who was lying wounded on the ground. He killed two of the Russians, and protected Lt-Colonel Carpenter until the arrival of some men of the 41st Regiment.'

The Sandbag Battery – Second Attack (6)
Colonel Hugh Henry Manvers Percy, 3rd Grenadier Guards
- 'At a moment when the Guards were some distance from the Sandbag Battery at the battle of Inkerman, Colonel Percy charged singly into the Battery, followed immediately by the Guards; the embrasures of the battery, as also the parapet, were held by the Russians who kept up a most severe fire of musketry.'

Captain Charles Russell and Private Anthony Palmer, 3rd Grenadier Guards
- 'On 5 November 1854, Brevet Major Russell offered to dislodge a party of Russians from the Sand-bag Battery, if any one would follow him; Sergeant Norman, Privates Anthony Palmer, and Bailey (who was killed) volunteered the first. The attack succeeded.'

Captain Robert James Lindsay, Scots (Fusilier) Guards
- 'At Inkerman, at a most trying moment, he, with a few men, charged a party of Russians, driving them back, and running one through the body himself.'

Captain William Peel and **Midshipman Edward St John Daniel, Naval Brigade**
- 'On 5 November at the battle of Inkerman joined some of the officers of the Grenadier Guards and helped to defend the colours of the regiment when they were hard-pressed.'

The assault on Home Ridge (4)

Lieutenant Frederick Miller, Royal Artillery
- 'For having, at the battle of Inkerman, personally attacked three Russians, and with the gunners of his division of the battery, prevented the Russians from doing mischief to the guns which they had surrounded.'

Sergeant Major Andrew Henry, Royal Artillery
- 'For defending the guns of his battery [G Battery, 2nd Division] against overwhelming numbers of the enemy at the battle of Inkerman, and continuing to do so until he had received twelve bayonet wounds.'

Sergeant John Park, 77th (East Middlesex) Regiment
- 'On 20 September and 5 November 1854 at the battle of the Alma, and at Inkerman, Sergeant Park showed great bravery.'

Lieutenant Henry Hugh Clifford, 2nd Rifle Brigade
- 'For conspicuous courage at the battle of Inkerman, in leading a charge and killing one of the enemy with his sword, disabling another, and saving the life of a soldier.'

The Lancaster Battery/Inkerman Caves (5)

Mate William Nathan Wright Hewett, Naval Brigade
- 'On 5 November, at the battle of Inkerman he again acted with great bravery.'

Seamen James Gorman, Thomas Reeves and **Mark Scholefield, Naval Brigade**
- 'On 5 November 1854 at the battle of Inkerman, when the Right Lancaster Battery was attacked and many of the soldiers were wounded, Seamen Gorman, Reeves and Scholefield mounted the defence work banquette and, under withering attack from the enemy, kept up a rapid, repulsing fire.

Their muskets were re-loaded for them by the wounded soldiers under the parapet and eventually the enemy fell back and gave no more trouble.'

Corporal John Prettyjohns, Royal Marines
- 'Reported for gallantry at the Battle of Inkerman, having placed himself in an advanced position; and noticed, as having himself shot four Russians.'

A Selection of Tributes and Commemorations

I have not included biographies for some of the men who took part in the assault because they went on to be among the most influential and best-known soldiers during the Victorian era, and their lives and careers have been considerably documented. They include Midshipman (later Field Marshal) Henry Evelyn Wood VC (1838–1919) of the Royal Navy; Lieutenant (later Major General) Charles George Gordon (1833–1885) of the Royal Engineers; and Captain (later Field Marshal) Garnet Joseph Wolseley (1833–1913), who was attached to the Royal Engineers at Sebastopol. Their names will be familiar to all students of Victorian military history.

Royal Navy (Naval Brigade)
Commander Henry James Raby VC
Henry James Raby was born on 26 September 1827, at Boulogne in France. He was one of six children of the well-known influential Llanelli industrialist, Arthur Tournour Raby (1789–1856), and his wife Henrietta Jane (1792–1880) of Llanelli in South Wales. A street in the town bears the family name. His grandfather Alexander Raby had invested his entire wealth in the local iron and coal industries, which failed during the depression after the Napoleonic Wars, and Henry's father had to travel to France after the family home, 'Plas Uchaf', (Upper Hall) in the village of Furnace was destroyed by fire. Henry was educated at Sherborne School in Dorset, where he was a member of Abbey House. He left Sherborne in 1838 and finished his education at Greenwich.

Henry Raby joined the Royal Navy on 8 March 1842 as a volunteer first class on HMS *Monarch*. He was one of the men put ashore at Xanthus, and helped with the removal and embarking of the Xanthian Marbles for the British Museum in 1842. He served as a mate from 7 March 1848 until 14 January 1850, at various times with HMS *Rodney*, HMS *Trafalgar*, HMS *Victory*, HMS *Ocean* and HMS *Terrible*. He was promoted to lieutenant on 15 January

1850 and from 2 October of that year he served aboard HMS *Wasp*, a 100hp screw steam sloop, carrying out anti-slavery operations along the west coast of Africa. He was then sent on active service to the East.

The award of a Victoria Cross to Commander Raby was announced in the *London Gazette* on 24 February 1857, and he was the first man to receive the medal at the first investiture. He also received the Crimea Medal with *Inkerman* and *Sebastopol* clasps, the French Legion of Honour, the Turkish Order of the Medjidie (5th Class), the Turkish Crimea Medal and the Sardinian Medal of Valour. Lieutenant D'Aeth, the son of an admiral, died of cholera at the Cossack Bay Hospital on 7 August 1855, and therefore did not receive the Victoria Cross for his part in the action.

Henry Raby was promoted to commander two days after the action at the Redan in recognition of his bravery. Described as 'A very active officer, with considerable knowledge of affairs on the coast of Africa,' Henry took command of HMS *Medusa* on 1 August 1856 and then HMS *Weber* on 12 October 1859. He commanded HMS *Alecto* from 27 January 1860, playing a prominent part in the suppression of the slave trade on the west coast of Africa, where he was present at the attack on, and destruction of, Porto Novo in Dahomey. He was wounded during these operations on 23 April 1861, and he was frequently mentioned in despatches. He received the thanks of the Foreign Office for the conclusion of a treaty with the African chiefs of the Old Calabar River, which had been one of the main centres for the slave trade. He was promoted captain for his services on 24 November 1862. He commanded HMS *Adventure* on the China Station from 22 June 1868 to 18 January 1871, when he retired from active service.

Henry married Judith (1831–1914), daughter of Colonel Watkin Forster of Holt Manor, Trowbridge, in Wiltshire, on 9 December 1863, at Bradford in Wiltshire. A son named Montague was born on 1 November 1865, followed by a daughter in 1867, Arthur in 1869 and a son named Henry who died at the age of 9 at Honfleur in France. Montague became a captain in the Royal Artillery and died in Bath on 21 September 1897. He is buried with his father.

In 1875 Henry was reported to be living at Crembourne House on Nightingale Road in Southsea, Hampshire. Four years later he moved briefly to Bath and then returned to Southsea, where he lived at 6 Clarendon Parade. The 1881 census records him as having settled at 8 Clarence Parade. He was made Companion to the Order of the Bath (CB) on 29 May 1875 and was appointed rear admiral on 21 March 1878. In July 1878 he returned for a nostalgic trip to Llanelli, where he visited Raby Street and Forge Row, and received a warm welcome from the residents. He also visited the burnt-out ruins of the old family home.

Henry and his wife were involved in various charitable duties in Southsea, and they were listed for various appointments concerning the Royal Seamen and Marines Orphanage in Queen Street, and the Home for Sick Children at 2 Ryde View. Henry was also chairman of the Portsmouth and Hayling Lifeboat Committee from 1885 until his death.

When Judith died, she was buried in St Mary's Churchyard in Bathwick, and Henry's name appears on her headstone. He died of senile decay at his home on 13 February 1907, aged 79, and he was buried at Highland Road Cemetery in Portsmouth. There is a headstone at his grave, a memorial plaque at Holt parish church, and a brass tablet dedicated to him at the entrance to Llanelli town hall. Having become a club member in 1871, he is one of four Crimean VCs named on the memorial in the corridor of the Royal Naval and Royal Albert Yacht Club in Portsmouth, which was unveiled by the Duke of Edinburgh in 2007. His medals were once displayed at the Royal Naval Museum, until being acquired by Lord Ashcroft in 2011, and they are now displayed on rotation at the Lord Ashcroft Gallery, as part of the 'Extraordinary Heroes' exhibition at the Imperial War Museum in London.

Captain William Peel VC
William Peel was born on 2 November 1824 at 12 Great Stanhope Street in Mayfair, London. He was the third son and fourth child of the statesman and ex-Prime Minister Robert Peel (1788–1850), who served two terms of office from 1834 to 1846, and was famous for establishing the Metropolitan Police force, and his wife Julia, daughter of Sir John Floyd. He was educated at the Reverend Francis Joseph Faithfull's boarding school at The Parsonage in Hatfield, and then, like his father, he was sent to Harrow School (1837–1838); he would become the first Old Harrovian to gain the Victoria Cross. His grandfather had become Member of Parliament for Tamworth in 1790, and the family home was at Drayton Manor in Tamworth.

William's father stated that the boy had wanted to go to sea from the age of 3, and at the age of only 13 he entered the Royal Navy, joining his first ship HMS *Princess Charlotte* as a midshipman on 7 April 1838. After serving on several ships in the Mediterranean, he took part in the Turko-Egyptian War of 1839–1841, being present at the bombardment and capture of Acre in November 1840, for which he received the Naval General Service Medal with *Acre* clasp and the St Jean D'Acre Medal. He then spent some time with the royal yacht *William and Mary*.

Britain wished to expand its commercial influence in China, but the Chinese authorities resented the use of opium by the merchants of the 'Fan Kwei' – foreign devils – and they destroyed about £2 million worth of the crop. This led to a declaration of war with China, and Captain Peel joined *Cambrian 36* for service in the First China War in June 1840. The British eventually reached the outskirts of the ancient city of Nankin on 9 August 1842, where a demonstration of force was enough to bring the Chinese to see reason, after which most of the main Chinese ports were opened to British trade and Hong Kong was ceded to Britain.

After returning to London, William enrolled in the Gunnery School at HMS *Excellent* on the Thames in Woolwich, for a fourteen-month course. However, he finished the course in only four months and his father had to make statements to prove that he had not used his influence to gain any advantages for his ambitious son. He received his commission as lieutenant on 13 May 1844, a week after he passed the course.

William was in the government steam yacht *Black Eagle* that brought Tsar Nicholas to the UK on a state visit. When the *America 50* was sent to investigate unrest between American and Canadian settlers in the Oregon Territory, Peel went with her and carried out the survey for the Hudson Bay Company to try to settle the dispute. He was promoted commander on 27 June 1846 and was given command of the twelve-gun sloop *Daring*, in which he went to South America. He was promoted captain on 10 January 1850. He applied unsuccessfully to join the expedition to try to find Sir John Franklin, and he published *A Ride through the Nubian Desert* in June 1852, which chronicles his travels there in 1851.

William purchased a somewhat neglected estate that stood between the villages of Sandy and Potton in Bedfordshire, where he oversaw the renovation and enlargement of the house, brought land under cultivation and laid out gardens. When the Great Northern Railway opened nearby in 1850, he decided to finance the construction of a new Sandy and Potton Railway branch line.

In October 1852 William commissioned the frigate HMS *Diamond*, which was attached to the Mediterranean Fleet, and when the Crimean War broke out he was sent to the Black Sea Fleet, and joined HMS *Leander* on 6 January 1855.

One of his ADCs, Midshipman Evelyn Wood of HMS *Queen*, who fought alongside Captain Peel in the Crimea, stated in his memoirs: 'I was evidently much struck with Captain Peel's appearance and manners, for I recorded in boyish language, "Captain Peel, very intelligent, sharp as a needle; I never saw a more perfect gentleman. His looks and bearing were greatly in his favour, for both in face and figure there was an appearance of what sporting men, in describing well-bred horses, call quality."' Wood went on to win the Victoria Cross during the Indian Mutiny, and rose to the rank of field marshal, being knighted for his military service.

Captain Peel was sent to the Therapia Hospital, but his wound would not heal and he was invalided home, where he was given a civic reception at Tamworth town hall. During this time the Sandy and Potton Railway, known locally as Captain Peel's Railway, was opened by his mother in 1857, and William named one of the steam engines *Shannon* after his ship. He was the first of nineteen Old Harrovians to be awarded the Victoria Cross when it was announced in the *London Gazette* for 24 February 1857. He was also entitled to the Crimea Medal with *Inkerman* and *Sebastopol* clasps, the French Legion of Honour (4th Class), the Turkish Order of the Medjidie (3rd Class), the Turkish Crimea Medal and the Sardinian Medal of Military Valour. He was also appointed Knight Commander, Order of the Bath (KCB). However, he did not live to wear the medals.

The 51-gun steam frigate HMS *Shannon* had been launched at Portsmouth in 1855, and she sailed for service in the China War under Captain Peel. However, she was diverted to Calcutta, where Peel formed a Naval Brigade from its sailors for active service during the Indian Mutiny, now referred to as the Sepoy Rebellion. British forces had marched to the relief of the Lucknow garrison in September 1857, only to find that the enemy forces were too strong and, as they could not break out again, they too came under siege.

A second relief force was sent in November, including Peel's unit, armed with eight heavy guns and two rocket-launchers mounted on carts. They fought their first action at Kujwa on 1 November, and as the British advanced through Lucknow they battered several strong masonry fortresses. This included a large stone compound known as the Sikandar Bagh, which contained about two thousand rebels. Captain Peel's unit played a major part in breaching the thick walls of the defences, and four members of Peel's Brigade received the Victoria Cross for their valour. The total number of Victoria Crosses gained for the storming of the Sikandar Bagh was seventeen, which is only surpassed by the twenty at the first assault on the Redan. Peel's Brigade followed Sir Colin Campbell's Oudh campaign, and at the final capture of Lucknow in March 1858 Captain Peel was severely wounded when a musket ball shattered his thigh and upper leg. He was transported to Cawnpore on a dhoolie that had previously been used to carry a smallpox victim, and in his weakened state he too contracted the disease. He was taken to the house of the Reverend Moore, where he and his wife did all they could to keep him comfortable. He said mournfully: 'If I were in England the Queen would send her own physician to look after me; here I can scarcely get any attention.'

Sir William died on 27 April 1858, aged 33, and was buried in the Old British Cemetery at Mirpur, Cawnpore (Kanpur). The inscription reads: 'To the memory of William Peel. His name will be dear to the British inhabitants of India, to whose succour he came in the hour of need. He was one of England's most devoted sons. With all the talents of a brace and skilful sailor, he combined the virtues of a humble, sincere Christian. This stone is erected over his remains by his military friends in India, and several of the inhabitants in Calcutta.' The walls and the gate of the cemetery still exist, but most of the interior has been built on.

William Peel's name is recorded on the family headstone in Deansgrange Cemetery in Dublin, where there is also a memorial to HMS *Shannon*. He has a statue at St Swithun's Church at Sandy, where there is also a Sir William Peel public house; copies of this statue are in Flagstaff House at Barrackpore in India and in the National Maritime Museum at Greenwich. A plaque placed at the headquarters of the RSPB at The Lodge in Sandy in 2008 commemorates the 150th anniversary of Captain Peel's death. There is a memorial to Captain Peel and the Naval Brigade of HMS *Shannon* on the seafront at Southsea. There is an anchor and chain inside one of the entrances to Tamworth Castle which is said to have been brought back from the Crimea by Sir William. The *Shannon* locomotive is preserved at the National Railway Museum in York. His Victoria Cross was sent home to his brother Sir Robert Peel, and his medals are now displayed at the National Maritime Museum, although the ribbon of his Victoria Cross is badly worn. The medals of Charles Lucas, William Hewett and John Sheppard are also at the museum.

In 2006 the Victoria Cross of Edward Daniel was brought from the Imperial War Museum to the National Maritime Museum for the filming of a BBC Television documentary. Thus it was the first time the medals had been together since they were originally struck and sent to India for presentation.

Lieutenant Osborne William Dalyell

Osborne William Dalyell was born in 1834 at Linlithgow in Scotland, the younger son in the family of four children, born between 1821 and 1834, of Captain Sir William Cunningham Cavendish Dalyell RN (1784–1865) of the Binns, 7th Baronet, a veteran of the French Revolutionary Wars and the Napoleonic Wars, and his wife Maria (1798–1886), a daughter of Antonio Texeira Sampayo, the Portuguese Consul in Ireland. Osborne had an older brother and two sisters. The *Illustrated London News* of 25 February 1865 stated: 'This family, in the male line, is one of the oldest in Scotland, representing the ancient Earls of Monteith; and in the female line, springs from the celebrated cavalier-general and rough-rider (celebrated by Sir Walter Scott in 'Old Mortality'), Sir Thomas Dalyell, commander of the forces in Scotland at the Restoration, who was created, in 1685, a Baronet, with limitations to his heirs of entails …'

An obituary in *Bell's Weekly Messenger* for 29 December 1862 stated that his father had been 'severely wounded and taken prisoner in an attempt to cut out the French lugger Vimereux, from St Valery, in 1805'. At the time of the first ever census (in 1841), the family were living with Maria's parents at Peterborough House in Fulham. On retiring from the navy, his father became governor of the Royal Hospital in Chelsea.

Dalyell became a mate in the Royal Navy on 21 October 1853, and served in the *Britannia*, flagship in the Mediterranean, from that date until he was appointed lieutenant of the *Leander* on 27 May 1854. He saw active service during the Crimean War, and on joining the Naval Brigade, he was seriously wounded during the assault on the Great Redan, when he had his left arm amputated. For his service he received the Crimea Medal with *Sebastopol* clasp, the French Legion of Honour and the Turkish Order of the Medjidie (5th class). He was granted a pension for wounds on 21 August 1856.

Subsequently Dalyell was lieutenant of the *Waterloo*, flagship at Sheerness, from September 1855 until he was appointed to the royal yacht *Victoria and Albert* in the following December, in which vessel he remained until he was promoted commander on 4 September 1857. He was appointed inspecting-commander in the coastguard service at Gravesend on 7 June 1861.

Having not fully recovered from his wounds, Commander Dalyell died on 22 December 1862 at North Aylesford near Maidstone in Kent, aged only 28, and was buried at Gravesend. One descendant was the former anti-war Scottish MP Tam Dalyell.

Lieutenant John Halliday Cave

John Halliday Cave was born on 12 November 1827 in Bristol, the second son of six in the family of ten children, born between 1824 and 1843, of George Cave (1797–1877) and his wife Anne (formerly Halliday, 1801–1888).

John Cave was appointed lieutenant in the Royal Navy on 10 April 1849. He saw active service in the Crimean War and joined HMS *Diamond* on 1 April 1855 for service with the Naval Brigade. He was promoted commander on 29 September 1855. For his service in the Crimea he received the

French Legion of Honour, the Turkish Crimea Medal and the Turkish Order of the Medjidie (5th Class). He was appointed Commander of the Bath (CB).

Cave was given command of HMS *Ardent* on 12 November 1857 and was sent to patrol the west coast of Africa as part of the Royal Navy's anti-slavery operations. He was promoted captain on 25 March 1863 and retired from the Navy with that rank on 22 February 1870. He was appointed Admiral in July 1889.

He married Louisa Ellis (1834–1933), and they had two sons and eight daughters, born between 1861 and 1874. He lived at Henbury Court in Bristol until 1897, and in 1901 bought the schooner *Hesperia*.

Admiral Cave died at 17 Palace Gate in Kensington, London on 30 March 1913, aged 85, and after a service at Kensington Church he was buried in Brompton Cemetery. Louisa Cave was in her one hundredth year when she died on 27 July 1933.

The *Clifton Society* journal for 14 May 1914 stated:

A tablet to the memory of Admiral Cave was unveiled by Mrs Cave at St Mary's Church, Henbury, on Sunday morning. The tablet, which is placed at the west entrance of the church, immediately over the door leading into the tower, contains the following inscription, 'In Memory of Admiral John Holliday Cave, CB, who resided for many years at Henbury Court, and took a deep interest in the restoration of the church in 1878, especially the baptistery and the west entrance. Born November 27 1827; died March 30 1913. This tablet is erected by his loving wife.'

At both morning and evening services, the Vicar, who was the preacher, made special reference to Admiral Cave's work in connection with the restoration of Henbury Church, more especially as regards the baptistery.'

Their youngest child, Louisa Catherine (1874–1961), married Colonel Percyvall Hart-Dyke (1872–1952), who was awarded the Distinguished Service Order (DSO) while serving with the Indian Army during the First World War; and one of their sons, Brigadier Trevor Hart-Dyke, was awarded the DSO while serving with the York and Lancaster Regiment during the Second World War. Other descendants include Captain David Hart-Dyke, who was the commander of HMS *Coventry* when it was sunk during the Falklands War of 1982, and he received serious burns; Miranda Hart, the popular comedian and writer; Tom Hart-Dyke, the world renowned horticulturist; and many more well-known distant relatives.

A Selection of Tributes and Commemorations

Lieutenant Thomas Osborne Kidd

Thomas Osborne Kidd was born in 1831, the son of Joseph Kidd (1801–1883) and his first wife Isabella (formerly Dickinson), although his monument mentions Joseph Kidd's second wife Mary Anne (formerly Morgill, 1803–1870). He had a half-brother named Edward Gambin Kidd. Joseph was a partner with his brother Osborne in Kidd Brothers, flour and oatmeal millers, bread and biscuit bakers of English Street in Armagh, and the family home was Ballinahone Manor in Armagh, which is now a hotel.

Thomas Kidd joined HMS *Albion* on 1 April 1855 and volunteered for the Naval Brigade for service in the trenches before Sebastopol. He was buried in the Royal Naval Brigade Cemetery near the 3rd Division camp, his headstone reading 'Sacred to the memory of Lieut. T.O. Kidd, RN, killed before Sebastopol on June 18 1855, aged 24 years.'

The circumstances of his death are detailed in the official dispatch from Captain Sir Stephen Lushington RN to Rear Admiral Sir Edmund Lyons GCB: 'It is with extreme regret I have to report the death of Lieutenant Kidd who fell on the 18th inst. After bringing the remains of his party safely into the trenches, he again returned to the open to recover some wounded men, and in this gallant act of devotion to his duty, he was shot through the body by a rifle ball, and died shortly after reaching the camp. Lieutenant Kidd was an honour to the brigade, and Her Majesty's service has lost one of its most promising young officers.'

There is a memorial dedicated to him at St Patrick's Cathedral in Armagh, Northern Ireland, that reads: 'SEBASTOPOL: Sacred to the memory of Thomas Osborne Kidd, RN, Lieut. of her Majesty's Ship Albion. (Son of Joseph Kidd, esq, and Mary Anne his wife) who fell pierced by a rifle ball whilst serving in the Naval Brigade, before Sebastopol, in the attack on the 18th June 1855, aged 24 years.

This monument is erected by the inhabitants of Armagh, to record their grief for his early death, and their admiration of the last act of his brief but distinguished career.'

Lieutenant William Brabazon Urmston

William Brabazon Urmston was born on 11 February 1828, at Woodlands in Chigwell, Essex, the second son of four in the family of five children, born between 1809 and 1829, of Sir James Brabazon Urmston (1785–1850), who was employed by the Honourable East India Company as president of Supercargoes of Canton from 1816 to 1827, and his wife Elizabeth (formerly Hanson, 1790–1863) of Killingbeck Hall near York. It is said that while on his way to China in 1816, Sir James's ship stopped at St Helena to drop off supplies for the garrison and Sir James 'partook of breakfast with Napoleon'. In 1823 a broad body of water in Hong Kong called Toon-Koo Bay was renamed Urmston Road after Sir James.

William passed his examination in the Royal Navy in August 1847 and was appointed on 8 September that same year. He served as mate in HMS *Collingwood*, the flagship of Sir George Francis Seymour in the Pacific, and was advanced to lieutenant on 29 September 1848. He joined the magnificent hundred-gun warship HMS *Queen* on 23 March 1853. The ship was engaged in the first bombardment of Sebastopol on 17 October 1854, when it was set on fire three times and had to withdraw from the action. He volunteered his service with the Naval Brigade. For his service in the Crimea he was awarded the Crimea Medal with *Sebastopol* clasp; was appointed the French Knight of the Legion of Honour and the Order of Corpus Christi of Portugal; and was awarded the Turkish Order of the Medjidie. He was appointed commander on 29 September 1855.

On 10 January 1856 he married Marion (formerly Higgins Burn-Murdoch, 1827–1914), and they had five boys and one girl, all born between 1857 and 1869, including twins.

William died on 18 December 1869, aged 41, at 'Rosehill' in the village of Bishop's Tawton near Barnstaple in Devon.

HMS *Queen*'s mascot was a spur-thighed tortoise named Timothy (however, it was actually a female). This animal was said to have been 160 years old when it died at Powderham Castle in Devon in 2004, the last survivor of the Crimean War.

Midshipman Edward St John Daniel VC

Edward St John Daniel was born in the family home at 1 Windsor Terrace, Clifton, in Bristol, on 17 January 1837, the first child of well-known Bristol solicitor Edward Daniel and his wife Barbara (1789–1855), the daughter of Henry Beauchamp St John, 13th Baron St John of Bletso. His distant maternal ancestry included Henry Tudor, King Henry VII. Edward was known by his middle name of St John (pronounced Sinjun). He had a younger brother named Henry, and three sisters named Barbara, Adele and Lucy. Their mother died of phlebitis (inflammation of a vein) soon after Lucy was born in 1850, and their father married a younger woman named Darkey Knight Cox, with whom he had another seven children, although two died in infancy.

Ten days before his 14th birthday Daniel enrolled as a cadet in the Royal Navy with HMS *Dauntless*, and it has been reported that he initially trained

A Selection of Tributes and Commemorations

on Lord Nelson's former flagship, HMS *Victory*. A year later he served briefly on HMS *Blenheim*.

In March 1852 he joined the flagship HMS *Winchester*, aboard which he got his first taste of naval action in the Second Anglo-Burmese War of 1852–1853. An expedition was sent to Burma (now Myanmar) to redress the grievances of British subjects in Rangoon. When Rangoon was occupied, an expedition was sent to Pegu (now Bagu), which was captured on 21 November 1852, and the province was annexed to the British crown. For his service Daniel received the Indian General Service Medal with *Pegu* clasp. During his time in Burma he developed chronic leg ulcers which affected him for the rest of his life.

Daniel joined HMS *Contest* in March 1853 and he began his long association with Captain William Peel when he joined HMS *Diamond* on 7 September 1853, and on the following day was appointed midshipman. The young teenager became devoted to his leader, and when the war with Russia broke out HMS *Diamond* was sent to join the Black Sea Fleet, where both Daniel and Midshipman Evelyn Wood became Peel's aides-de-camp. On the ship's arrival off the Crimean Peninsula, the two midshipmen joined the Naval Brigade with their captain.

Having been recommended for the Victoria Cross himself, Captain Peel put Midshipman Daniel's name forward too, and he was the youngest recipient of the medal at that time, and the first Bristol-born man to be awarded the Victoria Cross, when it was announced in the *London Gazette* on 24 February 1857. Daniel's medal, along with Captain Peel's, was forwarded from Hong Kong to India, where he received it from Captain Francis Marten, the new commander of the Shannon Brigade, during a special parade of the troops at Gyah in Bengal on 13 July 1858. He also received the Crimea Medal with *Inkerman* and *Sebastopol* clasps, the French Legion of Honour, the Turkish Order of Medjidie (5th Class), the Turkish Crimea Medal and the Sardinian Medal for Military Valour.

Daniel sailed to the East with Captain Peel on HMS *Shannon*, and served with distinction during the Indian Mutiny, for which he received the Indian Mutiny Medal with *Relief of Lucknow* and *Lucknow* clasps. However, when Captain Peel died of smallpox in 1858 it had a devastating effect on Daniel. He was promoted to lieutenant on 15 September 1859, and in April 1860 he was presented before Queen Victoria at St James's Palace, where the sovereign is said to have been 'much impressed' by him. However, his career declined drastically from then on.

On 24 May 1860, while serving on HMS *Wasp*, he was severely reprimanded for going absent without leave, and two weeks later he faced a court martial after being found drunk and incapable while on duty. On 25 June 1861, while serving on HMS *Victor Emmanuel* in the Mediterranean, he was taken into custody again for an unspecified offence which was described by the Secretary of War as 'disgraceful'; Captain Clifford stated that he had been arrested for 'taking indecent liberties with four of the subordinate officers'. He was due to be court-martialled at Corfu, but on the following evening he went missing from the ship and was designated a deserter.

In the following month his name was removed from the navy list, and in accordance with Clause 15 of the royal warrant, on 4 September 1861 Queen Victoria signed the warrant that made Edward St John Daniel the first man to be stripped of the Victoria Cross, the official reason being given as desertion. Seven other men have forfeited their Victoria Crosses since, but Daniel was the only officer and the only member of the Senior Service.

Having somehow got back to England undetected, on 16 September 1861 he boarded a clipper at Liverpool bound for Melbourne in Australia, where he is believed to have found work as a miner in the goldfields. In January 1864 he signed up at Melbourne for three years' service with the Taranaki Military Settlers, and arrived in New Zealand in the following month. He spent most of his service engaged in fighting the Maoris in South Taranaki. He was arrested in August 1864 and sentenced to intensive labour, and soon after serving his sentence he was arrested again and a court-martial sentenced him to two weeks in confinement. His unit was disbanded in May 1867.

Daniel enlisted as a constable in the New Zealand Armed Constabulary in November 1867, and seventy members of his division were sent to Hokitika on the South Island to deal with disturbances among the Irish Protestants and Catholics in the West Canterbury goldfields. He remained in Hokitika and on 16 May 1868, after being ill for some time, he was admitted to the Hokitika Hospital. He died of 'delirium tremens' on 20 May 1868, aged 31, and was buried with military honours at the Hokitika Municipal Cemetery. Cemetery records list his age as 37. A headstone was erected in 1972, and there is a plaque at the foot of a flagpole in the cemetery. A commemorative plaque was placed at his birthplace in Bristol in 2001.

Daniel's Victoria Cross was on display at the United Services Institute in Whitehall for some time, and then came up for auction in 1930. It was the first to appear at auction after the Second World War, on the anniversary of the assault on the Redan, 18 June 1947. It was purchased in 1990 and is now displayed on rotation at the Lord Ashcroft Gallery, as part of the 'Extraordinary Heroes' exhibition at the Imperial War Museum in London.

In 1981 a petition sought the restoration of his award, which was rejected on the grounds that 'the restoration of forfeited awards may only be made on a petition to the Sovereign from the former recipient himself. In Daniel's case this is not possible. Furthermore, as your proposal relates to events so long ago it is considered inappropriate to reverse the decision made in 1861 by Queen Victoria.'

A twist in the story of his life – and death – suggests that the man who died in New Zealand in 1868 may not have been Daniel, who some historians believe was living a destitute life in London in 1902.

In his book *The People of the Abyss*, published in 1903, the famous American author Jack London, writer of the classic book *The Call of the Wild*, which was published in the same year, tells of his experiences among London's poor people in 1902. The seventh chapter is entitled 'A Winner of the Victoria Cross'. He says that as he waited in the queue to get into Whitechapel Workhouse he met two men, one of whom he described as a short and stout old man (Daniel would have been in his 65th year if he had still been alive). The man seems to have kicked up a bigger fuss about his plight than anyone else in the line, and eventually began to tell the tale of his service in the same theatres of war as Daniel, and claiming that he had won, and lost, the Victoria Cross. He also states that a lieutenant had enraged him by calling him a bastard – a terrible degrading insult at the time – and he had attacked him with an iron bar and knocked him into the sea, after which he dived in and tried to drown both the officer and himself. For this he lost all his privileges and his Victoria Cross.

On reading the account I find it difficult to ignore a feeling of embellishment to the story, as if the man was well-rehearsed, and Jack London stated that he 'recited his sentence word for word, as though memorised and gone over in bitterness many times'. There are some obvious discrepancies, such as the fact that he says he was aged 87, which made him twenty-two years older than Daniel would have been; he had served for two score years and more, which is over forty years, and Daniel died when he was only 31; and he had received fifty lashes and served a two-year prison sentence, which Daniel had not. Jack London does not indicate any kind of West Country accent, which would have been noticeable to an American and worthy of remark, as Charles Beresford did when listening to the accent of Henry Curtis (see below). For all his grievances, the man did not mention the severe leg ulcers caused by his naval service, and he did not know the correct word for 'a sea trial', which is strange after being in the navy for so long. The story of Daniel's service and downfall would have been well-known in the navy, and possibly the incident the man described, although Captain Clifford states that the problem was with four lieutenants and not just one. He may have even known Daniel.

This man was not the only one to claim he had won the Victoria Cross when he had not, and it was common for Victorian ex-servicemen to romance about their battle and seafaring exploits. For instance, just in Liverpool alone there is a gravestone dedicated to 'A Hero of Rorke's Drift' for a man who was not there, and a Liverpool cab driver became quite famous in the city for saying that he rode in the Charge of the Light Brigade when he did not. Respectively, one may well have been with the force that relieved the Rorke's Drift garrison on the following day, and the other may have been at Balaclava on the fateful day of the charge, and a subtle twist in the tale was enough to get a man a free pint.

It was a time when the plight of many surviving Crimean War and other veterans who had fallen on hard times was being highlighted in the media, and several benefit concerts and charity organisations had been set up to give them financial assistance. The man was aware that Jack had some money with him, and it may have simply been an attempt by two down-and-outs to try to dupe the writer for a hand-out. The story of James Gorman is testament to how gullible writers and journalists were in the pursuit of a good story.

In recent times a photograph of a man in civilian clothes has come to light which is said to be Edward Daniel. It is believed to have been taken in London after 1865, and was compared to a known picture of Edward in uniform by a forensic pathologist, who was of the opinion that the two are the same person. It is said that Daniel may have stolen another man's identity so as not to be tracked down by the authorities on returning to England sometime around 1866 to 1868. If the switched identity is true, the other man is believed to have been a Robert Daniels, who enlisted at Melbourne on the same day as Edward Daniel, and apparently there is evidence in the New Zealand National Archives that information concerning the two men may have become mixed up. The pictures do look like the same man, although the one in civvies looks a bit older than Edward would have been at the time. However, the traumatic life he had led and his alcoholic problem might well have aged him. Nevertheless, I believe Edward Daniel is the man buried in New Zealand – but I leave it to the readers to make their own decision!

Captain of the Forecastle John T.N. Taylor VC

John Taylor was born in February 1822 in the parish of St Philip and St Jacob, Bristol, and later made his home in London. He entered the Royal Navy at the age of 19 as an ordinary seaman, being described as 5ft 9in tall, with a

A Selection of Tributes and Commemorations

fresh complexion, grey eyes and brown hair. He had a crucifix and the initials JTNT tattooed on his right arm and a tree on his left.

Taylor's first ship was HMS *Cornwallis*, which he joined in October 1841, and like Captain Peel he saw active service during the First China War of 1840–1842. He served on HMS *Eagle* from 1845 to 1848 and then transferred to the flagship HMS *Hastings*, and like Edward Daniel he saw active service in the Second Anglo-Burmese War in 1852. He left the ship as Captain of the Forecastle in May 1853 and joined HMS *London*. It seems he was marked as a deserter from 17 August to 18 October 1853. Having seen active service in China and Burma, he was perhaps the most experienced of all the twenty 18 June Redan Victoria Cross recipients, when he sailed for active service in the East.

John Taylor was later drafted to work with Florence Nightingale in the hospital at Scutari. However, his service in the Crimea had an adverse effect on his health. On his return to England he went to live in Woolwich, where he was a supernumerary boatswain with the Fishguard flagship. He was admitted into the Royal Marine Infirmary in Woolwich with difficulty in breathing and coughing up blood. He died of bronchitis and pulmonary congestion on 24 February 1857, aged 35, the day after his award of the Victoria Cross had been announced. He had only just been informed of it a few hours before he died. A notice in the *Army and Navy Gazette* stated: 'The deceased was much esteemed by the officers in the Dockyard, and by those who knew him, and although covered with honours so unassuming was his character that he could scarcely be prevailed upon to wear them ... unfortunately, this brave man has left a wife and family unprovided for.'

Taylor's widow Elizabeth wrote to the Admiralty in March 1857, informing them of his death and asking if she could represent him at the first investiture. A letter was sent back to her on 25 June stating: 'It would not be necessary for you to come to London ...' – and the Victoria Cross was sent to her from the Admiralty by registered post on 7 July 1857. John Taylor was buried in an unmarked grave at Woolwich Cemetery, and a new headstone was erected at the grave in February 1996.

Taylor's medals are at the Sheesh Mahal Museum in Patiala, Punjab, India. The group formed part of the Maharaja Bhupendra Singh's collection that was bequeathed to the museum on the death of the his son in 1947, and consists of the Victoria Cross, the Conspicuous Gallantry Medal (1st type), the China War Medal 1842, India General Service Medal 1835–54 with *Pegu* clasp, the Crimea Medal with *Inkerman* and *Sebastopol* clasps, the French

Legion of Honour and the Turkish Crimea Medal. The collection also includes the medals of Thomas Beach and George Fiott Day.

Botswain Henry Curtis VC

Henry Curtis was born on 21 December 1823 and although he gave Romsey in Hampshire as his place of birth on censuses and his naval record, it seems that he was actually born in the village of Awbridge in the parish of Michelmersh, near Romsey. The evidence for this is unclear, as his place of birth on the 1861 census looks like 'Awbury'. However, his father is recorded as living in Awbridge in 1841, where he worked as a carpenter, and there is a baptism of a Henry Curtis in the neighbouring parish of Lockerley dated 15 February 1824, the son of Robert and Sarah Curtis. Henry is recorded on the 1841 census in Embley, aged 18 and employed as a servant.

Apparently, Henry Curtis was a big man. He joined HMS *Victory* as a boy second class in June 1841 and after ten years' service he became a coast guard in August 1851. He stated that he was 'picked up' – usually meaning conscripted – to the ninety-gun, two-deck ship HMS *Rodney* in the following November. Midshipman (later Admiral) Kennedy, who joined the ship in the following month, described how crews were 'picked-up anyhow – long-shore loafers, jailbirds and such like, with a sprinkling of good seamen amongst them'. Henry Curtis was one such 'good seaman', who sailed for active service with the Black Sea Fleet as a boatswain's mate with HMS *Rodney*.

The award of the Victoria Cross to recently married Mate Curtis was announced in the *London Gazette* of 24 February 1857, and he received the medal at the first investiture. He also received the Crimea Medal with *Inkerman* and *Sebastopol* clasps and the Turkish Crimea Medal.

Henry left *Rodney* when she paid off in January 1856 and served aboard HMS *Ringdove* before joining the Coast Guard Service in November 1856. From March 1858 until his final discharge from the Navy in November 1864, he served as boatswain's mate on the flagship HMS *Marlborough*, known as 'the smartest ship in the Service'. Lord Charles Beresford (later Admiral) joined the ship in 1861 and he remembered Curtis as 'The great big Boatswain's Mate'; in return, Curtis remarked to another sailor, on seeing the young Beresford, 'Mate, 'ere's another orficer kim aboard jist in toime; but pore little beggar! – he aint long fur this world.' After four years' service in the Mediterranean Henry Curtis was paid off with a medal and a gratuity of 10 guineas. His next employment was as chief quartermaster on a cross-channel steamer sailing out of Southampton. Lord Charles came onboard one day and, on recognising him, shook his hand.

A Selection of Tributes and Commemorations

Henry married Maria Morley, a brewer's daughter who was fifteen years younger than him, on 7 February 1856 at St Mary's parish church in Alverstoke, Gosport, and they made their home at 19 Bailey's Buildings, St Paul's Parish in Portsea. They had a son named Henry William on 17 June 1857 and a daughter named Maria in 1859, both born in Alverstoke, Gosport, and another daughter, Victoria, born at Landport in Portsmouth in 1862. By 1871 they had moved to 123 Church Street, St Mary's Parish at Sholing in Southampton, where Charlotte was born in 1872 and Mabel followed in 1877. Henry was probably working on the cross-channel ferry and the three oldest children had moved away by 1881, leaving Maria and the two youngest girls living at 185 Botany Bay, Weston Common, South Stoneham, Southampton. Henry had retired by 1891 and they had moved to Portsmouth, where they settled at 82 Stirling Street, Buckland, Portsea.

The *Portsmouth News* of 7 April reported that on 1 April 1892 Henry had collected nearly £12 of his pension money, and on his returning home drunk, Maria asked him for some of it to buy food for the family. Henry refused, and set about punching her twice across her nose and threatening her with a 'loaded stick'. She was forced to seek the protection of her neighbours, who stated that he repeatedly shouted 'I'm a gentleman' as he attacked her. Maria said that her life was 'a perfect misery' because he came home drunk every night. A police officer was called and Henry was issued with a summons to appear in court, but he failed to comply. He had to be arrested and brought before the court, where he was sentenced to fourteen days' imprisonment with hard labour, and the bench advised him to behave better towards his wife when he came out of prison. There is no mention of him being a holder of the Victoria Cross.

Henry's drinking habits seemed to have had an adverse effect on his constitution, and he died of 'podagra [gout] and chronic Bright's uraemia [kidney failure]' on 23 November 1896, aged 74, and was buried at Kingston Cemetery in Portsea. Maria was buried with him. The grave had been reused for a lady whose family agreed to have her name put on a new stone which was erected in his honour at the grave in 1997.

His Victoria Cross was held at the British Steel Headquarters in Sheffield. Ironically, Mrs Freda McKay was working in the offices there when she was informed that her son Ian had been killed during the Falklands War, performing a gallant action for which he would be awarded the Victoria Cross. Curtis's medal was purchased by Lord Ashcroft in 1999, being the last Crimean War Victoria Cross to be sold at auction prior to this book going to publication. It is now displayed on rotation at the Lord Ashcroft Gallery, as part of the 'Extraordinary Heroes' exhibition at the Imperial War Museum in London.

Royal Regiment of Artillery
Gunner and Driver Thomas Arthur VC

Thomas Arthur was born on 28 August 1836 at Abbotsham near Bideford in Devon, and was baptised at St Helen's Church in the same year. He was the only son and second child of four of Thomas Arthur, a labourer, and his wife Jane. It seems that local parish records show the family name as 'Arthurs', and his father may have died before Thomas was born because parish records show the funeral of one Thomas Arthurs in 1836, and he is not named on the 1841 census. There were older twin sisters named Kitty and Fanny.

Thomas is believed to have worked as a labourer on the farm of John Becklick at Parkham before he ran away from home and enlisted into the Royal Artillery at Devonport in March 1853. He was 5ft 6in tall, with a fresh complexion, hazel eyes and brown hair. He sailed from Liverpool on the troopship *Niagara* for active service in the Crimea with the 1st company, 5th Battalion, on 1 December 1854. His award of the Victoria Cross was announced in the *London Gazette* of 24 February 1857, and he received the medal at the first investiture. He also received the Crimean Medal with *Sebastopol* clasp and the Turkish Crimea Medal.

On his return to Woolwich in March 1857, Thomas took two days off absent without leave, and found himself being court-martialled and serving a 28-day sentence at Weedon Military Prison in Northamptonshire. He was released only nine days before he attended the first investiture.

In the following year he served in the second Anglo-China (Opium) War of 1860, taking part in another dangerous assault at the Taku Forts on 21 August 1860. On this occasion the assault was successful. The attacking force had to cross a series of ditches and bamboo-stake palisades under heavy fire from the ramparts. Assault parties eventually breached the defences and forced entry into the fort. For his service he received the China Medal with *Taku Forts* clasp.

Thomas married Ann Goddard at Aldershot on 6 July 1859 and they went on to have eight children. He sailed to India in 1866, where his wife gave birth to several more girls. He changed his surname to McArthur and his wife changed her name to Britannia while they were in India. Sergeant Major Gower states in his memoirs: 'I had the pleasure of meeting him [Arthur] afterwards in India, with the cross upon his noble breast – "Gunner Arthur".'

The Charge of the Light Brigade became the most famous action of the Crimean War. The statement of Bugler McLaughlin of the 21st Regiment is the only unbiased account by a witness to the controversial discussion between Captain Lewis Nolan and Lord Cardigan which caused the action to take place.

Colonel John Campbell, seated (1807–1855) of the 38th (1st Staffordshire) Regiment volunteered to take part in the attack on the Great Redan, where he displayed 'a courage amounting to rashness, when he rushed out of the trenches and was shot through the head in the act of cheering his men on'.

A West Countryman, Colonel Lacy Walter Giles Yea (1808–1855) commanded the 7th Royal Fusiliers. He led from the front and was killed in action at the Great Redan.

Roger Fenton's picture of Colonel Lacy Yea (*left*) and Lieutenant James Hobson (*right*) in the camp of the 7th Royal Fusiliers. They both lost their lives during the assault.

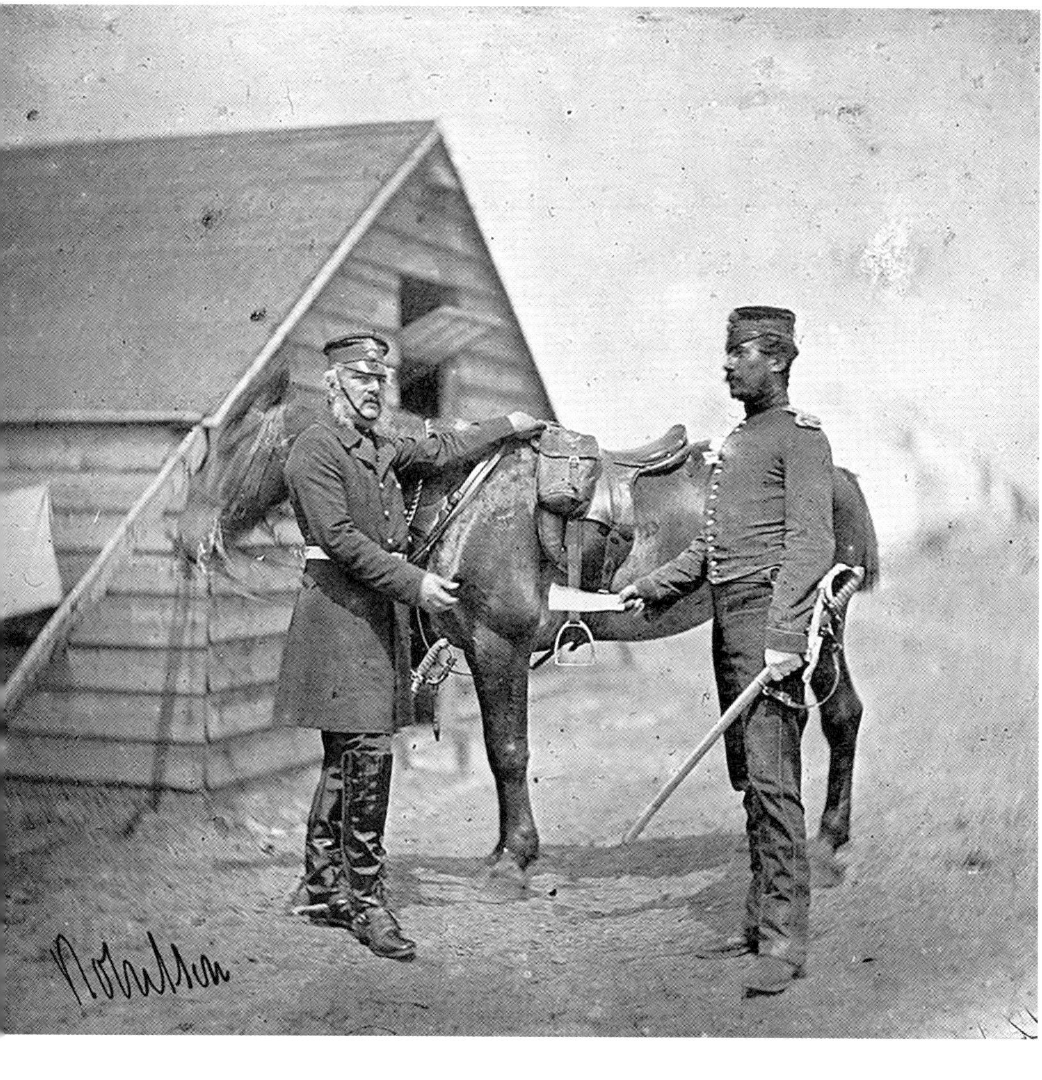

A native of Derbyshire, Colonel William Eyre (1805–1859) of the 73rd (Perthshire) Regiment commanded the 3rd Brigade, and later the 3rd Division, and was promoted to major general. For his service he received the Crimea Medal, the French Legion of Honour, the Turkish Order of the Medjidie (2nd class) and the Sardinian Crimea Medal, and was appointed Knight Commander of the Bath (KCB).

Major General Harry David Jones (1791–1866) assumed command of the Royal Engineers in February 1855. He became Governor of the Royal Military College at Sandhurst and played cricket for Middlesex CCC.

The son of a vicar, Lieutenant Arthur A'Court Fisher (1830–1879) of the Royal Engineers took part in a second dreadful assault against the Taku Forts in China in 1860, and in 1863 he published *A Personal Narrative of Three Years' Service in China*.

Lieutenant Gerald Graham (1831–1899) of the Royal Engineers was awarded the Victoria Cross for showing determined gallantry during the assault on the Great Redan.

The son of a vicar, Lieutenant Bradford Smith Hoskins (1833–1863) of the 44th (East Essex) Regiment was seriously wounded during the assault on the Great Redan. He became a soldier of fortune, joining the English Volunteer Legion in the army of Giuseppe Garibaldi, and was killed in action while fighting with the Confederate Army during the American Civil War.

The son of a Derbyshire MP, Lieutenant Francis Richard Hurt (1832–1855) of the 34th (Cumberland) Regiment was killed on 18 June but his body was not recovered.

Lieutenant William Hope (1834–1909) of the 7th Royal Fusiliers was informed that his fellow officer, Lieutenant James Hobson, was lying severely wounded outside the trenches. He went to search for him and found him lying in a ditch. He returned to the British lines and returned with a stretcher and four other men. All the time they were under continuous fire, and it seems that three men in the stretcher party were killed. Lieutenant Hobson later died of his wounds.

Corporal Philip Smith (1829–1906) of the 17th (Leicestershire) Regiment was awarded the Victoria Cross for 'repeatedly going out in front of the advance trenches against the Great Redan, on 18 June 1855, under a very heavy fire, after the column had retired from the assault, and bringing in wounded comrades'.

A *Punch* cartoon highlights the plight of the soldiers in the Crimea.

"Well, Jack, here's good news from home. We're to have a medal."
"That's very kind. Maybe one of these days we'll have a coat to stick it on."

One of twins who fought at Sebastopol, Captain John Lacy Croker (1820–1855) of the 17th (Leicestershire) Regiment was killed in action and was buried on Cathcart's Hill.

The camp of the 33rd (Duke of Wellington's) Regiment. The storming column which assaulted the right of the Redan originally consisted of 200 men of the 23rd (Welsh) Regiment and 200 men of the 33rd (Duke of Wellington's) Regiment, but the order was changed and these two regiments instead provided support troops for the attack.

The camp of the 34th (Cumberland) Regiment. The unit provided 400 men for the storming column on the right of the Redan.

Officers of the 57th (West Middlesex) Regiment were photographed several times by Roger Fenton. (*Left to right*): Major Inglis, Captain St Clair, Captain Hassard, Lieutenant Colonel Shadforth, Lieutenant Ashwin and Quartermaster Balcombe. Eight officers of the regiment were either killed in action or seriously wounded during the assault on the Great Redan.

(*Above*) Edinburgh-born Captain Arthur Maxwell Earle (*seated*) (1832–1863), commanded part of the assaulting column on 18 June. He became a leading light in the 4th Division's theatre productions, which helped to keep the troops' spirits up.

(*Opposite, above*) Soldiers of the 57th (West Middlesex) Regiment on parade. The column which assaulted the left of the Redan consisted wholly of men of the 57th Regiment under the command of Lieutenant Colonel Thomas Shadforth.

(*Opposite, below*) The interior of the Great Redan at Sebastopol after the Russians had evacuated the town on 9 September 1855.

A lone soldier pays his respects to the officers' graves on Cathcart's Hill.

Graves of the 33rd (Duke of Wellington's) Regiment, including those of Lieutenants Bennett and Heyland, who were killed in action during the assault on 18 June 1855.

The 57th (West Middlesex) Regiment memorial, 'erected by their brother officers', at St Paul's Cathedral.

(*Above*) The marble memorial dedicated to men of the 34th (Cumberland) Regiment at Carlisle Cathedral, which displays the names of the officers killed in action during the campaign.

(*Opposite: above left*) The memorial dedicated to the 33rd (Duke of Wellington's) Regiment at York Minster. (*Above right*) The memorial dedicated to Colonel John Campbell at the Church of St John the Evangelist in Edinburgh. (*Below left*) The impressive memorial dedicated to Colonel Lacy Walter Giles Yea at St James's Church in Taunton Deane, Somerset, which was erected by his eldest sister. (*Below right*) The memorial in the New Forest dedicated to Captain the Hon. Charles Welbore Herbert Agar. Mortally wounded when both his legs were carried off by a round shot, he died on the evening of 18 June 1855.

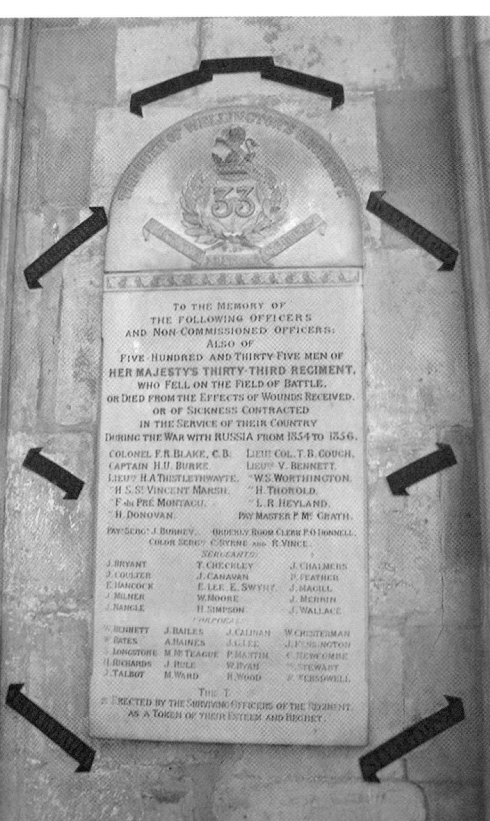

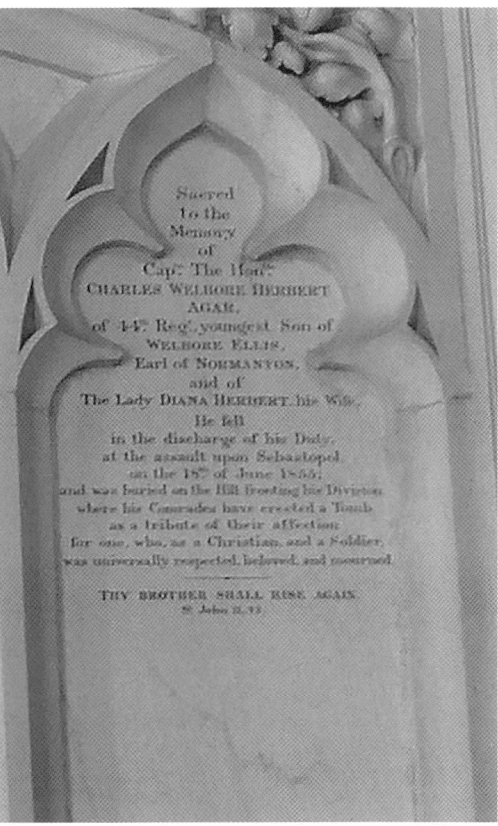

The grave of John Simpson Knox VC at Cheltenham Cemetery. The headstone was refurbished in 2002 after being found badly damaged. Knox was awarded the VC for two acts of gallantry, at the Battle of the Alma with the Scots (Fusilier) Guards, and with the Rifle Brigade at the assault on the Great Redan. (*Courtesy of Kevin Brazier*)

The Redan memorial at Sebastopol. (*Courtesy of John Grehan*)

The 1881 census states that he was living with his wife and five daughters, with the surname McArthur, at 7 Cadley Square in South Savernake, Wiltshire. The 1891 census describes him as a Chelsea Pensioner, and by 1901 he was back in Wiltshire, living at 28 Cadley in Savernake, with his wife, a daughter and a granddaughter.

Thomas died at Savernake on 2 March 1902, aged 67, and he was buried at Christ Church in Cadley near Savernake, where there was a headstone bearing the surname MacArthur. However, the church has been deconsecrated and is now a private house. His wife died in 1915. There is a stone plaque dedicated to him at the foot of the cross commemorating the war dead in St Helen's Churchyard, and his name is on the memorial at the Royal Artillery Chapel in Woolwich. His Victoria Cross was sold for £42 in 1902, and his medals are in the Royal Artillery Regiment Museum in Woolwich.

Corps of Royal Engineers
Major General Sir Harry David Jones

Harry David Jones was born on 14 March 1791 at Landguard Fort near Felixstowe in Suffolk, where his father John Jones was general superintendent. His mother was Mary, daughter of John Roberts of Landguard Fort, who was an officer in the 29th (Worcestershire) Regiment.

Harry became a cadet at the Royal Military Academy in Woolwich on 10 April 1805 and was gazetted as a second lieutenant in the Corps of Royal Engineers on 17 September 1808, being promoted lieutenant on 24 June 1809. He was employed on the construction of home fortifications at Dover and Flushing.

After his first tour of active service during the Walcheren expedition of 1809, he was posted to Spain, where he served in the defence of Cadiz. Having served during the relief of Tarragona in 1811, he joined the army under the Duke of Wellington, then engaged in the siege of Badajoz in 1812, and took part in all the ensuing campaigns until the termination of the Peninsular War in 1814. For his bravery at the battle of Vittoria he was recommended for promotion, and he was wounded and taken prisoner while leading the forlorn hope at the first assault of St Sebastian. Having been promoted second captain on 22 November 1813, he was sufficiently recovered to again take his place in the fifth division in the battle of Nivelle in 1813, and for his conduct then, and in the operations at the passage of the Bidassoa, at Nive and before Bayonne, he received the thanks of the Master-General of the Ordnance.

In February 1814 he was attached to Sir John Lambert's expedition against New Orleans at Dauphine Island, and in the following year he joined the

Duke of Wellington's army before the capture of Paris, was in command of the Engineers at Montmartre, and was made a commissioner to the Prussian army of occupation in 1816. He received the silver war medal with five clasps. On his return to England in 1818 he was employed in various routine duties at Plymouth, Jersey and Chatham.

In 1824 he married Charlotte, a daughter of the Reverend Thomas Hornsby, vicar of Ravensthorpe in Peterborough. They had six sons and five daughters. The eldest son, Harry Valette, died in 1863; their second son, Captain Arthur Jones, died on the coast of Africa while serving with the 2nd West India Regiment in 1861, and their fourth son, Montagu Hornsby, died in 1859 while serving as an ensign in the 84th (York and Lancaster) Regiment.

In the summer of 1826 Harry was promoted to the rank of captain and was sent to Malta, from where he was employed on services on the coast of Africa and on special duty at Constantinople in 1833–1834. Back home again, he was appointed commissioner for municipal boundaries in England in May 1835, and in November of that year he was employed in the improvement of the navigation of the river Shannon. On this commission he was engaged for several years, besides being First Commissioner for fixing the Municipal Boundaries in Ireland, and Secretary to the Irish Railway Commission, which latter office he held when elected a Member of the Institution of Civil Engineers on 25 April 1837. He was then for a short time Commanding Royal Engineer at Jersey, but he was soon again removed from the corps, to take up the appointment of Commissioner for the Improvement of the Navigation of the river Shannon, and in 1845 he became the Chairman of the Board of Public Works in Ireland, the duties of which office he continued to perform until 1850. He had been made brevet major on 10 January 1837 and attained the rank of lieutenant colonel on 7 September 1840.

In 1842 he communicated to the Institution some observations 'On the Forms of Breakwaters, with Suggestions for their Modification', which led to a very interesting discussion. In 1843 he consented to edit a third edition of the *Journal of the Sieges carried on by the Army under the Duke of Wellington in Spain, during the years 1811 to 1814*.

In 1849 he presented to the Institution a 'Description of the Bridge erected at Athlone, by the Commissioners for the Improvement of the river Shannon', for which useful record of a large work successfully executed he received a Telford Medal. In 1851 he was selected to fill the important position of Director of the Royal Engineer Establishment for Field Instruction at Chatham.

At the commencement of the war against Russia he was appointed brigadier general for particular service in the Baltic, and commanded the British forces at the siege operations against Bomarsund. For his conduct in the Baltic he was promoted to major general. In February 1855 he assumed the command of the Royal Engineers during the siege operations at Sebastopol, which he retained until the fall of the city, and in spite of his serious head wound he insisted on being carried to the trenches on a stretcher to witness the final assault on 8 September 1855. He was highly decorated for his services in the East, being awarded the Crimea Medal with *Sebastopol* clasp, the Baltic Medal, the Turkish Crimea Medal, the French Legion of Honour, the Sardinian War Medal for Military Valour, the Turkish Order of the Medjidie (2nd Class) and the Sardinian Military Order of Savoy, and he was appointed Knight Commander of the Bath (KCB).

In consequence of his wound and incessant fatigue, he returned to England in enfeebled health but he was sufficiently recovered in the following year of 1856 to return to duty.

As a recognition of his devotion to the varied and important trusts confided to him for forty-eight years, he was placed on the list of officers receiving rewards for 'Distinguished or Meritorious Services', and in May of the same year he was appointed Governor of the Royal Military College and of the Staff College at Sandhurst. He was appointed lieutenant general on 6 July 1860 and on 2 August he was appointed a colonel commandant in the Corps of Royal Engineers. He was appointed GCB in 1861.

His health continued to fail and he died at Sandhurst on 2 August 1866, aged 75, and was buried in the Royal Military Academy Cemetery. There is a memorial in the Chapel of the Academy which states: 'In Memory of Lieutenant-General Sir Harry D. Jones, G.C.B., Royal Engineers, who died as Governor of these Royal Military Colleges on the 2nd August 1866. This Tablet was erected by his brother officers in admiration of his character and distinguished services.'

Colonel Richard Tylden

Richard Tylden was born at Stede Hill in Harrietsham, Maidstone, Kent, on 22 November 1819, the youngest son of Colonel William Burton Tylden (1790–1854) of the Royal Engineers, and his wife Lecilena. He was educated at the Royal Military Academy in Woolwich and joined the Royal Engineers as ensign on 14 December 1847, gaining promotion to lieutenant on 19 March 1840. He was promoted captain on 9 November 1846 and in February 1848 he went for service at the Cape of Good Hope.

During the Eighth Cape Frontier War of 1850–1853 he led a small force against two thousand Xhosa warriors under Chief Sandile and completely routed them. In general orders dated 8 April 1852 it was stated that the exertions of Tylden and the burghers in this and similar affairs had been most conspicuous, and he was further mentioned both in general orders and in despatches during his service in South Africa. He was promoted to brevet major for his services on 31 May 1853.

Soon after returning home in 1854, he proceeded to Varna to serve on his father's staff as brigade major of Engineers. He took part in the battle of the Alma, and was with his father when he died of cholera two days after the battle. He resigned his staff appointment because he felt he needed to share the arduous duties with his men in the trenches before Sebastopol, and on 20 October 1854 he was given command of the forces forming the British right attack. From that time until he received his mortal wound he was never absent from duty, and he took part in every action which occurred near his batteries. For his distinguished service during these dangerous times he was promoted lieutenant colonel on 12 December 1854. He showed great gallantry during the attack and capture of the enemy's rifle pits on 19 April 1855, for which he was mentioned in despatches. During the attack on the Quarries on 7 June 1855 he commanded the Royal Engineers and Sappers and Miners.

Lieutenant Charles Gordon RE stated: 'A second after Murray had gone to the rear, poor Tylden, struck by grape in the legs, was carried back; and although very much depressed in spirits, he is doing well.' His wounds seemed to be getting better, and on 3 July 1855 he was appointed aide-de-camp to Queen Victoria, and made a Companion of the Bath, military division, two days later. However, while he was on his way to Malta he suffered an attack of diarrhoea. He arrived on the island on 1 August 1855 and died on the following day. He is buried in Malta.

A memorial dedicated to Colonel Tylden was erected in St Mary and the Holy Cross Church at Milstead in Swale, Kent:

> In memory of Colonel Richard Tylden of the Corps of Royal Engineers. Youngest son of William Burton Tylden, and Lecilena his wife; Companion of the Order of the Bath and aide-de-camp to Her Majesty Queen Victoria. Born Nov. 22nd 1819; died July 28th 1855. He served with distinguished courage and ability in the war on South Africa, AD 1851–1854; and in the expedition to the Crimea, AD 1854–5. At the siege of Sebastopol he held for some time the command of the right

attack of the British Army and was severely wounded on the 18th of June 1855. He departed this life at sea before he could reach England, to the inexpressible grief of his surviving relatives whose consolation it is to have been enabled through the devoted affection of Mary, his stepmother, to lay his remains at his mother's feet, and to hope in the mercy of his saviour and theirs in the resurrection of the last day.

Captain James Frankfort Manners Browne
James Frankfort Manners Browne was born on 23 April 1823 in Dublin, the eldest of two sons in the family of four children to the Very Reverend Henry Montague Browne (1799–1884), the Dean of Lismore, and his wife, the Honourable Catherine Penelope de Montmorency, who was a daughter of Lodge Evans Morres, 1st Viscount Frankfort de Montmorency. He was a grandson of the 2nd Baron Kilmaine.

James was educated at Epsom and at Mr Miller's Academy at Woolwich, before entering the Royal Military Academy at Woolwich on 15 May 1838. He gained a commission into the Corps of Royal Engineers on 1 January 1842.

After serving at Woolwich and in Ireland, he embarked for Halifax in Nova Scotia, Canada, in March 1845 and on 1 April was promoted lieutenant. In November 1846 he was transferred to Quebec. In June 1847 Lieutenant Browne was sent on special service to Fort Garry in the Red River Settlement, Hudson's Bay territory (now Manitoba), where a detachment of Royal Artillery, another of Royal Sappers and Miners, and three companies of the 6th (Warwickshire) Regiment had been quartered since the summer of 1846 in connection with the Oregon boundary settlement. Browne took two months to reach the inaccessible spot now known as Winnipeg, and was engaged in surveying, superintending the clearance of forest, and pioneer work generally. In August 1848 the force was withdrawn, and Browne went back to Quebec. In the autumn of 1851 he was in Ireland, doing duty first at Clonmel and then at Kilkenny.

On 24 April 1850 he married May, a daughter of James Hunt of Quebec, and they had six daughters between 1851 and 1868, but the four who were born in Bengal died very young. Emily May Elizabeth died aged 18 and was buried at Brompton; twins were born in 1854, but Augusta Amelia died in the following year, and Caroline Elinor Henrietta died aged 18, and was buried in Brompton; and Alice Augusta was born and died in 1857. Only the two born in the UK survived to old age. Annie Kathleen de Montmorency and Agnes Montague are both buried at Brompton.

Promoted second captain on 7 February 1854, he went to Chatham in July to take command of the 1st Company of Royal Sappers and Miners. He put the company through a course of field work instruction, and on 5 January 1855 embarked with it for active service in the Crimean War. On reaching Balaclava on 5 February, Captain Browne and his company were soon moved to the trenches of the British right attack on Sebastopol, and remained there until near the end of August.

On 22 March 1855 and again on 5 April Browne took part in the repulse of sorties made in force by the Russians. He was promoted first captain on 1 June and was the senior executive officer of engineers on 7 June, when he rendered conspicuous service in the successful attack on the Quarry outworks covering the Redan. The execution of the arrangements as well as the general superintendence of the work was in his hands. Browne was mentioned in the despatches both of Sir Harry Jones (8 June) and of Lord Raglan (9 June).

When Lieutenant Colonel Richard Tylden RE, director of the right attack, was fatally wounded on 18 June 1855, his duties devolved on Browne. On 24 August Browne was severely wounded and on 18 November he was invalided home. For his service in the Crimea he was mentioned in Sir Harry Jones's despatch of 9 September 1855, and received the Crimea Medal with *Sebastopol* clasp, the French Legion of Honour, the Turkish Crimea Medal, the Sardinian War Medal and the Turkish Order of the Medjidie (5th class), and he was created Commander of the Bath (CB), military division. On 17 July he received a brevet majority, and he was gazetted to lieutenant colonel on 26 December 1856.

Recovering his health at the end of 1856, Colonel Browne was quartered in Dublin until July 1859, when he went out to India to command the engineers in the Bombay presidency, with headquarters at Poona. In March 1860 he went on to Mauritius as commanding Royal Engineer, and in August 1861 he returned home to become superintendent of military discipline (now called assistant commandant) at Chatham, where he was second in command. He was promoted brevet colonel on 26 December 1864 and regimental lieutenant colonel on 2 May 1865. On 1 January 1866 he was moved to headquarters at the War Office, as assistant adjutant general for Royal Engineers, on the staff of the commander-in-chief, and five years later he was appointed deputy adjutant general. In July 1870 he was a member of the committee on the pay of officers of the Royal Artillery and Royal Engineers, and in January 1873 on the admission of university men to the scientific corps. He was awarded a distinguished service pension in October 1871. On 1 January 1876 Browne was appointed colonel on the staff and commanding Royal Engineer of the south-eastern district, with his headquarters at Dover, but his promotion to major general on 2 October 1877 (afterwards antedated to 22 February 1870) placed him on the half-pay list.

Browne was appointed Governor of the Royal Military Academy at Woolwich on 2 June 1880 and was promoted lieutenant general on 13 August 1881. He was placed on the unemployed list in 1887 and was promoted general on 12 February 1888. General Browne retired on a pension on 5 May 1888. On 6 April 1890 he was made a colonel commandant of Royal Engineers. He was appointed Knight Commander Order of the Bath (KCB) on 26 May 1894.

General Browne died on 6 December 1910, aged 87, at 19 Roland Gardens in South Kensington, and he was buried in Brompton Cemetery.

Brevet Major Eustace Fane Bourchier
Eustace Fane Bourchier was born on 25 August 1822 at Fareham in Hampshire, the only child of Commander William Bourchier (1791–1844) of the Royal Navy and his first wife Amelia (formerly Jackson), who had married in Canada on 8 April 1821 and made their home at The Briars in Jackson's Point, Ontario, Canada. Eustace had two step-sisters and a step-brother from his father's second marriage. He was educated at Bonn and the Royal Military Academy, from where he was commissioned as a second lieutenant in the Royal Engineers in January 1842.

Eustace quickly found himself employed on some memorable demolition duties, notably commanding a team of sappers detailed to blow up two large barges formerly used as foundations for the beacons at Blyth Sand in Sheerness. One of the explosions caused by his handiwork threw debris up in the air to a height of 200ft, at the same time blasting a column of water 80ft skyward. He was promoted to lieutenant in December 1844 and on being posted to the Cape of Good Hope he was employed with the 9th Company of Sappers and Miners in South Africa. The official history of the Corps recorded:

> On 23 April 1846, under Lieutenant Bourchier, RE, fifty-one non-commissioned officers and men repulsed an attack by the enemy on Farmer's Camp, near Fort Brown [on the Great Fish River]. The action lasted about four hours, and though the night was extremely dark, the sappers, serving both as infantry and artillery in charge of two field-pieces, beat off the enemy with the loss, as was afterwards acknowledged by the Chief, Stock, of thirty killed. The sappers *only* were engaged in this affair, and their spirited and gallant conduct was reported by Lieutenant Bourchier.

For his service he was mentioned in despatches and he received the South Africa Medal with *1834–53* clasp, and he was appointed second captain in August 1852.

While he was in South Africa he met and married South African-born Anne Jane (formerly Pillans, 1826–1868). Their first daughter was born at sea while they were on their way back to England, and they went on to have two sons and five daughters, born between 1850 and 1860. On the death of his wife, Eustace married on 25 August 1869 Maria (formerly Ramsey, 1820–1882), the widow of Wilmot Seton, who worked at the Treasury.

Eustace was serving at Gibraltar when he received orders for active service in the Crimean War, and landed at Kalamity Bay in mid-September 1854 as commanding officer of the 8th Company of Sappers and Miners. He was present at the battles of the Alma and at Inkerman, and he was made brigade major in April 1855. For his services in the East he received the Crimea Medal with *Alma*, *Inkerman* and *Sebastopol* clasps, the Turkish Order of the Medjidie (5th Class), the French Legion of Honour and the Turkish Crimea Medal 1855, and he was appointed Commander of the Bath (CB) on 5 February 1856. He was mentioned in despatches by General Sir Harry Jones and was also advanced to lieutenant colonel. From 1857 to 1860 he acted as Commanding Royal Engineer at Nassau in the Bahamas, gaining promotion to full colonel in August 1862. He was appointed AAG in Ireland between 1866 and 1868, in which latter year he became a major general. He retired in the late 1870s as a lieutenant-general.

Lieutenant General Bourchier died in Brighton on 16 January 1902, aged 79. His medals were sold at auction in 2002.

Captain Howard Crawfurd Elphinstone VC
Howard Crawfurd Elphinstone was born of a distinguished Scottish military and diplomatic family at his family's country seat of 'Kumenhoff' at Wattram in Livonia on 12 December 1829. He was the youngest of four sons to Captain Alexander Francis Elphinstone of the Royal Navy, a noble in Livonia, and his wife Amelia Anne (formerly Lobach). His great-grandfather was Captain John Elphinstone of the Royal Navy, who as an admiral was attached to the Russian Navy and commanded the Russian Fleet in the victory over the Turks at the sea battle of Tchesme Bay in 1770. He was named after his uncle, Major General Sir Howard Elphinstone, who commanded the Royal Engineers during the Peninsular War.

Howard was educated abroad and passed out of the Royal Military Academy at Woolwich as the head of his batch. He was commissioned as a

A Selection of Tributes and Commemorations

second lieutenant in the Royal Engineers on 18 December 1848, and became a lieutenant on 11 November 1851. He attended military reviews in Prussia in an official capacity in 1853, after which he worked in the Ordnance Survey in Scotland until March 1854, when he received orders for active service in the Crimea.

His award of the Victoria Cross was announced in the *London Gazette* of 4 June 1858, and he received the medal from Queen Victoria on Southsea Common in Portsmouth on 2 August 1858, along with fellow Redan hero Thomas Esmonde. He also received the Crimea Medal with *Alma*, *Inkerman* and *Sebastopol* clasps, the French Legion of Honour and the Turkish Order of the Medjidie (5th Class).

In March 1856 he went on an official mission to The Hague in the Netherlands, and reported on a public hospital in Rotterdam, and in September reported on the Koblenz siege operations. He was highly commended for these reports, and he received a promotion to brevet major on 26 December 1856. From 5 September 1857 he was employed in the topographical department of the War Office working on an official history of the Royal Engineers in the Crimea. In 1858 he was involved in the administration concerning the establishment of the 'The Prince Consort's Library' at Aldershot, which was a gift to the army from Prince Albert. He served in the North British Military District, and was promoted captain on 1 April 1862, brevet lieutenant colonel on 9 April 1968 and major on 5 July 1872.

He became a great friend of Prince Albert, who appointed him as governor to his seventh child, the young Prince Arthur, Duke of Connaught, on 24 January 1859. Howard seemed eminently suited for the job. He was an excellent linguist, had considerable talent for art and music, a pleasant personality and a reputation for integrity, discretion and tact – all highly necessary qualities for one entrusted with the care of the prince.

Howard gave a comforting hand to the Queen on the death of her beloved husband in 1861. He became a close confidant of hers, and he was appointed treasurer and comptroller of Prince Arthur's household in May 1871. Bagshot Park in Surrey was a residence of the Duke of Connaught, and as most of his military service now centred around nearby Aldershot, Howard had a house built in Bagshot, which was off College Ride and was named 'Pinewood'.

On 5 December 1876 he married Annie Frances (formerly Cole), who was twenty-six years younger than him, at the Church of St Anne in Bagshot. Annie was the daughter of William Cole of Woodhay House in Newbury, and one of her relations was the famous eccentric prankster, Horace de Vere Cole. They had four daughters: Victoria Alexandrina (1877–1952), Irene

Francis (1878–1957), Olive Margaret (1882–1968) and Mary Howard (1888–1965). Queen Victoria stood sponsor for Victoria, and all four daughters married army officers.

Howard was made Commander of the Bath (CB, civil division) on 23 August 1865, (CB, military division) on 20 May 1871, a Companion of the Order of St Michael and St George (CMG) on 28 July 1870, and Knight Commander of the Order of the Bath (KCB) on 3 July 1871. He was appointed aide-de-camp to Queen Victoria on 1 October 1877.

He commanded the Royal Engineers units at Aldershot from August 1873 until 30 December 1881, and was colonel commanding Royal Engineer at Aldershot from 31 December 1881 to 30 December 1886. He became a colonel on 3 May 1884, and during 1884–1885 he acted as temporary military attaché at Berlin. He was promoted major general on 29 January 1887, and on 1 April 1889 he was appointed to command the western military district. He was awarded the Queen Victoria Jubilee Medal in 1887 and he was also appointed Grand Officer of the Order of the Red Eagle (Prussia).

On 8 March 1890 he and his wife left Plymouth bound for Tenerife in the steamer *Tongariro* on leave for his health. He was walking on the deck near Ushant in the Bay of Biscay when he slipped, hit his head and fell overboard. He was 60 years old. His body was never recovered, and Queen Victoria, who was said to have been 'much upset, and cried at the news' of his death, stated: 'I am quite upset, the whole thing haunts me.' She wrote in her journal, and later in a letter to Lady Elphinstone, 'Words cannot be found to express all I feel – what a beloved and valuable friend he was. My tears flow fast while I write, in thinking of you both! My poor Arthur loses a second father, and he owes his success in life to him!' She demanded that a memorial service was held at Exeter Cathedral. His obituary in the *London Echo* read:

> In the circumstances of the death of Crimean hero, Sir Howard Elphinstone, there is something which appeals strongly to the imagination.
>
> It has its pathetic side also; the man who thirty-six years ago escaped alive from the fatal attack on the Redan, who survived the forlorn hopes, the diseases, and the iron showers of the famous siege, has lost his life in what appears to have been a casual, accidental manner. To perish in the discharge of a great duty is a form of the end which men may envy, but in death from what seems to have been a trifling avoidable casualty there is an element of fatality.
>
> Sir Howard Elphinstone left Devonport on Saturday, 8th March, on a voyage to Tenerife, where he was to meet his daughter, and to recruit his

health. On the very day of his departure he was swept overboard by a wave, and drowned. We know nothing about the construction of the *Tongariro*, in which he sailed to Tenerife, but if she is at all like some other vessels trading to the east and south, there must be considerable risk to her passengers on deck when heavy seas are running and the vessel is pitching and lurching. Low bulwarks are a frequent feature in the construction of many of these vessels. For all we know the *Tongariro* may be built quite differently.

It is merely announced that he was swept overboard and drowned. There will be genuine public sympathy for the widow and her children in their bereavement, and among those who knew Sir Howard Elphinstone keen personal regret. Sir Howard Elphinstone was still young enough for many years' useful labour in his profession. He was only 61.

Last year he was appointed to the command of the Western District, a post for which he was highly qualified by honourable service, wide knowledge of military affairs, to say nothing of his inborn faculty of winning the confidence, respect, and liking of all with whom he was professionally associated.

When the Crimean War broke out he had been already for some years an officer of Engineers. In the Crimea he won his Victoria Cross; and the terms in which the official despatch spoke of his claims to the distinction were flattering in the highest degree. He volunteered on the most desperate enterprises before Sebastopol; and on one occasion he succeeded in bringing away twenty wounded men almost from the very muzzles of the Russian guns. This last exploit performed, not in the excitement of actual combat, but with deliberation and for a purely humane object, made a great impression upon his superiors at the time.

With all this, Sir Howard Elphinstone was modest and unassuming in the extreme. When the Queen appointed him to take charge of the military education of her son, the Duke of Connaught, it was said that her Majesty could not have made a wiser choice. He held his post of tutor, or governor, for twelve years. He turned out a capital pupil. At any rate, we have heard Lord Wolseley himself say so. 'If there's a man in the Army that knows his business it is the duke of Connaught.' Of course, the Duke has learned his business in the practical work of camps, barracks, and battlefields; but he owes a great deal to Sir Howard Elphinstone.'

Annie, his wife, died in 1938, and there are brass plaques and a memorial window dedicated to them by their daughter at St Anne's Church in Bagshot and at St Lawrence's Church in Newbury. There is a memorial at Exeter Cathedral; a memorial plaque at Devonport Chapel; a memorial at St George's Garrison Church in Aldershot; and Howard is named on the 'For Valour' commemoration board at the Royal Engineers Museum in Chatham. A locomotive nameplate bears his name at the Museum of Army Transport in Beverley, Yorkshire. His Victoria Cross is now displayed on rotation at the Lord Ashcroft Gallery, as part of the 'Extraordinary Heroes' exhibition at the Imperial War Museum in London. It is the only one of the four 18 June Redan Royal Engineers Victoria Crosses not in the regimental museum.

'The Queen Thanks Sir Howard'
In 1945 Sir Howard's youngest daughter, Mary Howard McClintock, wrote a biography of him, which she entitled *The Queen Thanks Sir Howard: The Life of Major-General Sir Howard Elphinstone, VC KCB CMG*. She chose the title because that was the form with which at least half of Victoria's 600 or so letters to him began. They were replies to his letters to her, over a thousand of which were discovered late in 1942 among twenty huge volumes of confidential family papers which had been stored at Bagshot Park, the Duke of Connaught's home. Published by royal permission, the letters form the basis of the biography, which at the same time serves to give an extraordinarily intimate and human picture of the relationship between the Queen and her 'favourite' son. The first of these volumes dates back to 1857, the year in which the Prince Consort began to look around for an army officer to act as governor in charge of young Prince Arthur, for whom a military career was planned.

Sir Howard also had a great deal of influence over Queen Victoria. It did not extend to affairs of state, but in all family matters, from the royal children's whooping cough to their matrimonial alliances, he was her confidant and councillor. It was to Sir Howard that the Queen confided her domestic troubles, problems and sorrows; to him she poured out her worries, fussed endlessly about the health, manners, habits and character of her four sons and five daughters, and later her brood of grandchildren. 'Why, the Queen can't even choose a carpet without consulting him!' was the somewhat acid comment once passed on Sir Howard. How complete was the Queen's dependence on Sir Howard not merely for advice (which, need it be added, she did not always take) but also for a sympathetic audience is evident from the hundreds of letters that passed between them during his long association with the Court.

The Queen admitted to Albert, 'This child is dear, dearer than any of the others put together, thus after you he is the dearest and most precious object to me on earth. The bare thought of his growing out of my hands and being exposed to danger makes the tears come to my eyes.' Inevitably her Majesty was bound to regard with jealous suspicion whoever was entrusted with the upbringing of her 'precious angel'. To win both the boy's affection and respect and the anxious mother's confidence would not be an easy task. However, the appointment, which the captain accepted in January 1859, was intended to be only for twelve months. It lasted for thirty years.

As his governor, Sir Howard had to teach Prince Arthur to be steady under fire and how to stand, sit, eat, speak and dress. He had to help choose the Prince's friends, and take him into society. He had to see that all the Prince's apartments were kept at the Queen's favourite temperature of 60 degrees, and nurse him when he was sick because the Queen would have no female nurses. He had to keep the Prince away from the influence of his two elder brothers, supervise his correspondence, and report to the Queen by letter anything from three times a week to five times a day. When the Prince visited the courts of Europe in search of a bride, Sir Howard was there with advice. When the Prince went on honeymoon, Sir Howard went too. When the Prince was to live at Bagshot Park, the house was reconstructed according to detailed drawings, interior and exterior, by Sir Howard.

Holidays were practically impossible. Victoria wrote: 'The Queen wishes Sir Howard to accept her very sincere congratulations on his engagement to Miss Cole, which she trusts will secure his happiness. She feels sure that Sir Howard is far too conscientious ever to let his private affairs interfere with his services to herself and her dear son, of which she has had so many proofs during the last 17 years.'

Sir Howard's great day came when the Prince sailed off in command of the Guards Brigade for a short campaign to put down a native rising in Egypt. When the Guards charged at Tel-el-Kebir, the Prince was more than steady under fire. He led the attack and behaved, according to a general, 'like a veteran'. Soon he was given the important Bombay command, and Sir Howard attended him in India.

Captain William Howard Jesse
William Howard Jesse was born on 13 November 1821 at St John in New Brunswick, Canada. Educated at the Royal Military Academy at Woolwich, he was commissioned as an ensign into the Royal Engineers in June 1841, being promoted lieutenant in December 1844. He saw active service against Xhosa natives in South Africa during the Seventh Cape Frontier War of 1846–1847, serving on the staff as an Assistant Quarter-Master General and gaining

advancement to second captain in April 1852. For his service in South Africa he received the South Africa Medal with *1834–53* clasp.

While he was serving in South Africa he met Catherine Jemima, the daughter of Lieutenant Donald Moodie RN (1794–1861), and they married and had one daughter named Mary Louise. Unfortunately Catherine died of tuberculosis in Natal in 1860 and Mary died at the age of 17.

Leaving his family in South Africa, Jesse sailed for active service in the trenches before Sebastopol. Lieutenant Fisher RE stated in his report that his senior 'was shot through the head whilst in the act of speaking to me'. Lieutenant Charles Gordon RE likewise reported: 'Jesse was killed at the abbatis, shot through the head.' For his service he was entitled to the Crimean Medal with *Sebastopol* clasp.

At the time of his death the Jesse family home was in Bayswater. His two medals were sold at auction in 2000.

Lieutenant Gerald Graham VC

Gerald Graham was born at East Acton in West London on 27 June 1831, the only surviving son of Doctor Robert Hay Graham, who practised in London although his main residence was Eden Brows at Armathwaite near Carlisle, and his wife Frances, who was a daughter of Richard Banner Oakley of Oswaldkirk in Yorkshire. Gerald had an older sister named Joanna, to whom he was devoted. His father was a director of various railway companies, but suffered from gout, and in 1844 he prepared a paper entitled *Graeffenberg: or a True Report of the Water Cure*, in which he devalued the claims of Vincent Priessnitz that the use of a water compress was a cure for the disease.

Gerald grew to be 6ft 4in tall and despite his height was stockily built. He and his sister were ardent readers of the classics, and he read and later befriended Charles Kingsley. However, he showed his prowess early in life when he is said to have jumped onto the back of a colt that was being difficult in a field at Eden Brows, and stayed there despite the horse's wild efforts to throw him off. It raced into the farmyard and smashed into a gatepost and nearly broke Gerald's leg, while several local farm lads looked on in astonishment at his 'fearless audacity'.

Gerald was educated in Wimbledon, at Dresden in Germany and at the Royal Military Academy in Woolwich. After completing his training at the School of Military Engineering in Chatham, he was commissioned as a second lieutenant in the 11th Company, Royal Sappers and Miners, on 19 June 1850, becoming a lieutenant on 17 February 1854. He embarked for active service in the East with his company at Southampton on 24 February 1854 on the

A Selection of Tributes and Commemorations

steamship *Himalaya*. He was employed on constructing fortifications at Boulair in Gallipoli before moving on to Varna. A letter from Lieutenant Charles Gordon RE (later Gordon of Khartoum) states: 'Lieutenant Graham, RE, was rather severely wounded by stones from a round shot on Sunday night – a good deal cut in the face.' After the fall of Sebastopol, Gerald was engaged in the destruction of the docks, when he and Major Nicholson made a gallant attempt to rescue a man who was poisoned by the toxic air at the bottom of a shaft.

His award of the Victoria Cross was announced in the *London Gazette* on 24 February 1857, and he became the first member of the Corps of Royal Engineers to wear the medal when he received it at the first investiture. It is a known fact that Victoria pierced the skin of Commander Raby, but she must have done this more than once, as Gerald wrote to his father: 'We were formed in a line and then advanced singly to the Queen, who remained on horseback. She pinned the medal (cross) with her own hand to our coats. She stuck the pin fairly into me, so that I keenly realised my momentary interview with Royalty.' He also received the Crimea Medal with *Alma*, *Inkerman* and *Sebastopol* clasps, the French Legion of Honour, the Order of the Medjidie (5th Class) and the Turkish Crimea Medal.

Doctor Graham died at Eden Brows on 12 December 1859 and Gerald took over his estate. After being employed in Scotland and at Aldershot, he was posted to India in August 1858 to take command of the 23rd Company, Royal Engineers, but the mutiny there was almost over. He was promoted captain on 8 October 1858.

His next tour of active duty was in China in 1859–1860, where he served in the Second Anglo-China (Opium) War, taking part in another dangerous assault at the Taku Forts on 21 August 1860. On this occasion the assault was successful. The attacking force had to cross a series of ditches and bamboo-stake palisades under heavy fire from the defences. Assault parties eventually breached the defences and forced entry into the fort. Gerald was seriously wounded when he was hit by a ball from a jingal fired from the ramparts. He received the China Medal with *Taku Forts* and *Pekin* clasps. Newspapers reported:

> Major Graham was in China with Gordon, and led the sappers, whose duty it was to lay the pontoon across the wet ditch surrounding the great northern fort.
>
> While superintending this operation he was on horseback, and being almost the only mounted officer present, afforded an easy mark to the

Chinese matchlock men, who had already picked off 15 of his sappers. During the height of the uproar caused by the firing of the great guns and small arms, Lieutenant-Colonel Wolseley, who was attending by Major Graham, having some remark to make, placed his hand on that officer's thigh to draw his attention.

'Don't put your hand there!' exclaimed Graham, wincing under the pain. 'There's a jingal-ball lodged in my leg.' It was the first notice he had taken of the wound.'

For the next sixteen years he was commanding engineer at various stations throughout England and Montreal, and he was promoted captain on 4 August 1864, major on 5 July 1872 and lieutenant colonel on 27 September 1876, and he was appointed Commander of the Bath (CB) on 6 April 1867.

He served as brigadier general in Egypt in 1882 with his old friend Garnet Wolseley, commanding the second brigade of the first division through out the campaign. He was in the thick of the action as usual in the victories at El Magfar, Kassassin and Tel-el-Kebir. He commanded the Saukin Field Force in the Sudan, 1884–1885, where he was in charge of the troops trying to relieve his friend, Charles Gordon, at Khartoum. For his service in North Africa he received the Egypt Medal with *Tel-el-Kebir, Saukin, 1884, El Teb-Tamaii* and *Saukin, 1885* clasps, the Order of the Medjidie (2nd Class) and the Khedives Bronze Star. He wore on his breast a total of ten medals with nine clasps.

Lord Wolseley, who had known and witnessed the deeds of many gallant soldiers, described him as 'perhaps the bravest man I have ever met'. He also stated that he was 'a man with the heart of a lion, and the modesty of a young girl'. On his return to England he was one of the 'Sudan celebrities' who became the subjects of waxworks models in the Madame Tussaud Exhibition soon after it moved to its present location in London in 1884. He rose to the rank of lieutenant general on 21 May 1884, and received the thanks of both Houses of Parliament on three occasions.

On a short summer tour of the north-east he was presented with a sword of honour by the 1st Newcastle and Durham Engineer Volunteers of Jarrow on 22 July 1884. In January 1887 he contributed an article to *Fortnightly Review* magazine entitled 'Last Words with General Gordon', in which he recalled his service and friendship with Gordon of Khartoum. He was offered the position of Governor of Bermuda in 1888 but turned it down. He retired on 14 June 1890, being appointed Knight Commander of the Grand Cross (GCB) on 20 May 1896 and Knight Commander of St Michael and St George (GCMG).

For the last six years of his life he lived at a house called 'Springfield' in Northam near Bideford in Devon. He was suffering with a cold when he went out to read telegrams about the Boer War and caught a chill which developed into inflammation of the lungs. He died on 17 December 1899, aged 68, and was buried at East-the-Water Cemetery in Bideford, where there is a headstone. The mayor and corporation of Bideford were present at his funeral. Graham Close at Chatham in Kent is named after him; there is a painting of him in the Royal Engineers Officers' Mess in Chatham; he is named on the 'For Valour' commemoration board at the Royal Engineers Museum in Chatham; and he had an army locomotive named after him. His medals are with the Royal Engineers Museum.

Lieutenant Arthur A'Court Fisher

Arthur A'Court Fisher was born on 16 January 1830 in the village of Poulshot near Devizes in Wiltshire, the third son of six in the family of eight children, born between 1825 and 1838, of the Reverend William Fisher (1801–1874) and his wife Elizabeth Reed (formerly Cookson, 1801–1853), who had married at Salisbury Cathedral in 1824. William was the vicar of St Peter's Church in Poulshot from 1823 until his death.

Arthur was educated at the Royal Military Academy and was commissioned into the Royal Engineers on 1 October 1847. He worked on fortifications at Gibraltar prior to the Crimean War.

On 11 September 1851, at St Clements Church in Leigh-on-Sea, Essex, he married Caroline (1832–1918), a daughter of the Reverend Robert Eden (1804–1886), Bishop of Moray, Ross and Caithness, and his wife Emma. They had three boys and three girls, born between 1853 and 1873.

After the Crimean War they lived for a time at Beyton in Suffolk, and the 1861 census has the family living with Caroline's parents at Capel House on The Green in Kew, Richmond.

Arthur was promoted major in 1859 and took part in the second dreadful assault against the Taku Forts in China in 1860, and in 1863 he published *A Personal Narrative of Three Years' Service in China*.

Their sixth and last child was born at Reay House in Inverness in 1873, and Lieutenant Colonel Fisher died there on 2 November 1879, aged 49.

Lieutenant Thomas Molyneux Graves

Thomas Molyneux Graves was born on 22 March 1831 in Whitehall, London. He was the eldest son of five in the family of thirteen children, born between 1828 and 1852, of John Samuel Graves JP (1800–1861), a barrister, and Maria (formerly Molyneaux, 1802–1875). They had married on

15 February 1827 at Charlton King's in Cheltenham. The main family home was at 15 Burlington Street in Bath, and they also owned property at Castle Dillon House in County Armagh, Ireland.

Thomas's name appears on the obelisk at Bath Abbey Cemetery which is dedicated to all those from Bath who lost their lives during the Crimean War, and also includes Major General Sir John Campbell. There is also a memorial dedicated to Lieutenant Graves at St Nicholas Church in the Devonshire village of Combe Raleigh near Honiton, which reads: 'In memory of Thomas Molyneux Graves, Ltn, RE. Born 22 March 1831. Killed in the assault on the Redan, 18 June 1855; and Thomas Molyneux Graves, Ltn, 76th Punjabis, Indian Army. Born 1 June 1890, at Woodbine Hill, Combe Raleigh. Killed at Sanna-i-at, Mesopotamia, 22 April 1916. The eldest son and grandson of J S Graves, Esq, of Woodbine Hill, Combe Raleigh. These were men who put their duty above all else.'

Lieutenant James Murray
James Murray was born on 3 July 1829, one of three sons in the family of five children of Vice Admiral James Arthur Murray RN (1790–1860), and his first wife Harriet (formerly Coupland). They had married on 13 December 1821, but sadly Harriet died soon after James was born. He was a great-grandson of the 3rd Duke of Athol.

James attended the New Cross Naval School, being one of six men who were killed in action in the Crimea whose names appear on the Crimean War memorial tablet at the New Cross Old Royal Naval School Chapel in Greenwich: 'Lieutenant James Murray, RE, mortally wounded whilst leading his company to the assault in the Redan, 18 June 1855. In remembrance and appreciation of their gallant and meritorious services. A few former pupils and friends of the Institution have erected this monument [in 1858].'

The names of Captain Jesse, Lieutenant Graves and Lieutenant Murray are among the 274 which appear on the Triumphal Arch at Brompton Barracks in Chatham, which is dedicated to members of the Corps of Royal Engineers who were killed in action during the Crimean War: 'To their comrades who fell in the war with Russia MDCCCLIV–V. Ubique, Quo Fas Et Gloria Ducunt Ubique [Everywhere Where Right and Glory Lead].

Colour Sergeant Peter Leitch VC
Peter Leitch was born in August 1820 at Milnathort, Orwell, Kinross-shire, Scotland. On 28 August 1843 he enlisted into the 2nd Company, Royal Sappers and Miners at Glasgow, which was the same company as John Ross. In February 1844 he was posted from the Hospital Company to the

3rd Company at Chatham. At an unknown date he was charged for breaking his spitting cup when in the House of Correction at Cold Bath Fields in Southampton. He returned to the 2nd Company for active service in the Crimean War.

Peter Leitch and John Ross were with the 2nd Company sent to the Baltic theatre of war, taking part in the capture of the Aland Islands and the demolition of the fort at Bomarsund. They returned to England on HMS *Cumberland*, arriving at Woolwich on 16 October 1854, only to be sent back on active service to the Crimea before the end of the year.

Leitch's award of the Victoria Cross was announced in the *London Gazette* of 4 June 1858, and he received the medal from Sir James Outram at Natal in South Africa on 2 November 1858, being the last of the 18 June Redan Victoria Cross men to receive it. At the age of 35, Colour Sergeant Leitch was the oldest of all the 18 June Redan Victoria Cross recipients. He also received the Baltic Medal, 1854–55, the Crimea Medal with *Sebastopol* clasp, the French Legion of Honour (5th Class) and the Turkish Crimea Medal.

He was promoted to sergeant major, and on 14 January 1858 he was injured in the back by a fall of earth at Chatham. Later in that year he sailed for service at the Cape of Good Hope, where he remained for nine years. He married an Irish girl named Clarissa, and they had a son named Malcolm Peter there in 1860, who became a civil engineer. He served in Gibraltar for six years prior to his discharge at Gravesend on 14 March 1872, having served over twenty-eight years. He had two good conduct badges, had never been in the defaulters' book and his conduct was described as very good. He was awarded the Long Service Good Conduct Medal. He went to live at Milton Barracks in Gravesend, Kent, and in 1881 he was living at Dover Castle with his wife and 7-year-old grandson named Malcolm, being described as a foreman of works.

Leitch died at Durville Road in Fulham, West London, on 6 December 1892, aged 72, and was buried at the Margravine Road Cemetery in Hammersmith. His grave was not marked and the cemetery has now been partially levelled. Leitch Row in Chatham is named after him; he is named on the 'For Valour' commemoration board at the Royal Engineers Museum in Chatham; and an army locomotive was named after him. His medals are in the Royal Engineers Museum.

Sapper John Pirie VC
John Perie was born on 7 April 1821 at Huntly in Aberdeenshire, Scotland. His father was a farm servant living at Gartly in 1821. Apparently, all local

pupils were guided to go to the sixth form comprehensive Gordon School in Huntly, which was founded in 1839. John was a mason by trade, and joined the Royal Artillery at Aberdeen on 8 January 1848, aged 18. He transferred to the 8th Company, Royal Sappers and Miners, on 1 March 1848, and it seems that he pronounced his name in the local dialect, 'Peerie', and the English clerk wrote his name on the roll as Pirie. He thus sailed for active service in the Crimea as 854 Sapper Pirie.

After the assault on the Redan, Lieutenant Graham acknowledged 'the steady conduct of the party of sappers under Sergeant Coppin of the 4th company', and drew attention to the valiant behaviour of Private John Pirie. Speaking of Private Pirie at another time, Lieutenant Graham wrote, 'He was invaluable to me on that day, as he followed me everywhere, and was always ready when I wanted anything done.' His cool determination in taking a message to Lieutenant Murray in front during the thick of the fight, and returning with an answer, was one of the instances which called for Lieutenant Graham's special commendation.

His award of the Victoria Cross was announced in the *London Gazette* on 24 February 1857, and he received the medal at the first investiture. He also received the Crimea Medal with *Alma, Balaclava, Inkerman* and *Sebastopol* clasps, the French Military Medal and the Turkish Crimea Medal.

Regarded as 'an unlettered man, but a first class sapper and leader', Sapper Pirie was tried by a regimental court martial at Sebastopol on 31 January 1856 for habitual drunkenness, and he was sentenced to twenty-eight days in prison with hard labour.

Perie went on to serve in Gibraltar for five and a half years before sailing for active service in the second Anglo-China (Opium) War of 1860, taking part in the second dangerous assault at the Taku Forts on 21 August 1860. On this occasion the assault was successful. The attacking force had to cross a series of ditches and bamboo-stake palisades under heavy fire from the ramparts. Assault parties eventually breached the defences and forced entry into the fort. For his service he received the China Medal with *Taku Forts* clasp. On his return from the East he was discharge at Chatham on 3 September 1860, and returned to Scotland.

It would seem that his excessive drinking habits continued and eventually had a bad effect on his constitution, because he was aged only 53 when he died of liver disease and general debility in his home at 69 East North Street in Aberdeen on 17 September 1874. He was considered a pauper and was buried in the 'Strangers Ground' at St Peter's Cemetery in Aberdeen. The grave was not marked and the burial register records his name as 'Pirie'. A new

A Selection of Tributes and Commemorations

headstone bearing the surname 'Perie' was erected against a wall at the cemetery in 2001 near to where he is believed to be buried, which gives his date and place of birth as '7 April 1821 in Gartly'. He is named on the 'For Valour' commemoration board at the Royal Engineers Museum in Chatham; Perie Row in Chatham is named after him, as is an army locomotive; and a new Territorial Army centre in Huntly was named after him. His medals are with the Royal Engineers Museum.

4th (King's Own) Regiment

Colonel Henry Clermont Cobbe

Henry Clermont Cobbe was born on 20 December 1811, the eldest child in the family of five sons and five daughters of Colonel Thomas Alexander Cobbe (1788–1836), who was in the service of the Honourable East India Company, and his wife Nuzzeer Begum Khan, who was known as 'Trigger'. Henry's nephew was General Alexander Stanhope Cobbe (1870–1931), who was awarded the Victoria Cross for gallantry while serving with the King's African Rifles in Somaliland in 1902.

Colonel Henry Cobbe was buried on Cathcart's Hill: 'Sacred to the memory of Colonel HC Cobbe, CB, 4th King's Own Regiment; who died August 6 1855, of wounds received when in command of the trenches, Left attack, June 18 1855. Deeply regretted by his brother officers.'

Ensign Edward Bromhead

Edward Bromhead was born on 21 March 1832 at Sligo, although the family home was at Thurlby Hall near Lincoln. The Bromhead Baronetcy was established in 1806 as a reward for the family's highly distinguished military service. His father was Major Sir Edmund de Gonville Bromhead (1791–1870), the 3rd Baron, who lost an eye while on active service during the Battle of Waterloo in 1815. Two of his younger brothers saw active service in the Zulu War in 1879, and one of them, Gonville, was awarded the Victoria Cross as the officer in command of B Company, 24th Regiment, during the immortal defence of Rorke's Drift – the battle made famous in the motion picture *Zulu!*

Edward was commissioned into the 4th (King's Own) Regiment as an ensign on 15 February 1855 and joined the unit while it was on active service at Sebastopol in the Crimea. He was promoted lieutenant on 21 December 1855 and captain in 1866. He left the King's Own in 1867 to join the 76th (West Riding) Regiment, and went with that regiment to Burma in January 1868. Captain Edward Bromhead died at Thyetmyo in Burma on 9 January 1869, aged 37, and was buried there. A memorial stone was erected at his grave 'by his brother officers'. As the eldest son, his death deprived him of becoming the 4th Baron Bromhead in the following year.

7th Royal Fusiliers
Colonel Lacy Walter Giles Yea

Lacy Walter Giles Yea was born on 20 May 1808 at Park Row in Bristol. He was the eldest son of Sir William Walter Yea (1784–1862), 2nd Baronet, of Pyrland Hall in Cheddon Fitzpaine near Taunton, and his wife Anne (formerly Heckstetter), who died in 1846. The Baronetcy was created on 18 June 1759, a date which was to become significant in the family a hundred years later.

Lacy Yea was educated at Eton College, where Lord Salmesbury remembered that at the age of 13 he had a desperate fight with a boy who was three years older, which he won by 'sheer pluck'. He is said to have borne a resemblance to Napoleon I, and that he once went to a fancy dress ball held in Bath dressed as the emperor, with some of his fellow officers as his suite.

He was commissioned as an ensign in the 37th Regiment on 6 October 1825, transferring to the 5th Regiment on 13 March 1827. He began his long service with the 7th Royal Fusiliers on 13 March 1828, serving in the Mediterranean and North America. He was promoted to captain on 30 December 1836, major on 3 June 1842 and lieutenant colonel on 9 August 1850. He gained a reputation as a strict disciplinarian. For his gallantry in the Crimea he received the praise of the colonel of the regiment, Sir Edward Blakeney. He was mentioned in despatches several times and was made brevet colonel.

Colonel Yea was buried in the 1st Brigade, Light Division Cemetery near Sebastopol: '7th Royal Fusiliers. To their Colonel Walter Lacy Yea, who was killed on 18 June 1855, whilst gallantly leading the storming party against the Great Redan, aged 47 years.'

His eldest sister, Charlotte Mary, erected an impressive memorial dedicated to him at St James's Church in Taunton Deane, Somerset:

> In memory of Colonel Lacy Walter Giles Yea, Lieut-Col of the Royal Fusiliers. Aged 47; Eldest son of Sir William Walter Yea of Pyrland Hall in this county. He was killed on 18 June 1855 at the head of his regiment while leading the assaulting Division which he commanded with dauntless intrepidity in a desperate attack on the Redan during the siege of Sebastopol, after nearly 30 years service.
>
> On the commencement of the war with Russia, up to the moment of his heroic death, he lost none of the many opportunities of distinction

offered on the battlefields of the Alma and Inkerman, and by the arduous duties of the trenches; exertions honourably recognised in the despatches of Field Marshal, Lord Raglan. He was no less conspicuous throughout the severity of his memorable campaigns for the parental attention which he successfully bestowed on the condition of his regiment. A solicitude requited by their most devoted respect and affection. He was buried in the Crimea in the presence of the Brigade he commanded. This monument is erected by his eldest sister.

The town of Muddy Creek in Victoria, Australia, was renamed Yea in his honour.

Lieutenant, Viscount, the Honourable Edward FitzClarence
Edward FitzClarence was born on 8 July 1837 in Upper Belgrave Street in Westminster, London. He was the youngest of four sons in the family of seven children, born between 1820 and 1837, of George Augustus Frederick FitzClarence (1794–1842), 1st Earl of Munster, and his wife Mary (1792–1842), the daughter of George Wyndham, 3rd Earl of Egremont. George was a veteran of the Peninsular War.

Prince William, Duke of Clarence (1765–1837) the future King William IV, had at least ten children with his mistress Dorothea Bland (1761–1816), an entertainer who was better known by her stage name, Mrs Jordan. She became his mistress in 1791 and when George III appointed the Duke as the ranger of Bushy Park in 1797, Bushy House became their home. 'Dora' eventually took the surname FitzClarence. Edward's father was believed to be the first-born child of this relationship.

Edward entered the 7th Royal Fusiliers as an ensign in November 1854 and while on active service in the Crimea in January 1855 he was promoted lieutenant. The *London Evening Standard*, and several other newspapers of 28 July 1855, reported,

> Death of Lieutenant, The Hon. E Fitzclarence – We regret to announce that telegraphic intelligence of the death of this gallant and promising young officer was received in town yesterday. Lieutenant Fitzclarence died Wednesday last, from the effects of his wounds at the English Hospital at Constantinople, to which place he had been conveyed from Balaclava. The gallant deceased was serving as aide-de-camp to his colonel, the late Yea, and with him took part in the unsuccessful attack on the Redan on the 18th, ult, when he was very dangerously wounded. He suffered amputation of the left leg and the right hand, which

operation he bore with great fortitude, and, at the date of the last letters he was considered to be progressing most favourably, so that the receipt of the news of his death has occasioned much grief to his relatives.

The deceased was the fourth and youngest son of the late Earl of Munster, and was born on 8 July 1837. He entered the 7th Regiment as ensign in November 1854 and in January last obtained his lieutenancy. In the spring he accompanied the depot of his regiment to the seat of war, and he had only been a few weeks before Sebastopol when he was called upon to assist in the attempt on Redan.

The families of the Earl and Countess of Erroll; the Countess (Dowager) of Erroll; Lord Adolphus Fitzclarence; Viscount and Viscountess Campden; Mr Duff MP, and Lady Agnes Duff; Lord Frederick and Lady Augusta Gordon Halyburton; Viscount and Viscountess Falkland, etc, are placed in mourning by the premature death of the gallant deceased.

Edward's nephew was Captain Charles FitzClarence of the 7th Royal Fusiliers, known as the 'Hero of Mafeking' for his gallantry on defending that town during the Boer War, and for which he was awarded the Victoria Cross. He was killed in action in 1914 serving with the Irish Guards during the First World War.

Lieutenant Charles Hawiton Malan
Charles Hawiton Malan was born on 19 August 1837 in Brighton, one of six sons and a daughter of Solomon Jean Caesar Malan (1812–1894), a native of Geneva in Switzerland, and his wife Mary (formerly Marsh-Mortlock, 1813–1840), who bore him three children before she died of consumption. Solomon became the vicar of St John the Baptist Church in the village of Broadwindsor, Dorset, in 1845, and was known to have spoken twenty-seven languages. An inscription at Broadwindsor Church states that he was 'the most accomplished Oriental linguist in England'. On 16 July 1878 he donated a collection of over a thousand birds' eggs of nearly 300 different species to the Royal Albert Memorial Museum in Exeter.

Charles served in the Crimea from 12 June 1855. Despite being wounded four times at Sebastopol, he later travelled extensively and was twice married – firstly to Edith Mary Josephine (formerly Maryatt, 1838–1866), and then to Caroline Georgiana Monk (formerly Mason, 1836–1924). He had a daughter with his first wife, named Evelyn Mary Georgiana (1864–1954).

He had reached the rank of major, and was head of the British Army Contingent in Singapore, when he decided to devote his life to Christianity.

He resigned his commission in 1872 and became a missionary in South Africa, including Zululand and Natal, and in the Eastern Cape, where he set up 'Malan's Store'. He recorded his experiences in two books: *A Soldier's Experience of God's Love and of his Faithfulness to his Word* (1874) and *South African Missions 1876* (1876). He was involved with the establishment of a ladies' college in London, along with Constance Maynard (1849–1935) and Ann Dudin Brown (1822–1917).

Major Malan died on 17 May 1881, aged 43, at 42 Stanhope Gardens in South Kensington, London, and was buried in Brompton Cemetery. His wife Caroline was buried with him. Westfield College for Ladies in Hampstead was established in the following year.

Lieutenant Napier Douglas Robinson

Napier Douglas Robinson was born on 3 December 1836 in Macao, China, the youngest of four sons in the family of five children, born between 1826 and 1836, of Sir George Best Robinson (1797–1855) and his wife Louise (formerly Douglas, 1800–1843). They had married on 5 December 1825 at St Peter's Church in Dyrham, Gloucestershire. George was the 2nd Baronet and Chief Superintendant of British Trade in China. At the time of the 1841 census the family lived at Dyrham House in Chipping Sodbury, and in 1851 they were living at Belle View House in High Street, Cheltenham.

Napier Douglas passed out of the Royal Military College at Sandhurst as a gentleman cadet in August 1854 and was soon sent for his first tour of active service in the Crimea. Lieutenant Robinson received the Crimea Medal with *Sebastopol* clasp and was promoted captain in August 1857.

In 1857 his brother Douglas, a captain in the 72nd Highlanders, had married Matilda, a daughter of the Reverend William Scott Robinson (1804–1875), who was Rector of Dyrham for forty-seven years, and on 14 March 1865, at St Peter's Church in Dyrham, Napier married Sophia Jane (1848–1927), another daughter of the Reverend Robinson. They had two daughters, Sophia Edith, born at Lucknow on 28 June 1868, who only lived for three months, and Ethel Sophia Napier, born at Kisser in India on 16 November 1869, after the death of her father.

Captain Robinson retired in 1866 and died at Cawnpore on 9 October 1869, aged 32. His widow Sophia married William Strachen in 1881.

Lieutenant William Hope VC

William Hope was born at 20 Moray Place in Edinburgh on 12 April 1834, the only surviving son of the Right Honourable John Hope PC FRSE (1794–1858), the Lord Chief Justice Clerk of Scotland from 1841 to 1858, and his wife Jesse Scott, the daughter of Thomas Irving of Shetland. They had married in August 1825. William was educated by private tutors and matriculated at Trinity Hall in Cambridge before he entered the 7th Royal Fusiliers on 12 April 1855 for active service in the Crimea.

William's award of the Victoria Cross was announced in the *London Gazette* of 5 May 1857 and he received the medal at the first investiture. He also received the Crimea Medal with *Sebastopol* clasp, the Turkish Crimea Medal and the Sardinian Medal of Military Valour, the citation for which states:

> At the great explosion of the French siege train, on the 15th of November, 1855, Lieutenant Hope was conspicuous for his coolness and activity, when in charge of a fatigue party, to cover the mill with wet blankets; the roof had been blown off, and one hundred and sixty tons of gunpowder were exposed to the fire of burning materials, rockets, etc.; he mounted the mill, and by his courage and example saved the magazine, which was momentarily expected to explode, and preserved the lives of probably hundreds of the light division. His conduct received the marked encomiums of the authorities. He had previously distinguished himself at the assault and taking of the Quarries.

In 1893 a submission was made to the War Office that he should receive a bar to his Victoria Cross for this action, but it was rejected.

The 7th Fusiliers landed at Portsmouth on 26 July 1856 and Lieutenant Hope retired from the regular army on 3 March 1857. However, he was a supporter of the Volunteer movement and became colonel of the 1st (City of London) Artillery Volunteer Corps when it was formed in 1863.

In 1857 he married Margaret Jane, the daughter of Robert Cunningham Cunninghame Graham of Gartmore in Fife. Their first child, Adrian, was born in Washington DC in the following year, and they had three boys and three girls between 1858 and 1873. They lived at Parsloes Manor in Dagenham, Essex (now Greater London) from 1867 to 1878. A painting of the manor commissioned by Hope is now in the Valence House Museum collection in Dagenham. The house was demolished in 1925.

Hope became military attaché to the celebrated diplomat Lord William Napier, who visited him several times at Parsloes. He was involved in various business ventures, notably being the inventor of the shrapnel shell for rifled guns. In 1862 he was described as general manager of the International Financial Society, and he was also director of the Lands Improvement Company, through which he had been involved in reclamation and irrigation work in Spain and Majorca, and reclaiming marshland in Essex. With Lord Napier

A Selection of Tributes and Commemorations

he proposed a scheme to convey sewage from the northern outfall of Joseph Bazelgette's London sewer system some 44 miles across Essex to reclaim 20,000 acres of land from Dengie Flats and a similar area from Maplin Sands, off the shore of Foulness Island. The estimated cost of the project was over £2 million, and although work started in 1865, a crisis in the banking system, when the Overend Gurney bank failed, made it difficult to obtain finance and the scheme foundered.

In October 1879, as a member of the Wanderers Gentlemen's Club in Pall Mall, London, he was present at a special dinner held in honour of fellow members Major John Chard VC and Surgeon Major James Reynolds VC, who were two of the heroes of the defence of Rorke's Drift during the Zulu War, the battle depicted in the motion picture *Zulu!*

The Hopes lived at 40 Brondell Road in Fulham, but when Margaret died, aged 75, on 11 December 1909, Colonel Hope was taken into a nursing home at 211 New King's Road in Fulham, where he died on 17 December 1909, aged 75. After a service at Fulham Church he was buried with Margaret in Brompton Cemetery. He was the last survivor of the 18 June Redan Victoria Cross holders, and he is one of twelve Victoria Cross holders who are buried at Brompton. His medals were sold at auction in 1997 and are at the Royal Fusiliers Museum in the Tower of London. A blue plaque commemorating his name was placed at the Bowling Pavilion at Parsloes Park in Dagenham, and a painting by Louis Desanges depicting his Victoria Cross action is in the Royal Fusiliers Museum.

Private Matthew Hughes VC
Matthew Hughes was born in Bradford on 31 March 1822, the son of Samuel and Alice Hughes. His father was a comber/cutter in a cotton mill. Standing only 5ft tall, he joined the 7th Royal Fusiliers at Leeds, aged 18, as 1879 Private Hughes. He discharged by purchase in January 1844, only to re-enlist in June of the same year. He spent a month 'in custody of the Civil Powers' in 1845. He sailed for active service in the Crimea, where he was promoted corporal before his Victoria Cross achievements.

His award of the Victoria Cross was announced in the *London Gazette* of 24 February 1857 and he received the medal at the first investiture. He also received the Crimea Medal with *Alma*, *Inkerman* and *Sebastopol* clasps and the Turkish Crimea Medal.

Hughes retired to pension from the army on 1 October 1861 and married a Bradford girl named Elizabeth, the daughter of William Roberts, on 16 November 1861, at St John's Church in Bradford. Unfortunately,

Elizabeth died and he later married Eliza, the daughter of Richard Wilson, a comber in a cotton mill, on 7 March 1866 at St Peter's, Bradford Cathedral. Hughes was described as a labourer and Eliza as a spinster, but she had a daughter, Harriett, who was born in Bradford on 21 August 1852. At the time of their marriage they lived in Horton, Bradford, and by the time of the 1871 census they were living at 15 Cross Frederick Street, Bradford East End.

Hughes became a beer-house keeper, of the 'Gardener's Arms' at 147 Wapping Road in Bradford, and was believed to be in his 59th year when he died of cirrhosis and exhaustion at the pub on 9 January 1882. He was buried at Undercliffe Cemetery in Bradford. His daughter died in 1894 and his wife died two years later. A new headstone was erected at his grave in 1997 and his medals are in the Royal Fusiliers Museum at the Tower of London.

9th (East Norfolk) Regiment

Captain Frederick Smith

Frederick Smith was the fifth son of Major Smith of Weston-super-Mare. Captain Smith was buried in the Officers' Burial Ground, The Quarries, 3rd Division camp: 'Sacred to the memory of Captain Frederick Smith, IXth Rgt. Died of his wounds, June 20 1855.'

There is a memorial dedicated to him at St John the Baptist Church in Weston-super-Mare:

> This tablet records the heroic death of Captain Frederick Smith of Her Majesty's 9th Regiment of Foot who fell mortally wounded at the siege of Sebastopol on the 18th day of June 1855, in the 31st year of his age. The crowning act of his brief but gallant career lives in the hearts of the good and brave. When engaged in administering to the wants of a dying brother officer in the heat of action, a shot from the enemy guns pierced his body, from which he suffered manfully and then died.

Captain Henry Ralph Browne

Henry Ralph Browne was born on 29 December 1828 at Gosport House in Northumberland and baptised on 1 February 1829 at Gosport. He was the eldest son of Thomas Henry Wagner Browne KCH (1785–1855) of Bronwylfa in Flint, North Wales, and his second wife Elizabeth (formerly Brandling, 1799–1860) of Thorpe, Rothwell, Yorkshire. He had a younger brother named Ralph Charles (1830–1922). His father held the office of Knight Commander of the Hanoverian Guelphic Order.

Henry was commissioned as an ensign in the 9th (East Norfolk) Regiment in April 1846. He purchased a lieutenancy on 23 September 1848 and became

A Selection of Tributes and Commemorations

captain in December of the following year. In 1852 he married Frances Mary Anna (1835–?) of Sidmouth in Devon, who was a daughter of Admiral W.R. Parsons.

The following appeared in the *Eastern Daily Press* for 2 November 1903, at the time of his appointment as colonel with the Norfolk Regiment:

> He served as ADC to brigadier-general Ridley, and during the Crimean War as brigadier-major of Division. He also took part in the second attack on the Redan on 8 September 1855, and for his services he was mentioned in despatches, was awarded the Crimean Medal with *Sebastopol* clasp, the French Legion of Honour, the Turkish Crimea Medal, the Turkish Order of the Medjidie (5th class), and he was promoted brevet-major.
>
> He was transferred from the unattached list to the Military Train (a forerunner of the Army Service Corps), attaining the rank of lt-colonel in June 1858. In November of the following year he transferred to the 87th (Royal Irish) Fusiliers, being placed on half-pay in August 1861. In June 1863 he was recalled for special service in Canada with the 20th (East Devon) Regiment, commanding the 2nd Battalion for over nine years, during which he was for various periods commandant in Japan, Hong Kong and Natal. He obtained the brevet of lt-colonel in September 1864. In January 1873 he transferred to the 37th (North Hampshire) Regiment, and in December 1874 he joined the 63rd (West Suffolk) Regiment. He next obtained a brigade command in India, and held the appointment of brigadier-general in Bengal from June 1875 to July 1880, during which time he was promoted to major-general in October 1877. He commanded a brigade with the Kuram division in the Zalmusht Expedition, during the Afghan War of 1878–80.

Browne commanded troops in the West Indies in 1884 and in January 1885 he was appointed lieutenant general; in July of that year he retired, being granted a distinguished service award of £100 a year. He was appointed colonel of the Dorsetshire Regiment in October 1894 and colonel of the Norfolk Regiment in 1903. At the time of the Jubilee of the Crimean War in 1905 he was appointed to be Ordinary Member of the military division, 3rd class, Companion of the Bath (CB).

In 1915 he was invited to the luncheon of senior surviving officers who saw active service in the Crimean War, held at the United Services Club in London to commemorate the 60th anniversary of the assault on the Redan.

However, he did not attend due to ill health. Major General Browne died on 23 December 1917 at Vancouver in Paignton, Devon, aged 89.

17th (Leicestershire) Regiment
Captain John Lacy Croker
John Lacy Croker was born one of twins in May 1820 at Croom Glebe in Limerick, Ireland, the son of the Reverend Edward Croker (1788–1863) of Croom Glebe and his wife Mary (formerly Copley, 1800–1848). His twin brother was named Edward. Their uncle, Colonel William Croker, had seen active service in Afghanistan with the 17th (Leicestershire) Regiment, and John was gazetted to that regiment on 5 June 1839. Edward followed him into the regiment on 21 October the same year. They served together in India, being involved in the wreck of the transport *Hannah* in 1840.

Subsequently the twins sailed for active service in the Crimea, and they were both involved in the first major action of 1855, on 22 March, when Russian troops attacked the British trenches. The regimental history describes Captain Croker's death, and describes his conduct as 'beyond praise'.

Captain Croker was buried on Cathcart's Hill: 'Sacred to the memory of Captn J.L. Croker 17th Regt who fell in action 18th June 1855.' His name is recorded on the Crimean War memorial tablet in the chapel of St Mary's Church at RMA Sandhurst.

Corporal (Felix) Philip Smith VC
Philip Smith was born on 5 October 1825 at Lurgan, Virginia, County Cavan, Ireland. His father was named Thomas. He enlisted into the 17th (Leicestershire) Regiment on 17 May 1847 in Dublin. After seven years of Home service, the regiment was posted to Gibraltar, before receiving orders for active service in the Crimea.

The award of the Victoria Cross to Corporal Smith was announced in the *London Gazette* on 24 February 1857 and he received the medal from Brigadier General Sir Charles Trollope at the Citadel in Quebec, Canada, on 1 August 1857. He also received the Crimea Medal with *Sebastopol* clasp, the French Military Medal and the Turkish Crimea Medal.

He was an in-pensioner at the Royal Hospital in Kilmainan from 1 October 1871 to 1 June 1876; again from 1 December 1881 to 1 February 1883; and in 1903. He died of bronchitis and pneumonia at Our Lady's Hospice, Harold's Cross in Dublin on 16 January 1906, aged 80. He was buried in St Bridget's section at Glasnevin Cemetery in Dublin, in a burial plot which was later purchased by his son-in-law, John Scully, who was High Sheriff of Dublin in

A Selection of Tributes and Commemorations

1913. Smith's name was not included on the memorial stone, but in 2003 five generations of the Smith family joined veterans from the Royal Leicestershire Regimental Association in a service to place a footstone at the graveside. His name appears on the Lurgan War Memorial.

Smith's medals were the first complete Victoria Cross group to appear at auction, and were sold in 1886 as part of the Captain E. Hyde Greg collection. The sale was considered exceptional, and it was the first time a catalogue included details about the recipient. It was bought by 'regular dealer' Mr Partridge. The medals are now with the Royal Leicestershire Regimental Museum.

18th (Royal Irish) Regiment
Captain Thomas Esmonde VC
Thomas Esmonde was born on 25 May 1829 at Pembrokestown House in County Waterford, Ireland, the son of Sir Thomas Esmonde, 9th Baronet, and his first wife Mary (formerly Payne). His father represented Wexford in the British Parliament. The Esmonde family home was at Ballynastragh House at Killinierin in County Wexford, which was burnt down by the Irish Republican Army in 1923.

Esmonde entered the 18th (Royal Irish) Regiment and served in India. The Royal Irish played a major part in the operations during the Second Anglo-Burmese War of 1852–1853, being in the forefront of the troops which captured the Golden Pagoda in Rangoon. Disease and heatstroke took a terrible toll, and the Royal Irish lost 365 men, mainly to disease. For his service Esmonde received the Indian General Service Medal (1854–1895) with *Pegu* clasp. Therefore he was the only soldier of the 18 June Redan Victoria Crosses who had seen previous active service.

The award of the Victoria Cross to Captain Esmonde was announced in the *London Gazette* of 25 September 1857, the last to be announced for the assault on the Redan, and he received the medal from Queen Victoria at Southsea Common in Portsmouth on 2 August 1858, along with Edward Bell, Henry Ramage, James Mouat, Henry MacDonald, Matthew Dixon and Howard Elphinstone. He also received the Crimea Medal with *Sebastopol* clasp and the Turkish Crimea Medal.

His mother had died in 1840 and after his return from the Crimea in 1856, his father had married again. He reached the rank of lieutenant colonel.

While following the 'Kildares' – a local hunt at Bruges in Belgium – late in 1872, he was trying to jump a thorn fence when he was struck in the eye by a branch. The eye became badly inflamed. The other eye also became infected, and the injury got worse. He died from his injuries on 14 January 1873, aged 43, at Bruges, and was buried in the Bruges Town Cemetery, where there is a headstone. His medals are in the Imperial War Museum in London, but they are not part of the Lord Ashcroft Collection.

33rd (Duke of Wellington's) Regiment
Lieutenant Colonel George Valentine Edward Mundy
George Valentine Edward Mundy was born the sixth son of seven in the family of nine children of General Godfrey Basil Meynell Mundy (1776–1848), and his wife Lady Sarah Brydges (formerly Rodney, 1780–1871). The family home was at 1 Hobart Place in Eaton Square, Belgravia, London.

Mundy served with the Coldstream Guards from 1835 to 1841, and the National Army Museum holds some items concerning him, comprising two diaries from 1837; a journal of his service in Canada in 1840; letters written from St Vincent, Barbados and St Lucia, from his service in the West Indies, 1842–1843; four diaries from 1854 to 1856; and letters to his mother from February 1854 to July 1856, describing his service in the Crimea.

Colonel Mundy was awarded the Crimea Medal, the French Legion of Honour and the Sardinian Medal, and having been appointed Commander of the Bath (CB) on 5 August 1856, he served with the 1st Battalion, 19th (Yorkshire) Regiment from 28 November 1857 until his death, being promoted to colonel in the army on 24 April 1860.

Colonel Mundy died on 14 May 1863, aged 44, at 42 Bryanston Street near Portman Square, London, and was buried in Brompton Cemetery.

Lieutenant Colonel John Douglas Johnstone
John Douglas Johnstone was born on 13 December 1836, the son of Major General John Douglas Johnstone (1807–1863), of the 33rd (Duke of Wellington's) Regiment, and his wife Caroline (1805–1878), the daughter of the Reverend Andrew O'Beirne.

Captain Fanshawe stated that Colonel Johnstone had lost his left arm. Despite the severity of his injuries he saw active service in the Abyssinian campaign of 1868, and gained the rank of colonel in the Royal Sussex Regiment.

He was appointed Companion of the Bath (CB, military division) on 27 July 1855, and retired on full pay on 17 April 1860.

On 20 January 1869 he married the Hon. Augusta Anna Margaretta, daughter of Thomas Oliver Plunkett, 12th Baron Louth, and they had two daughters and a son. They lived at Snow Hill in Lisbellaw, County Fermanagh, Ireland. He was a Justice of the Peace and a deputy lieutenant for County Fermanagh, and he held the office of High Sheriff of County Fermanagh in 1899.

Colonel Johnstone died on 10 January 1906, aged 69. The *Fermanagh Herald* of 20 January 1906 reported:

> At the meeting of the Fermanagh County Council on Friday, the following resolution was unanimously passed, on the motion of the Viscount Corry, seconded by Mr William Teele – 'That we, the County Council of Fermanagh have heard with the deepest regret of the death of Colonel John Douglas Johnstone, DL, who for three years was a valued member of the Council, and we desire to express our heartfelt sympathy with the Hon. Mrs Johnstone and her family in their sad bereavement.
>
> The funeral of Colonel Johnstone, DL, Snowhill, who died in Dublin last week, took place on Saturday. The remains were interred at Lisbellaw.'

Captain Thomas Basil Fanshawe

Thomas Basil Fanshawe, known to his family as Basil, was born on 3 December 1829, the second son of three in a family of six children, born between 1822 and 1831, of the Reverend Thomas Lewis Fanshawe (1792–1858), an Old Etonian and vicar of Dagenham from 1819 to 1857, and his wife Catherine Stevens (formerly Le Marchant, 1796–1881). Her father, Major General John Le Marchant, was killed in action in 1812 while leading the Heavy Brigade in the charge at Salamanca during the Peninsular War. The family owned Parsloes Manor, but lived at the vicarage in Dagenham village.

Captain Fanshawe had only recently arrived in the Crimea from England, when he joined the 33rd on the night of 17 June 1855. He wrote numerous letters home to his mother, and in one he stated:

> We had to cross, on leaving the trenches, 150 yards of open ground, exposed to a very heavy fire of grape-shot from the enemy ... Our loss, I regret to say, was very considerable, having had 50 men killed and wounded. Lt-Colonel Johnstone has lost his left arm, Mundy is hit in the leg with a bullet; Bennett, I am sorry to say, is killed; Quayle shot in the elbow and arm. Wickham is so hit in the foot that he is likely to be disabled for some time to come; Collings was stunned by a blow for a moment. I have had a bruise in the shoulder from a stone or spent ball which has made it stiff. The rest of our fellows have escaped unhurt. The loss our Division has sustained is frightful. The Rifle Brigade is almost annihilated! Out of 130 men, 35 only survive. The 23rd nearly cease to

exist! Poor Sir John Campbell, in rushing out of the trenches, fell in the act of cheering on his men ... It seems the general opinion we shall never take the place by assault, and therefore we are going to attack the Redan and Malakoff by sap.

Captain Fanshawe later made a visit to the British Hotel set up by Nurse Mary Seacole, and another to the hospital at Scutari administered by Florence Nightingale. He later served in India, and rose to the rank of lieutenant colonel.

In March 1864 Fanshawe married Emily Catherine (formerly Gosselin, 1835–1926) and they had three boys and three girls born between 1865 and 1874. On his retirement, they lived at 23 Park Street in Walcott near Bath. One of his sons was Major Gerard Lewis Fanshawe, who was serving with the Royal Engineers when he died of fever in Malta in 1904, aged 38.

Colonel Fanshawe died on 4 May 1905, aged 74, at Bath in Somerset, and was buried at Locksbrook Cemetery in Bath. The Fanshawe family donated their extensive archive to the Valence House Collection in Dagenham in 1963.

Captain John Edward Taubman Quayle

John Edward Taubman Quayle was born on 24 April 1824, the son of John Quayle of Rushen House in Castletown, Isle of Man. He entered King William's College near Castletown in September 1834 and left on 30 June 1839. From there he went to the Royal Military College in 1840, and was gazetted as an ensign into the 33rd (Duke of Wellington's) Regiment on 7 September 1841, being promoted lieutenant on 5 December 1843.

Captain Fanshawe recorded that Captain Quayle was shot in the elbow and arm. For his service he received the Crimea Medal with *Alma*, *Inkerman* and *Sebastopol* clasps, the French Legion of Honour and the Turkish Order of the Medjidie.

Despite his injuries he served as captain during the Indian Mutiny, being promoted to brevet major on 5 August 1856. Brevet Major Quayle died of sunstroke at Surat in India on 29 May 1859, aged 55.

A memorial to Captain Quayle was placed at the Kirk Malew Church in Ballasala on the Isle of Man:

> In memory of John Edward Taubman Quayle, Esq, of Castletown. Brevet-Major and senior Captain of the 33rd Duke of Wellington's Regiment; who died at Surat on the 29th May 1859, aged 35 years, from the effects of sunstroke received whilst in command of a field force sent against the mutineers. He served in the West Indies and North America,

was at the battle of the Alma, and siege of Sebastopol, where he was shot through the body on the 18th June 1855. For his service he received the Crimea Medal with *Alma*, *Inkerman* and *Sebastopol* clasps; the French Legion of Honour; and the Turkish Order of the Medjidie. A mourning mother erected this monument to a most affectionate and dutiful son.

Lieutenant Valentine Bennett
Valentine Bennett was the third son of Valentine Bennett of Thomastown House in King's County (now Offaly), Ireland.

Lieutenant Bennett was buried in the 1st Brigade, Light Division cemetery: 'Sacred to the memory of Valentine Bennett, Lieut. 33rd The Duke of Wellington's Regt. who was killed in the attack on Sebastopol on the 18th June 1855. Aged 27 years. Erected by his brother Frederic Philip Bennett and Officers of the 33rd The Duke of Wellington's Regiment.'

His name was originally reported on casualty lists as 'Bellew'. It would seem that a memorial service was held for him because a memorial paper was sold at auction, and his Crimea medal was sold at auction in 1994.

Lieutenant Langford Rowley Heyland
Langford Rowley Heyland was born at Azimgurh, Bengal, India, on 17 July 1837. He was the youngest child of Alexander Charles Heyland (1807–1894), of the Bengal Civil Service, and his wife Anne Alexander (formerly Montgomery, 1808–1839), a vicar's daughter. Both his parents were Irish, and sadly his mother died when he was 2 years old.

Lieutenant Heyland was aged just 17 when he died and was buried in the 1st Brigade, Light Division cemetery: 'Sacred to the memory of Langford R Heyland 33rd Regt. who fell in the assault on the Redan on the 18th June 1855.'

The *Dublin Evening Mail* of 9 July 1855 published the following from letters to his family from brother officers of the 33rd Regiment: 'We found him close to the abbatis of the Redan, pierced with six wounds, some from grape shot, some from rifle bullets. We had him carried up to the camp the same evening and buried.' Another letter states: 'He fell, poor fellow, sword in hand whilst leading on his men, and one of the foremost in the attack.'

34th (Cumberland) Regiment
Captain John Robinson
John Robinson was aged 29 when he was killed in action. He was the eldest son of the Reverend William Robinson, preceptor of Christ Church in Dublin.

The *Dublin Evening Mail* of 13 July 1855, stated:

> He was one of the first who advanced from the trenches, and in the middle of the attack was heard to exclaim 'I am hit, God help me!' On the evening of the next day, during the armistice, his body was found within 80 yards of the Redan fort, lying on its back. A grapeshot had passed through the middle of his body, and another had shattered his left ankle. His countenance was calm and composed, and it was evident his death had been immediate. His sword, pistol and cap had been taken by the enemy, and his pockets had been rifled; in other respects his person was intact. Near him lay the body of Colonel Yea and Captain Shiffner of his own regiment, and a heap of the bodies of the brave fellows of the 34th Regiment. His remains were brought into camp and buried the same evening, by the chaplain of the division, between Captain Shiffner and Lieutenant Alt, who had fallen at the same time. His family have to lament the loss of an affectionate and dutiful son, and a kind brother, the service has lost a gallant and promising officer, and society an honest man in every sense.

There is a memorial dedicated to him at the Portstewart Church of Ireland Church in Coleraine, Londonderry:

> Sacred to the memory of Captain John Robinson of the XXXIIV Regiment, who was killed by a grapeshot, whilst leading the storming party of his regiment against the Redan fort at Sebastopol, on the XVIII June MDCCCLV. He had completed his XXXIII Years, eleven of which had been spent on active service with his regiment. He was the eldest son of the Reverend William Robinson, grandson of the Reverend Sir John Robinson, Baronet, and the Hon. Susanna Sophia, eldest daughter of Henry Jeffery Mower, 4th Viscount Ashbrook. He was an affectionate and dutiful son and kind brother and a faithful friend. A tablet has been erected over his grave at Sebastopol by the officers of his regiment.

Captain John Shiffner

John Shiffner was born on 15 September 1824, the second son of four in the family of six children of the Reverend Sir George Shiffner (1791–1863), vicar of St Mary's Church in Amport near Andover in Hampshire, and his wife Elizabeth, the daughter of the Reverend Croxton Johnston; they had married on 10 July 1817. The Reverend Shiffner held the office of Canon Residentiary of Chichester, and succeeded as the 3rd Baronet Shiffner of Coombe in Sussex on 18 March 1859. The family home was at Coombe House in Lewes.

The baronetcy was created on 16 December 1818 for George Shiffner, Member of Parliament for Lewes from 1812 to 1826.

John was commissioned into the 53rd (Shropshire) Regiment on 15 October 1841, becoming a lieutenant on 31 March 1843. He transferred to the 34th (Cumberland) Regiment as a captain on 3 August 1849. He arrived with his regiment at Balaclava on 9 December 1854 and played a prominent part in the Russian sortie of 22 March 1855. His death at the Redan on 18 June 1855 was announced in the *London Gazette* of 4 July 1855 and he received a posthumous mention in the despatches of Lord Raglan, *London Gazette* of 25 June 1855. His Crimea Medal without a clasp was sold at auction.

Major John Gwilt
John Gwilt was born on 22 January 1817 in Chelsea, the son of Robert Gwilt (1780–1861) of the Chelsea Hospital and of Icklingham in Suffolk, and his wife Mary (1780–1859), a daughter of Henry Williams of Nassau in the Bahamas, who had married on 23 November 1808 at St Andrew's Church in Holborn. John was christened at St Martin's in the Field, Westminster, on 29 March 1817 and his siblings were Robert, Mary and Elizabeth Anne. There are several memorials dedicated to the Gwilt family at All Soul's Church in Icklingham.

John entered the 34th (Cumberland) Regiment as an ensign on 25 November 1836, being promoted lieutenant on 10 August 1838, captain on 14 February 1845 and brevet lieutenant colonel on 6 June 1856. He served in the Crimea from 9 December 1854 to 18 July 1855, during which time he was promoted brevet major on 17 July 1855. He received the Crimea Medal with *Sebastopol* clasp, the French Legion of Honour and the Turkish Crimea Medal, and he was appointed to the Turkish Order of the Medjidie (5th class) on 4 August 1856.

He then saw active service in the Indian Rebellion, being present at the actions at Cawnpore on 26–28 November 1857, the capture of Meangunge, the siege and capture of Lucknow, and the defeat of the rebels under Bala Rao near Bootwal on the Nepal border. For his service he was mentioned in despatches, received the Indian Mutiny Medal with *Lucknow* clasp, and was appointed Commander of the Bath (CB). He was appointed colonel on 22 October 1863 and lieutenant colonel on 28 October 1864. Colonel Gwilt died on 18 October 1877, aged 60, at 8 Regent Street in London.

Lieutenant Francis Richard Hurt
Francis Richard Hurt was born on 12 July 1832 at Yeldersley near Ashbourne in Derbyshire and was christened on 20 November 1832. He was the first son

of eleven, and second child of sixteen, born between 1834 and 1854 to Francis Hurt (1803–1861) and his wife Cecelia Emely Norman (1809–1891), a niece of the Duke of Rutland. They had married at Bakewell in Derbyshire on 22 August 1829 and their home was Alderwasley Hall near Matlock in Derbyshire, which had belonged to the family since 1690. His father was Member of Parliament for South Derbyshire from 1837 to 1941 and Lord of the Manor from 1854 to 1861. His grandmother was the granddaughter of the inventor Richard Arkwright.

Francis was educated at Eton College, where he is known to have suffered a severe illness. He was sent to a military academy in Edinburgh, from where he was commissioned into the 34th (Cumberland) Regiment at Fort William. He was stationed in the West Indies until receiving orders for active service in the Crimea, being promoted to lieutenant on 25 November 1853. His brother Henry was mortally wounded at the Battle of Inkerman on 5 November 1854 while serving with the 21st (Royal Scots) Fusiliers, and his brother Albert Frederic (1835–1907) served in the Royal Navy aboard the *Hannibal* in the Baltic Sea, the Black Sea, the Sea of Azov and in the capture of Kertch.

The *Derby Mercury* for 27 June 1855 reported:

> It is with sincere regret that we see among the list of officers killed in the attack of the 18th upon the Redan battery the name of Lieutenant Francis Richard Hurt of the 34th Regiment. This gallant officer was the eldest son of Francis Hurt of Alderwasley in this county. The second son of the same gentleman fell at the battle of Inkerman in November last, and he is now followed by his elder brother. Mr Hurt, who has thus lost two sons before Sebastopol, has still, we believe, a third in the Black Sea if not in the Crimea. Deeply and heartily do we sympathise with this esteemed gentleman in his cruel bereavement.

Lieutenant Hurt's body was not recovered. His name appears on the Eton Memorial and on the Royal Garrison Church memorial in Portsmouth (as Hunt), dedicated to Old Etonians killed in the Crimean War. There is an impressive stone cross memorial at All Saints Church in Alderwasley:

> To the precious memory of the two eldest, beloved, and deeply regretted sons of Francis and Cecelia Emely Hurt of Alderwasley. This monument is erected by their parents as an expression of unceasing sorrow, but of future hope. Francis Richard – Lieutenant in the 34th Regiment, fell in the attack in the Redan, Sebastopol, June 18th 1855, in the 23rd year of his age.

A Selection of Tributes and Commemorations

Henry Francis Eden – Lieutenant, 21st Fusiliers, was mortally wounded at the battle of Inkerman on the 5th November 1854, and died the day after, in the 21st year of his age.

Ensign Robert John Browne-Clayton

Robert John Browne-Clayton was born in 1834, the eldest son in the family of six children of Richard Clayton Browne-Clayton (1807–1886) and his wife Henrietta, daughter of Sir Richard Clayton, 1st Bt. The family home was Adlington Hall near Chorley in Lancashire, and they also owned land at Browne's Hill in County Carlow, Ireland. Robert was educated at Harrow.

Robert's brother, Lieutenant Charles Henry Clayton (1836–1889) was wounded in action while serving with the 97th (The Earl of Ulster's) Regiment in the Crimea.

There is an impressive memorial dedicated to Robert at St Paul's Church in Adlington near Chorley in Lancashire:

> Erected by the inhabitants of Adlington and its vicinity to the memory of Robert John Browne Clayton, Esq. Lieut. 34th Regt. Only son of Richard and Catherine Browne Clayton, of Adlington Hall in this Parish, and Carigbyrne, County of Wexford, who died on the 12th July 1855 of wounds received at the siege of Sebastopol, aged 20 years, at the memorable assault on the Redan Battery 18th June, when he was mortally wounded.
>
> At his country's call, and in obedience to the clades of Honour and Duty, he accompanied his regiment to the Crimea. On landing he was attached to the Light Division. He performed the duties in the siege in the advance trenches, was twice called to lead with the officers of his regiment, a storming party, first at the attack and capture of the Quarries and Rifle Pits on the 7th June; the second time at the memorable assault on the Redan Battery, 18 June, when he was mortally wounded.
>
> He resigned himself in peace and hope into the hands of his maker, humbly trusting through the merits of his saviour Jesus Christ, to inherit the joys of eternity. May this reminiscence of him prove consolation to his family and friends; and this tablet to his memory a proof, 'if such were needed', that the man who sacrifices private interest to the public welfare will ever live in the affection of a grateful country.

There is also a brass plate memorial dedicated to him in the Harrow School Chapel, and he is named on the memorial at the Royal Garrison Church in Portsmouth dedicated to Old Harrovians killed in the Crimean War.

Private John Joseph Sims VC

John Joseph Sims was born in February 1836 at Bloomsbury in London, the son of John Francis Sims and his wife Sarah Ann (formerly Manning). Little is known of his early life except that his father died when he was about 14 years old, and he worked as a labourer trying to help his destitute family, before he entered the 34th (Cumberland) Regiment as 3482 Private Sims at Westminster on 4 January 1854. He was aged only 18 when the regiment was serving in the Mediterranean and received orders for active service in the Crimea.

Sims's award of the Victoria Cross was announced in the *London Gazette* of 24 February 1857 and he received the medal at the first investiture. He also received the Crimea Medal with *Sebastopol* clasp and the Turkish Crimea Medal.

On his discharge from the army in 1857 it was stated that 'his character has been good'. In 1861 he lived at 33 William Street North in Islington, with his wife Janet, and was working in the goods yard of the local railway.

He died of phthisis (tuberculosis) on 6 December 1881, aged 46, in the Union Workhouse at Thavies Inn, in the City of London, and he was buried in a common grave at the City of London Cemetery at Manor Park. There is no headstone, but a plaque was erected in the memorial garden at the cemetery in 2003, and he is named on the Victoria Cross memorial at Carlisle Cathedral. The location of his Victoria Cross is not known, but he may have lost or pawned it, as a replacement medal which had been awarded to him was auctioned in 2015.

38th (1st Staffordshire) Regiment
Major General Sir John Campbell

John Campbell was born in Perthshire on 14 April 1807, the second son of Sir Archibald Campbell (1769–1843), 1st Baronet of New Brunswick, and his wife Helen, daughter of Captain John McDonald of Garth in Perthshire. The Campbells were members of the Smalls of Dirnanean in Perthshire. His elder brother was the Reverend Archibald Campbell, who died unmarried when serving in India in 1831, and John became the heir to the baronetcy. John showed a talent as an artist at an early age, producing pictures of events in New Brunswick, which still survive in the Provincial Archives of New Brunswick.

Newspaper reports of his death at the time stated:

> This veteran officer, who fell in the unsuccessful assault on the Redan on 18th, entered the army as ensign in the 38th Regiment, and proceeded to

A Selection of Tributes and Commemorations

India with his father, the late Lt-General, Sir Archibald Campbell, GCB, the same year. On their way out, Sir Archibald, then Colonel Campbell KCB, assumed the command of the 38th, at the Cape. In 1824, Sir Archibald being selected for the command of the forces sent to Burma, his son was placed on his staff, and though very young, his conduct during the whole of the Burmese War elicited such frequent notices in general orders that, at the conclusion of the war in 1826, he received the thanks of the Right Hon. the governor-general in council. He remained in the ceded provinces till 1829, when he returned to England, and shortly after joined the depot of his regiment.

On his father's appointment to the governor of New Brunswick in 1831, he was again placed on Sir Archibald's staff, and in 1837 returned to England, and joined the 38th Regiment, in which he subsequently served in the Mediterranean, West Indies and Nova Scotia, returning from the last-named place in 1851, in command of the regiment, which he retained till the opening of the present war when he was appointed a brigadier-general, and from the hour when he first set foot at the scene of duty he was ever at his post. He was made a major-general by a late brevet, and placed on the list of officers receiving rewards for distinguished service.

Endowed with an activity and energy of mind and body not often granted to younger men, his loss as general officers is to be deeply deplored at this moment while his career throughout every relation of life endeared his memory to all who knew him, and renders his premature loss irreparable to his family and friends. He leaves a widow and eight children to mourn their loss. The eldest son, Archibald Ava, now aged eleven years, succeeds to the baronetcy.

Major General Campbell was buried in the cemetery on Cathcart's Hill near Sebastopol on 20 June 1855: 'Sacred to the memory of Major-General Sir John Campbell, Bart, killed in action, 18 June 1855.'

There is a memorial dedicated to him in the Church of St John the Evangelist in Edinburgh: 'Sacred to the memory of Major-General, Sir John Campbell, Baronet, KCB, who served throughout the first Burmese War under his distinguished father Lt-General, Sir Archibald Campbell, GCB – KCTS. He commanded the 38th Regiment for fourteen years, and as a brigadier-general fought at Alma and at Inkerman. He fell while gallantly leading on at the assault of the Redan, 18 June 1855. His remains were laid in the cemetery on Cathcart's Hill near Sebastopol. His widow dedicates this tablet near the remains of his revered parents to the memory of a beloved husband.

A monument has also been erected in Winchester Cathedral by the 38th Regiment in which he served for thirty-three years 'As a Testimony of respect, sincere affection and esteem.'

Colonel John Jackson Lowth

John Jackson Lowth was born on 20 June 1804 at Hinton Ampner near Winchester in Hampshire. He was the second son of seven in the family of twelve children, born between 1797 and 1818, of the Reverend Robert Lowth (1762–1822), rector of All Saints Church at Hinton Ampner, and a grandson of Bishop Robert Lowth (1710–1787), the former archdeacon of Westminster, and his wife Frances Sofia (1773–1860), who was the daughter of the Reverend Dr John Harrington of Thruxton in Wiltshire, who conducted the service when they married in Thruxton on 20 January 1794. His elder brother was Major General Robert Henry Lowth, who served in the Indian Mutiny with the 86th (Royal County Down) Regiment. Hinton Ampner Church stands in the grounds of the mysterious Tudor Hinton Ampner Manor.

John was educated at Twyford School and Winchester College before going on to the Royal Military Academy at Sandhurst, from where he was commissioned as an ensign in the 38th Regiment on 3 July 1824 and posted to India. He was promoted lieutenant on 11 September 1825, captain on 23 March 1832 and major on 12 June 1840. He served with the 38th Regiment throughout the Burmese War of 1825–1826. He then saw service at various times at Home, in North America and in the Mediterranean.

On 12 August 1841, at Cork, he married Katherine (1809–1892), youngest daughter of Richard Hull Lewis and widow of Captain Sandys of the 24th Dragoons. In 1852 John Lowth was in command of the military guard on the convict ship *Lady Harwood*, which took 200 prisoners to New South Wales in Australia. His wife accompanied him on the journey.

On the outbreak of the Crimean War the 38th Regiment's commanding officer, Sir John Campbell, was appointed to the command of a brigade, and Colonel Lowth took over the regiment. He was appointed Companion of the Bath (CB) on 5 July 1855.

Colonel Lowth died upon landing at Portsmouth and was buried with military honours at Winchester Cemetery, not far from the college where he was educated. His name appears on the memorial at Winchester College that is dedicated to Old Wykehamists who were killed during the Crimean campaign.

A Selection of Tributes and Commemorations

The *Portsmouth Times and Naval Gazette* of 11 August 1855 published a detailed obituary:

> The public will have learnt with regret the death, caused by a wound received at Sebastopol on 18 June, of a distinguished officer of the British army, Colonel John J Lowth of the 38th Regiment.
>
> Colonel Lowth was the third son of the Reverend Robert Lowth, who was for many years the rector of the parish of Hinton Ampner, in this county, and Canon of St Paul's, London, and was a grandson of the erudite Hebrew scholar and ornament of the church in the see of London, Dr Lowth. Colonel Lowth was educated at Winchester College, and at Sandhurst, where he signalised himself by his attainments in military drawing and fortification.
>
> From Sandhurst he was appointed to an ensigncy in the 38th Regiment, and at once joined it in India; and he was with it in the principal part of the Burmese War in 1825–26, and to the close of it, being present in the actions at Sembike and Nepadie, and in the attack and capture of Melloon and of Pegham Mew, obtaining the Ava Medal.
>
> He returned with the 38th to England in 1836, and served with it subsequently in Canada, the West Indies, and in the Mediterranean, rising step by step in it until he commanded it at various times in the absence of his senior officer, the late Sir John Campbell. It is not too much to say that Colonel Lowth, wherever he was quartered, whether at home or abroad – And he was never away from his regiment – proved himself by the common consent of all, to be a most able officer, at the same time that he knew how to attach to him and gain the confidence of both officers and men, and by an admirable mixture of decision and of kindness.
>
> On the breaking out of the war Colonel Lowth took out the 38th Regiment to Varna under his command, Sir John Campbell having been appointed to a brigade, and subsequently, on this officer being made a major-general, Colonel Lowth succeeded to the full command. He led it up the heights of the Alma, was in the reserve at the battle of Inkerman, and took his full share, with his gallant regiment, of all those most severe and most trying labours in the trenches during the terrible winter of the siege of Sebastopol.
>
> Here may be mentioned two circumstances which show more than words the character of this officer, and that unfailing attention which so marked him to those under his care. In one letter, written in the depth of

the winter to a member of his family, he said: 'I have drained and paved my camp, to keep my men dry and clean, and their health is much improved by it.' And again, in another letter: 'I have built a hut for my horses and another for my servants, and now I shall think about one for myself.' But he never did build this hut for himself, passing the whole winter under canvas.

The 18th June arrived, and the 38th, forming part of the brigade of the Third Division, under General Eyre, Colonel Lowth, with his regiment, aided on that memorable but unfortunate day in the attack on the Cemetery and the suburb of the town, which that brigade victoriously carried, and held, as is well known, for many hours.

While in this suburb, and in one of the houses, Colonel Lowth was struck down by a stone in the head, and immediately afterwards was wounded very severely in the right leg above the knee by the bursting of a shell – the same shell which killed Lieutenant Davies of the 38th Regiment, and a corporal, besides wounding, in addition, three or four of his men. At once Sergeant McFarren and a party of his men volunteered to carry out and to the rear their fallen colonel; but they were unable to do so for two hours, during which time Colonel Lowth lost a great deal of blood. At dusk this party of brave fellows carried him on a sofa mattress, taken from the house where he fell, for nearly half a mile over the open country through a terrible fire of grape and round shot and musketry, when, to the astonishment of all of them, there was but one of this little party touched, and that slightly. The wound of the leg was found to be very severe, and it weakened him materially. But it went on well, and a medical board after a time announced Colonel Lowth able to proceed to England.

At this time, in recognition of his services the Queen conferred on Colonel Lowth the distinguished honour of an appointment as aide-de-camp to Her Majesty, promoting him at the same time from the rank of lieutenant-colonel to a full colonel in the army; and shortly afterwards the Sovereign again honoured Colonel Lowth by conferring on him the Order of the Bath.

Captain Honourable Charles John Addington
Charles John Addington was born on 17 March 1832, the ninth child of thirteen of William Leonard Addington (1794–1864), 2nd Viscount Sidmouth, and his wife Mary (1795–1894), the daughter of the Reverend John Young, who had married on 20 April 1820. His grandfather Henry,

A Selection of Tributes and Commemorations

1st Viscount Sidmouth, served as the British Prime Minister from 1801 to 1804, and had houses at Bulmershe Court and Woodley Lodge in Reading.

Addington later served in the Indian Mutiny, and for his service he received the Indian Mutiny Medal with *Lucknow* clasp. On 5 August 1862 he married Nelly Hindmarsh, daughter of Arthur Miller Mundy of Shipley Hall in Derbyshire.

He was a lieutenant colonel in the 100th (Prince of Wales's Royal Canadian) Regiment from 1871 to 1877, colonel of the 35th Sussex Regimental District from 1877 to 1883, Quartermaster General from 1884 to 1884 and colonel of the troops at Shorncliffe from 1885 to 1886. He gained the rank of colonel in the Devonshire Regiment and retired as a major general.

Major General Addington died on 11 September 1903, aged 70. His series of letters were edited by his sister-in-law, the Hon. Mrs Hiley Addington, as 'The Crimean and Indian Mutiny Letters of the Hon. Charles John Addington, 38th Regiment', published in the *Journal of the Society for Army Historical Research* in 1968.

Lieutenant Owen Gwyn Saunders-Davies

Owen Gwyn Saunders-Davies was baptised on 14 May 1834 at Pentre in Maenordeifi, Dyfed (now Pembrokeshire). He was the second son of three in the family of six children of David Arthur Saunders-Davies (1792–1857), Conservative MP for Carmarthenshire from 1847 to 1857, and his wife Elizabeth Maria, daughter of Owen and Elizabeth Phillips.

Owen was educated at Eton College and was appointed ensign by purchase in the 38th (1st Staffordshire) Regiment on 12 December 1851, being promoted lieutenant on 18 October 1853.

Lieutenant Davies was buried on Cathcart's Hill: 'To the memory of Lieut Owen G. Saunders Davies 38th Regt who fell in action on the 18th June 1855. Erected by his brother officers as a testimony of their high esteem.'

His name appears on the Royal Garrison Church memorial in Portsmouth, which is dedicated to Old Etonians who were killed in the Crimean War.

41st (Welch) Regiment

Lieutenant Colonel Julius Edmund Goodwyn

Julius Edmund Goodwyn was born on 21 February 1824 at Blackheath in Middlesex, the son of Thomas Wildman Goodwyn (1788–1830), a partner in a brewers named Goodwyn and Company, and his wife Elizabeth. They had married at Woodford in Essex on 17 August 1809. Elizabeth was a daughter of Sir Charles Flower (1763–1834), who was Mayor of London in 1808–1809 and was created Baronet Flower of Lobb and Woodford in 1809. At the time of the first ever census in 1841 they were living in Bentinck Terrace in Marylebone.

Goodwyn entered the 1st Battalion, 41st Regiment, as an ensign on 5 January 1844, becoming lieutenant in June 1845, and by May 1850 he had attained the rank of captain by purchase. His first tour of active service was in the Crimean War, where he fought in the Battle of Alma, after which he was promoted to major. During the battle at Inkerman he found himself in an isolated position surrounded by Russians. He immediately drew his pistol and by the accuracy of his fire and the coolness of his judgement, put his enemies to flight. He was present at both the assaults on the Redan, on 18 June, when he was wounded, and on 8 September, when he succeeded to the command of the regiment upon the death of Colonel Eman in that action. For his services in the Crimean War he received the Crimea Medal with *Alma*, *Inkerman* and *Sebastopol* clasps, the French Legion of Honour, the Turkish Order of the Medjidie (5th class) and the Turkish Crimea Medal, and he was created a Companion of the Order of the Bath (CB) on 2 January 1857. Goodwyn served in the West Indies from 18 May 1857 to 30 April 1860, and in March 1858 he was promoted colonel. During his posting in the West Indies he married Euphemia Alexandrina Victoria (1836–1884), a daughter of Captain Kent RN, on 29 September 1858 at Port Royal in Jamaica. They had five children: Julius Henry, born 9 October 1859, Norton James, born 7 October 1861, Elizabeth Madlan, born 18 November 1862, Alfred Hunter, born 19 August 1864 and Walter Meredith, born 6 May 1871. Julius Henry became a colonel in his father's old regiment.

On 14 March 1866 he was appointed to the command of a brigade in Bengal and on 6 March 1868 he received the rank of major general. He vacated his Indian command on 28 February 1870, which was his last active military employment. He became a lieutenant general on 1 October 1877 and was appointed colonel-in-chief of the 28th (North Gloucestershire) Regiment on 5 November 1880. On 10 January 1881 he was promoted to general, and on 20 January 1883 was transferred back to the 41st Regiment as colonel.

General Goodwyn died on 4 March 1890 at Bath in Somerset, aged 66. He was buried in the churchyard of All Saints Church in East Budleigh, and there is a memorial dedicated to him and his wife which states: 'In memory of General Julius Edmund Goodwyn CB, colonel, 41st The Welch Regiment, of Stoneborough, Budleigh Salterton. Born 21 February 1824, Died 4 March 1890. Also of Euphemia, his wife. Born 1 October 1836, and who died at Stoneborough, 17 October 1884.' His set of five Crimea medals was sold at auction in 2016 and several other letters and articles related to him have also survived.

44th (East Essex) Regiment
General Sir Charles William Dunbar Staveley

Charles William Dunbar Staveley was born on 18 December 1817 at Boulogne-sur-Mer in northern France. He was the eldest son of Lieutenant General William Staveley (1784–1854), a veteran of the Peninsular War and the Battle of Waterloo, and his wife Sarah, a daughter of Thomas Mather, who had married in 1817.

Charles was educated at the Scottish Military and Naval Academy in Edinburgh and was commissioned as a second lieutenant in the 87th (Royal Irish) Fusiliers on 6 March 1835, being promoted to lieutenant on 4 October 1839 and captain on 6 September 1844. From July 1840 to June 1843 he was aide-de-camp to the Governor of Mauritius, part of the time in the service of his father. He was quartered at Glasgow, and had not fully recovered from a serious attack of measles when he saved a boy from drowning in the river Clyde.

He exchanged to the 18th (Royal Irish) Regiment on 31 January 1845 and then to the 44th (East Essex) Regiment on 9 May 1845, becoming a major on 7 December 1850. When the regiment embarked for the invasion of the Crimea he was to have been left behind on account of illness, but he hid himself on board till the vessel sailed. He was present at Alma and at Balaclava, where he acted as aide-de-camp to the Duke of Cambridge, and on 12 December 1854 he was promoted to lieutenant colonel. He was mentioned in despatches on 4 July 1855, and for his service he received the Crimean Medal with *Alma*, *Inkerman* and *Sebastopol* clasps, the Sardinian and Turkish Crimea medals and the Turkish Order of the Medjidie (fifth class). He was also appointed Commander of the Bath (CB).

Lieutenant Colonel Stavely commanded the regiment from 30 June 1855. It embarked for Madras in August 1857 and went on to China in March 1860. He became a colonel on 9 March 1858 and on 28 April 1860 he was made brigadier general and was given command of a brigade in Michel's Division during the Anglo-French expedition to Peking. He was present at the capture of the Taku Forts, was mentioned in despatches on 4 November 1860 and received the China Medal with *Taku Forts* clasp. He was left in command of the British troops remaining in China in 1862. The Taeping insurrection was then in full spate. The rebels had broken their promise not to come within 30 miles of Shanghai and were threatening that city itself. In April Staveley marched against them with a force of about two thousand men, of whom about one-third were French and English seamen and marines. He shelled the rebels out of their entrenched camp at Wongkadze, and stormed Tsipu, Kahding, Tsingpu, Nanjao and Cholin in the course of April and May. However, the Chinese imperial troops were unable to hold all the towns recovered, and Staveley had to withdraw the British garrison from Kahding. In the autumn Kahding and Tsingpu were again taken, and the 30-mile radius cleared of the rebels.

In December he was asked by Li Hung Chang to name a British officer to replace the American Burgevine as commander of the disciplined Chinese force which had been formed by Frederick Townsend Ward. Staveley named Charles George Gordon, who had been chief engineer under him in the recent operations, and had surveyed all the country round Shanghai. They had served together before Sebastopol and Staveley's sister was the wife of Gordon's brother. The appointment had to be approved from England and was not taken up till the end of March 1863. At that time ill-health obliged Staveley to resign his command and go home.

In March 1865 he was appointed Knight Commander of the Bath (KCB) and was given command of the 1st Division of the Bombay army. On 25 September 1867 he was promoted major general.

In November 1867 Sir Robert Napier expressed his desire for Staveley to be given command of the 1st Division of the force sent to Abyssinia. He showed his energy to good purpose in the organisation of the base at Annesley Bay, and he conducted the fight on the Arogye plain, which immediately preceded the capture of Magdala. Napier said in his despatches of 16 and 30 June 1868 that Staveley had afforded him most valuable support and assistance throughout the campaign. He received the thanks of parliament and the Abyssinia Medal with *Magdala* clasp.

Staveley commanded the troops in the western district for five years from 1 January 1869. He was commander-in-chief at Bombay from 7 October 1874 to 7 October 1878, with the local rank of lieutenant general, which became his substantive rank on 29 April 1875. On 1 October 1877 he became general. He was given the colonelcy of the 36th (Herefordshire) Regiment on 2 February 1876 and transferred to his old regiment, the 44th (which had become the 1st Battalion, Essex Regiment), on 25 July 1883. He was placed on the retired list on 8 October 1883 and was appointed Knight Grand Cross, Order of the Bath (GCB) on 24 May 1884.

Because of failing health, General Staveley had wintered in Egypt in 1895 and he died on 23 November 1896, aged 78, at Aban Court North, Malvern

Road, Cheltenham; he was buried in Brompton Cemetery. A memorial plaque at Capel le Fern in Kent states:

> To the glory of God, and Sacred to the Memory of General, Sir Charles William Dunbar Staveley, Knight, Grand Cross of the Order of the Bath, Commander-in-Chief of the Bombay Army, Colonel of Her Majesty's Essex late 44th Regiment. Born at Boulogne Sur Mer, France, December 18th 1817; Died at Cheltenham November 23rd 1896, leaving five sons, William, Charles, Henry, Arthur, Cecil, and three daughters Rose, Leila, Susan. In Reverence and Love This Tablet was Placed by his Widow.

General Sir Augustus Almeric Spencer

Augustus Almeric Spencer was born on 25 March 1807 at Blenheim Palace in Oxfordshire, the ancestral home of the illustrious Spencer family, whose members have included the Dukes of Marlborough, Winston Spencer Churchill and Diana, Princess of Wales. He was the third son of six in the family of eight children, born between 1801 and 1824, of Francis Almeric Spencer MP (1779–1845), 1st Baron Churchill of Whichwood, and Lady Frances Fitzroy (1780–1866), a daughter of the 3rd Duke of Grafton.

Augustus was commissioned as an ensign in the 43rd (Oxfordshire) Light Infantry, being promoted lieutenant on 15 July 1827, captain on 6 April 1831 and major on 21 July 1843. He transferred to the 44th (East Essex) Regiment and was given command of the regiment in 1845.

On 6 February 1836 he had married Helen Maria, daughter of Lieutenant General Sir Archibald Campbell, 1st Baronet of Ava, and they had five daughters and a son, born between 1843 and 1864.

He was present at the battles of the Alma and Inkerman and in the siege of Sebastopol. For his service he received the Crimean Medal with *Alma*, *Inkerman* and *Sebastopol* clasps, the French Legion of Honour and the Turkish Order of the Medjidie (5th Class). He was appointed Knight Grand Cross, Order of the Bath (GCB).

He became commander of a brigade at Aldershot in 1856. Having been promoted major general on 13 February 1860, he became general officer commanding a division of the Madras Army that year. He was general officer commanding the Western District in the UK in 1866. He was promoted lieutenant general on 9 May 1868 and became commander-in-chief of the Bombay Army in 1869. On 14 September 1875 he was appointed brevet general, and soon retired.

General Spencer died on 28 August 1893, aged 86, at 51 Ennismore Gardens in South Kensington and was buried in Brompton Cemetery.

Captains Fenwick, Agar, Mansfield and Caulfeild

There is a memorial at St Peter's Church in Colchester that reads:

> Sacred to the memory of Captains B. Fenwick, Hon. C. Agar, W.H. Mansfield & F.W. Caulfeild who were killed 18th June 1855. Lieutenants R. Eyre died at Balaklava 15th October 1854, M. Bradford, died 1856, Assistant Surgeon J. Thomson, died at Balaklava, 5th October 1854 and 18 Sergeants 12 Drummers and 420 rank and file who were killed or died of wounds or disease during the war in the Crimea doing their duty under the Colours which hang over this stone.'

Bowes Fenwick joined the Ceylon Rifle Regiment and transferred to the 44th Regiment as a lieutenant on 22 October 1844.

Charles Welbore Herbert Agar was born on 12 November 1824 at Ditchley House in Oxfordshire, the youngest of three sons in the family of four children of Welbore Ellis Agar (1778–1868), 2nd Earl of Normanton, and Diana (1790–1841), daughter of General George Augustus Herbert, 11th Earl of Pembroke, and his wife Elizabeth. They had married on 17 May 1816. Charles entered the army as an ensign by purchase in the 44th Regiment on 29 March 1844 and was promoted lieutenant by purchase on 27 February 1846.

The *Dublin Evening Mail* of 11 July 1855 reported on his death:

> June 18, before Sebastopol, of wounds received the same day in the attack upon the cemetery, beloved and respected by his brother officers, Captain, The Hon. Charles Welbore Herbert Agar, 44th Regiment, of whom his colonel, reporting his fall, writes, 'Charles Agar, of my regiment, was severely wounded in the assault, and died a few hours afterwards. Poor fellow! Both his legs were carried off by a round shot. The service has lost a most gallant officer, and we, his brother officers, a universal favourite.'
>
> Another officer writes: 'I heard myself from the men of his company that Captain Agar led them on like a hero, and that they all admired him as much in action as they had previously liked him.'

He was buried in All Saints Churchyard at Harbridge in the New Forest, and a memorial in the church is dedicated to him.

William Henry Mansfield was the son of Alexander John Mansfield of Morristown-Latin in County Kildare, Ireland, and his wife Paulina, who were the executors of his will.

A Selection of Tributes and Commemorations

Francis William Thomas Caulfeild was born on 21 April 1826 at Upper Pembroke Street in Dublin and was baptised at St Peter's Church in Dublin. He was the eldest of five sons in the family of twelve children of Colonel John James Caulfeild (1792–1865) and his wife Anna Lovell (1800–1888), daughter of James Bury of St Leonards, Nazing, Essex. They had married on 17 May 1824. The family is descended from Viscount Charlemont of Dunamon Castle, County Roscommon, Ireland, and has a long tradition of military service. His brothers were Colonel St George Caulfeild (1837–1898), who served for nineteen years in India; Captain Robert Caulfeild (1829–1905), who also served in India; and Henry Caulfeild (1831–1869), who went to Cheltenham College and also served in India.

Lieutenant Bradford Smith Hoskins

Bradford Smith Hoskins was born in 1833 at Bishop's Tachbrook near Warwick, a son of the Reverend William Edward Hoskins (1799–1875), who was rector of Chiddingstone near Sevenoaks in Kent for twenty-three years, and his wife Jane Maria. Memorials in Chiddingstone Churchyard record: 'Jane Maria, wife of William Edward Hoskins, died 26 January 1885. Fanny Cherisa Hoskins, born 24 December 1836, died 19 February 1902. William Edward Hoskins, Rector of this Parish for 23 years, born 3 May 1799, died 6 February 1875', and also 'Elizabeth Hoskins, born 14 January 1811, died 17 January 1886.'

Bradford joined the 65th (2nd Yorkshire, North Riding) Regiment as an ensign and was posted as an ensign in the 44th (East Essex) Regiment on 7 September 1852, being appointed lieutenant on 17 February 1854. He was placed on half-pay on his return to England, and was promoted captain on 9 October 1857. He retired from British Army service in 1858 and became a soldier of fortune. In 1860 he joined the English Volunteer Legion in the army of Giuseppe Garibaldi during the struggle to unify Italy, and served as a major during his expedition to Sicily.

Bradford then went to Canada and then on to the United States, and in March 1863 he joined the 43rd Battalion, Virginian Rangers, in the Confederate Army under Major John Singleton Mosby. On 30 May 1863, after his unit had derailed a supply train at Catlett station in Prince William County, Virginia, they were chased through Greenwich by Federal forces and made a stand 2 miles west of the town. Apparently, during the fighting a Union trooper rode up to Captain Hoskins, who, wearing his British red tunic and wielding his sabre, threatened the man with his weapon and cried out, 'Surrender, you damn Yankee!' The Union soldier replied, 'The hell I will,' and shot Hoskins in the neck and back, mortally wounding him. He died on 2 June and was buried in the Greenwich Presbyterian Church Cemetery, where there is a headstone. A fellow Ranger named James J. Williamson paid tribute to him with the words, 'He was a brave soldier, and had made many friends while with the command.' His death was announced in several British newspapers of the time, and his Turkish Crimea Medal was sold at auction in 2000.

Sergeant William McWheeney VC

William McWheeney was born in 1830 at Bangor in County Down, Northern Ireland. He entered the 44th (East Essex) Regiment as 2802 Private McWheeney.

The award of the Victoria Cross to Sergeant McWheeney was announced in the *London Gazette* of 24 February 1857 and he received the medal at the first investiture, thus becoming the first holder of the Victoria Cross of the Essex Regiment. He also received the Crimea Medal with *Sebastopol* clasp, the Turkish Crimea Medal and the Distinguished Conduct Medal for his action on 5 December 1854.

At the end of the Crimean War the 44th Regiment disembarked at Spithead from the steamship *Colossus* on 18 July 1856 and a special train was laid on to take them to Aldershot, where Sergeant McWheeney was among about eight hundred men of all ranks to be inspected by Queen Victoria and Prince Albert on 31 July 1856.

He later sailed for active service in the Second China (Opium) War of 1860 as part of the Anglo-French expeditionary force. The 44th Regiment played a major part in the capture of the North Taku Fort on 21 August 1860. The attacking force had to cross a series of ditches and bamboo-stake palisades under heavy enemy fire. When an attempt to gain entry by the main gate failed, the 44th were in the vanguard of an assault party which climbed the wall to an embrasure and forced entry into the fort. The 44th Regiment gained two more Victoria Crosses during this engagement, and Sergeant McWheeney received the China War Medal with *Taku Forts* clasp.

Having been promoted to colour sergeant and stationed at Dover Citadel, William was only 36 years old when he died on 17 May 1866. He was buried in the consecrated section of St James's Cemetery, where the headstone reads: 'In Honoured Memory of C/Sgt William McWheeney VC, 44th Regiment of Foot. Died 17th May 1866, aged 36 years. The First VC of the Essex Regiment.' His name is one of four which appear on the Dover War Memorial, a project commemorating Victoria Cross recipients who are buried in Dover.

His Victoria Cross was sold for the then record amount of £50 on 17 June 1893 and the *Dover Express* for 16 February 1894 reported:

> Perhaps it cannot be otherwise, but there is something incongruous about selling the Victoria Cross; yet two of these decorations were offered in auction in London the other day. The first offered was that presented to Sergeant McWheeney, 44th Regiment, by the Queen, and was earned by valour in three actions in the Crimea – on 20 October and 5 December 1854, and June 18, 1855. With the cross were included the same soldier's Crimea, Taku Fort, Distinguished Conduct in the field, and Turko-British Crimea medals. The lot sold for £50.

His medals are with the Essex Regiment Museum in Chelmsford. There is a cannon displayed in Oaklands Park, Chelmsford, described as 'The Sevastopol Cannon, 1855'.

57th (West Middlesex) Regiment
Lieutenant Colonel Thomas Shadforth

Thomas Shadforth was born on 24 July 1808 in Gibraltar. He was the second son of three in the family of four children, born between 1803 and 1810, of Lieutenant Colonel Thomas Shadforth (1771–1862) of the 57th Regiment, a native of Newcastle-upon-Tyne, and his wife Frances (formerly Hinson, 1771–1850). His brothers Henry John Tudor and Robert William were also officers in the 57th Regiment, and his brother Edward worked with their father.

Thomas arrived in Sydney with his father's regiment in 1825 and Lieutenant Colonel Shadforth arrived in Sydney with his wife and daughter in the following year, when he began working for Sir Ralph Darling, the Governor of New South Wales. When the 57th Regiment was posted to India in 1831, all the family but Edward remained in Australia, and Thomas became a director of several companies.

In 1831 he married Elizabeth Eliza Powell and they had five children: Maria Cornelia (1832–1915), Caroline Esther (born in India in 1837, died in 1913), Thomas (born at Brompton Barracks in Chatham in 1839, died young), Louisa Frances (born in Sydney in 1840, died in 1910), and Eliza (born in Madras in 1842, died in 1927).

Colonel Shadforth seems to have felt some presentiment of his approaching fate, for he took leave of his wife and children the night before the assault in the following terms:

Before Sebastopol, 17 June, pm.

My own beloved wife and dearly beloved children. At 1 o'clock to-morrow morning I head the 57th to storm the Redan. It is, as I feel, an awfully perilous moment to me, but I place myself in the hands of our gracious God, without whose will a sparrow cannot fall to the ground. I place my whole trust in Him. Should I fall in the performance of my duty, I fully rely in the precious blood of our Saviour, shed for sinners, that I may be saved through Him.

Pardon and forgive me my beloved ones, for anything I may have said or done to cause you one moment's unhappiness. Unto God I commend my body and soul, which are His; and, should it be His will that I fall in the performance of my duty, in the defence of my Queen and country, I most humbly say, 'Thy will be done.' God bless you and protect you; and my last prayer will be, that He, of His infinite goodness, may preserve me to you. God ever bless you, my beloved Eliza, and my dearest children; and, if we meet not again in this world, may we all meet in the mansion of our Heavenly father, through Jesus Christ, God bless and protect you; and ever believe me, Your affectionate husband and loving father – Thomas Shadforth.

Colonel Shadforth was buried on Cathcart's Hill: 'Sacred to the memory of Lieut. Colonel Thomas Shadforth Commanding 57th Regiment. Killed in action June 18th 1855.'

It was stated on behalf of Queen Victoria:

Her Majesty, with that anxious consideration for those who have suffered in her service which has always distinguished her, has already signed a warrant granting a pension of £200 a year to Mrs Shadforth, and has intimated that she will take advantage of any future opportunity which may occur to manifest her appreciation of Colonel Shadforth's services. Colonel Shadforth had a hereditary connection with the 57th, his father, who was severely wounded at Albuera, having served in it for 32 years, and two of his brothers being also officers in the same regiment.

The following letter from Lieutenant Colonel Henry Warre of the 57th Regiment is dated 'Camp before Sebastopol, 18 June':

My dear Mrs Shadforth, I trust the report from other sources will have prepared you to receive the painful intelligence it becomes my duty to convey to you.

A Selection of Tributes and Commemorations

When I look to the sincere regard all the officers and men of the 57th Regiment felt for our lamented colonel, it is with unfeigned grief that I am obliged to inform you that he is no more. His gallant spirit fled while leading his men to the unfortunate and unsuccessful attack on the Redan this day.

As a soldier, his 30 years' service in the 57th Regiment has endeared him to officers and men, and the recollection of his devoted attachment to the regiment has spread a gloom through our camp, showing how beloved he was in life and how respected in death. His remains were brought up by his attached men, and they will be interred tomorrow in the cemetery attached to the division, where our late Colonel Goldie and Lieutenant General Cathcart already rest in a soldier's grave.

Pray accept my deepest sympathy and heartfelt condolence for your irreparable loss, and believe me your faithful servant,

Henry T. Warre,

Lieutenant-Colonel, 57th Regiment.

The Times of 10 August 1855 reported: 'The following letter from the acting sergeant-major of the 57th to the widow of Colonel Shadforth, who was killed in the attack on the Redan on the 18th of June, affords a most affecting testimony to the esteem with which the colonel was regarded by his regiment, and the courage with which he led them to the assault':

Camp before Sebastopol, July 14.

Madam – I trust you will pardon me for presuming to address you while in the midst of such distress, but I consider it my duty to convey to you the deep regret of the non-commissioned officers and men of the regiment at the loss of our late Colonel. He was our father and friend, and watched over the regiment and its wants in a manner that gained for him the adoration of his men; and never did I see more genuine grief among a body of men than what was seen in the 57th Regiment for the poor Colonel, and the memory of his many acts of kindness, of his unflinching courage at the head of his own 'Die-hards', and of his glorious death, will long be a theme in the 57th Regiment.

Such are the feelings of the men of the regiment, they have lost their best friend; but I have lost, if possible, more than any of them, for I never experienced such kindness as he invariably showed to me and my welfare. He lost no opportunity in advancing me in my profession, and not only did he look after my temporal, but my spiritual welfare, and if ever a man died a Christian he did.

I spoke to him a few minutes before he fell; the last words I heard him say were, 'Now, Colonel Warre, you mind the right, I will take the left, and Major Inglis the centre.' This was said amidst a shower of missiles of every kind, and he was then as cool and collected as if on parade. Poor Colonel, it was the last order I heard him give, and the last time I saw him alive. He could not have suffered much pain from the nature of his wound.

I would have written to you before, but I did not like to intrude upon your grief. If there is any service I can do for you, or any information I can furnish, I will do so with pleasure; and Boakes knows that if there is anything to be done which he cannot properly manage, I will give him all the assistance in my power.

In conclusion, I beg respectfully to assure you of my best wishes for the welfare of yourself and the young ladies, and I trust you will not consider me too forward in thus addressing you.

I remain, Madam, your very humble servant,

George Cumming, Colour-Sergeant and Acting-Sergeant Major,

57th Regiment.

The *Fifeshire Journal* for 20 December 1855 reported: 'The Queen has signified her desire that Mrs Shadforth, widow of the late Colonel Thomas Shadforth, 57th Regiment, who fell in the attack on the Redan on 18 June, should reside in one of the royal cottages in Hampton Court Park.'

Colonel Henry James Warre

Henry James Warre was born on 12 January 1819 at Cape Town in South Africa, son of Lieutenant General Sir William Warre (1784–1853), a veteran of the Peninsular War, and Selina Anna, the youngest daughter of Christopher Thompson Maling. Henry was baptised on his first birthday at St Nicholas Church in Brighton.

He was educated at the Royal Military College at Sandhurst and was commissioned as a lieutenant in the 54th (West Norfolk) Regiment in 1837, and served as aide-de-camp to the commander-in-chief of the forces in British North America from 1839 to 1845. He transferred as a captain into the 57th (West Middlesex) Regiment in 1847. While employed on the staff in Canada in 1845–1846, he examined and reported on the river communications between Montreal and the Red River settlement, a total of 2,300 miles, with a view to the transport of troops, and he was also engaged in surveying and reporting upon the various settlements in the Oregon territory and on various islands on the coast of the Pacific. He was promoted major in 1854 and lieutenant colonel in 1855.

Lieutenant Colonel Warre arrived in the Crimea in March 1855. Lieutenant Joshua Cunliffe Ingham of the 57th Regiment seems to have harboured some discontent against him, and commented,

> Warre has joined out here, he wrote to Colonel Shadforth to say that he could neither ride nor walk, but when he heard from the Horse Guards that he would not get his lieutenant-colonelcy until he joined here he came out, and looks as well and strong as anyone. This morning he tried to drill the regiment but made a total failure, in fact, I could have done it much better myself. If he commanded for two months we would be worse than a Militia; from what I have seen of him I like him very well as a man, but as a soldier he is nothing.

Nevertheless, Warre was subsequently mentioned in despatches for his role in the attack of 18 June, and was also present in the attack of 8 September. He was also present at the bombardment and surrender of Kinburn. For his service he received the Crimea Medal with *Sebastopol* clasp, the Turkish Medal and the Turkish Order of the Medjidie (5th class), and was appointed Commander of the Bath (CB).

Having been promoted to colonel in 1858, he saw active service during the Indian Rebellion. He commanded the regiment on the line of posts on the Taptee river in cooperation with the Central Field Force. He then took part in the New Zealand (Maori) War of 1861 and was appointed commander-in-chief of the Bombay Army from 1878 to 1881.

Colonel Warre died on 2 April 1898, aged 79, at 36 Cadogan Place in south-west London.

Major William Inglis
William Inglis was born on 8 July 1823. He was the son of the famous Peninsular War veteran General Sir William Inglis (1764–1835) and his wife Margaret Mary Ann, the daughter of General William Raymond. General Inglis commanded the 57th Regiment at the Battle of Albuhera in 1811. Despite being seriously wounded, he refused to leave the battle and encouraged his men with the famous cry 'Die hard 57th! Die hard!' The regiment duly rallied and held their ground, and later became known as 'The Die-Hards!'

William junior was commissioned into his father's regiment on 6 March 1840, being promoted captain in 1849. He served at Balaclava and Inkerman, and in the expedition to Kinburn. While on active service in the Crimea he was promoted to major in 1854 and to lieutenant colonel in 1855. His younger brother Major Raymond Inglis (1826–1880) served in the Crimea with the 5th Dragoon Guards.

On 19 September 1860 William married Mary (1833–1895), the daughter of Hector William Bower Munro, 2nd Baron Edmondsham of Dorset. They lived at Hildersham Hall near Cambridge and had two children. Their son William Raymond was commanding the 33rd Battalion of the 7th Royal Fusiliers when he died in 1916, and was buried with his father.

William was later created Commander of the Bath (CB). He retired with the rank of general in 1882. General Inglis died on 2 September 1888, aged 65, at Blackheath, Lewisham (now in Greater London), and was buried in All Saints Churchyard at Rickling, Uttlesford District, in Essex.

Captain Arthur Maxwell Earle
Arthur Maxwell Earle was born in Edinburgh on 9 November 1832, the son of Charles Earle. He joined the 57th Regiment as an ensign by purchase on 18 January 1850 when he was 17 years old. He was promoted lieutenant in 1853, captain in December 1854 and brevet major in 1856.

During the Crimean War he served as aide-de-camp to Brigadier General Thomas Goldie. He was wounded in the trenches on 3 November 1854 and was with General Goldie when the latter was killed at Inkerman two days later. He did not have much respect for General Philip McPherson, the man who replaced General Goldie, and stated: 'Had I but a Goldie for a Brigadier instead of an old nonentity who, were I to put his own death warrant on his desk, he would sign it.'

He was with Sir Colin Campbell commanding the assaulting column on 18 June, with Major General Spencer in the assault on 8 September, and with Lord West at the capture of Kinborn. He became brigade major with the 4th Division. For his service he was three times mentioned in despatches, received the Crimea Medal with *Balaclava*, *Inkerman* and *Sebastopol* clasps, was made a Knight of the French Legion of Honour and received the Turkish Order of the Medjidie (5th Class). He was promoted brevet major on 5 August 1856. His Crimea Medal is in the collection at the National Army Museum.

Plays and musicals were a firm favourite with the troops in the Crimea, and Captain Earle became a leading light in the 4th Division's theatre, sometimes giving two performances in one night. In January 1856 he wrote to his father:

> Our theatre, a handsome building, is nearly completed and we hope to give another performance early next week. The 2nd Battn of the Rifles

performed two days ago, and gave great satisfaction especially to one person, a little more vulgar than the rest, who stood up in the middle of the performance and declared that 'It was much better than the 4th Divn.'

Earle is the subject of a photograph taken in Naples in 1861, with Captain Rowley Lambert of the Royal Navy. Major Earle died on 27 March 1863, aged 30, on the island of Corfu.

Lieutenant James Collins Ashwin

Lieutenant Ashwin was buried on Cathcart's Hill: 'Sacred to the memory of James Collins Ashwin Lieut. 57th Regiment. Killed in Action June 18th 1855.'

There is a memorial at St Leonard's Church in Bretforton, Worcestershire: 'Sacred to the memory of Lieutenant James Collins Ashwin of the 57th Regt. He was killed before Sebastopol in the assault on the Great Redan June 18 AD 1855 aged 21.'

The *Worcester Journal* in Evesham for 30 June 1855 reported:

> Amongst the many brave fellows who fell before Sebastopol on the 18th inst., was Lieutenant James Collins Ashwin, 57th Regiment, eldest son of James Ashwin of Bretforton Hall, an active and much respected magistrate and deputy lieutenant of this county. This promising young officer fell before the Redan, together with his gallant colonel, Thomas Shadforth, between whom the warmest friendship had existed, from the time the young soldier had joined the regiment. Often in playful parlance, Lieutenant Ashwin had been heard to tell his colonel that if ever he received his bullet, he would find him at his elbow, and most nobly did this brave youth justify his promise.
>
> It is a curious fact that on the 16th, only two days before the fall of these two heroic brothers in arms, we inserted a letter in this journal from a corporal of the 57th to his brother in this city, in which he says: 'Lieutenant Ashwin and Colonel Shadforth are both well. They are two as good officers as ever drew a sword and perfect gentlemen in every sense of the word, just such men as can win the hearts of every man in their command. Yes indeed, we would face anything for such men and will either take Sebastopol, or every man will leave his dead body beneath the walls.'
>
> It must be a great consolation to their mourning friends to see them thus spoken of. Lieutenant Ashwin was only in his 22nd year, and Colonel Shadforth in a letter to the father in March last says: 'If you try

to get a Staff appointment for your son, I shall be proud to certify that there is no finer fellow or smarter officer in her Majesty's service.'

On the following 15 December 1855 the same newspaper stated:

It will be remembered that Sir John Campbell chose the 57th to lead the storming party on the disastrous attack on the Redan on the 18th June last, where they bore the brunt of the day, and lost Colonel Shadforth and Lieutenant Ashwin killed, Captain Norman received his death wound, five other officers were severely wounded, whilst all the colour-sergeants, with 112 rank and file, out of 400 of this gallant regiment, were stretched on the ground.

Lieutenant Ashwin fell from a round shot which struck him on the breast, and he lies buried on Cathcart's Hill, between Captains Stanley and Norman of the 57th. The surviving officers and privates of his regiment have erected a monument over his grave in testimony of their respect for him.

In a letter to his relatives dated 'Heights of Alma, April 23rd 1855', the gallant deceased enclosed a photograph of a group taken in front of Colonel Shadforth's tent, containing portraits of Major Inglis, Captain St Clair, Captain Hassard, Colonel Shadforth, Lieutenant Ashwin and Quartermaster Balcombe. The party are represented in their trench dresses. Captain St Clair and Major Inglis are sitting down, the others standing round. In the background is one of Colonel Shadforth's servants picking a duck at the kitchen door. We understand it is intended to take copies of the likeness of the deceased hero from the photograph thus preserved; by which means those of his friends who wish to possess themselves of a memorial of the departed may be enabled to do so.

The fatal assault on the Redan, in which Lieutenant Ashwin fell, was thus graphically described in a letter to *The Times*, under date 'Camp before Sebastopol, July 19':

Eighteen officers and 400 men of the 57th Regiment (the old 'Die Hards') covered by 100 rank and file of the 2nd Battalion, Rifle Brigade, under the command of Lt-Colonel Shadforth, were told off as the assaulting party. On the signal being given they advanced to the attack (led by Sir John Campbell in person), under a storm of grape which Lord Raglan truly termed 'terrific'. They had not gone more than 50 yards (it being 280 to the nearest point of the Redan, when their gallant leaders fell. Captains Norman, Lea, St Clair; Lieutenants Ashwin and Venables, and at least 80 non-commissioned officers and men were hors-de-combat. Of the remainder, many ran forward towards the abattis in front of the Redan; the others were driven back by a shower of projectiles it was impossible to face, poured in upon their flank from a small battery, which our artillery had never even condescended to notice.

By an unfortunate accident their gallant leader mistook in the first instance the real point of attack; but most nobly did the remnant of the 57th respond to the call of their officers to renew the attack and attempt to turn the unprotected flank of this battery, which had dealt such destruction in its ranks. It was in vain that the 57th Regiment and the Rifles advanced to the very abattis, [where] they found themselves without support.

The result is well-known.

Captain George Herman Norman
George Herman Norman was christened on 25 September 1831 at Bromley in Kent. He was the eldest child in the family of six boys and two girls, born between 1831 and 1847, of George Ward Norman (1793–1882), a director of the Bank of England from 1821 to 1872, and a magistrate, land and fund owner, and his wife Isabella (formerly Stone, 1808–1887). They had married on 12 October 1830 at St George, Hanover Square, London. At the time of the 1851 census George was described as 'Ensign 57 Army', and the family home was at Bromley Common Turnpike Road in Bromley.

George Norman was promoted captain on 28 December 1854. He was buried on Cathcart's Hill: 'Sacred to the memory of George Herman Norman, Captain 57th Regiment. Wounded June 18th. Died in Camp June 30th 1855.' There is a memorial at Holy Trinity Church, known as Bromley Common Church:

> Sacred to the memory of George Herman Norman, Capt. 57th Regt. Wounded June 18th Died in camp June 30th 1855. Eldest son of George Warde Norman, of this parish and Sibella, his wife. Born at Bromley 26th July 1831, educated at the Royal Military College, Sandhurst. He was wounded in the head by a musket ball, while gallantly leading his company to the assault of the Redan on the 18th June 1855 and died in the British Camp before Sebastopol, June 30th 1855.

Colour Sergeant George Gardiner VC
George Gardiner was born in 1821 at Clonallon, Warrenpoint, in County Down, Ireland. All four soldiers of the Middlesex regiments who gained the

Victoria Cross in the Crimea were from Ireland, and George enlisted into the 57th (West Middlesex) Regiment, being posted to Lifford Barracks in 1846. The regiment had earned the nickname the 'Die Hards' after the bloody battle of Albuera, fought during the Peninsular War on 16 May 1811, when their colonel, having been struck down and wounded, urged his men on by shouting: 'Die Hard, the 57th, Die Hard!'

Gardiner's award of the Victoria Cross was announced in the *London Gazette* of 4 June 1858 and he received the medal from Brigadier General William Marcus Coghlan, the British representative in Aden, on 5 October 1858. He also received the Crimea Medal with *Inkerman* and *Sebastopol* clasps, the Distinguished Conduct Medal and the Turkish Crimea Medal. He subsequently saw service during the Maori Wars, for which he received the New Zealand Medal, 1860–66. He discharged from the regular army in 1861 and enlisted in the Prince of Wales's Own Donegal Militia.

His wife Elizabeth and their children travelled to the Crimea with him, but their 2-year-old son Arthur Trafalgar died in Trafalgar Bay on 29 November 1854. Another tragedy devastated the family in 1869 when their only daughter, Elizabeth Jane, died on 7 April, aged 12, and their only surviving son, Richard, died a week later, aged 3. In consequence of this, Gardiner retired as a sergeant major from the Militia on 17 July 1869. For his service he received a 'railway clock' at Lifford Barracks, with the inscription: 'as a token of appreciation of the zealous and impartial manner in which he performed his military duties, and of his most obliging conduct in civil life …'

Elizabeth died on 12 June 1882, aged 52, and George passed away on 17 November 1891, aged 70, at his home, Lifford House in County Donegal. He was buried at the Clonleigh churchyard in Lifford, where there is a headstone. His medals are with the Princess of Wales's Royal Regiment and Queen's Regiment RHQ in Canterbury.

77th (East Middlesex) Regiment
Sergeant John Park VC

John Park was born in February 1835 in Londonderry, Ireland. He joined the 77th (East Middlesex) Regiment, the 'Die Hards', as 2600 Private Park.

Park's award of the Victoria Cross was announced in the *London Gazette* for 24 February 1857 and he received the medal from the General Officer Commanding at Sydney in Australia in March 1858. He also received the Crimea Medal with *Alma*, *Balaclava*, *Inkerman* and *Sebastopol* clasps, the French Legion of Honour and the Turkish Crimea Medal.

A Selection of Tributes and Commemorations

John died of heat apoplexy (sunstroke) while still serving with the regiment at Allahabad in India on 16 May 1863, aged 28, and was buried in an unmarked grave in the Church of Scotland section of Allahabad Cemetery. His medals are at the Newarke Houses Museum in Leicester.

73rd (Perthshire) Regiment

Colonel Sir William Eyre

William Eyre was born on 21 October 1805 at Carlton in Derbyshire. He was the younger of two sons in the family of eight children born to Vice Admiral Sir George Eyre (1769–1839) and his wife Georgiana, a daughter of Sir George Cooke, 7th Baronet, of Wheatley. They had married at Doncaster on 1 November 1800. His father was a veteran of the American War of Independence, the French Revolutionary Wars and the Napoleonic Wars.

William was educated at Rugby School until 1817 and was commissioned as an ensign in the 6th Regiment on 17 April 1823, being promoted lieutenant on 5 November 1825. He gained a half-pay captaincy on 20 November 1827 and remained unemployed until 21 May 1829. On that date he received a company in the 73rd (Perthshire) Regiment, stationed in the Mediterranean. The regiment remained in the Mediterranean for a decade until 1839, when he was promoted major.

In 1841 he married Georgiana Lucy (1808–1898), third daughter of the Hon. John Bridgeman-Simpson.

In 1845 the regiment received orders for active service in the Cape Frontier War in South Africa, and he was promoted to lieutenant colonel in that same year. In the Cape Frontier War of 1851 he defeated the Xhosa at the battles of Quibigui River and Committees Hill. In 1852 he commanded the right wing in the punitive attack on Moshoeshoe at Berea in Basutoland. For his service in South Africa he was appointed Companion of the Bath (CB). He served as aide-de-camp to Queen Victoria and was promoted to colonel.

In the Crimea he commanded the 3rd Brigade and later the 3rd Division, and was promoted to major general. For his service he received the Crimea Medal, the French Legion of Honour, the Turkish Order of the Medjidie (2nd class) and the Sardinian Crimea Medal, and was appointed Knight Commander of the Bath (KCB).

In 1855 he accepted the appointment as commander in British North America – Canada. The *Quebec Mercury* for 1 September 1856 reported:

> Narrow Escape of General, Sir William Eyre – One of the most miraculous escapes we have ever heard of occurred to Lieutenant-General

Eyre and staff, and a number of pleasure seekers in the Saguenay River the day before yesterday.

As usual the gun on the forward promenade deck was fired in front of Cape Eternity, to give the passengers an idea of the echo, but, unfortunately and from some unaccountable cause, the gun burst in going off, and was blown to atoms, barely a fragment of the carriage remaining to view when the smoke cleared away. The majority of the passengers, including several ladies, as well as the Commander of the Forces, were congregated on the front deck admiring the stupendous rocks overhead, when the gun was loaded, and they merely retired a pace or two in different directions to see it fire. The man who fired it was knocked down, but not hurt, and, though portions of the gun flew in four different directions, not one of the companies was injured ...

Eyre's health had been broken during the Crimean War, and he resigned from the army due to ill-health in June 1859. He retired to the family home at Belton Hall near Rugby, but died on 18 September 1859, in his 54th year. There are several memorials to the Eyre family in St Mark's Church, Belton, including one to Sir William, which reads: 'History will gratefully record his services for his country, and affection cherish his memory in the hearts of his friends and relatives.' Another memorial honours his son Arthur Adolph, who was killed in action during the Ashanti campaign in 1874.

88th Regiment (Connaught Rangers)
Captain George Richard Browne

George Richard Brown was born on 10 June 1834, the only son of Captain the Hon. Richard Howe Browne (1811–1888) of the 8th Hussars and his first wife Elizabeth (1818–1876). The family home was at Crouch Oak in Addlestone, Surrey.

Browne was commissioned as an ensign by purchase in the 88th Connaught Rangers on 17 June 1851, being promoted lieutenant in 1854 and captain in April 1855. He was wounded dangerously, and was awarded the Crimea Medal with *Alma*, *Inkerman* and *Sebastopol* clasps, the Turkish Crimea Medal and the French Legion of Honour on 16 June 1856.

On 13 June 1857 at St Nicholas Church in Glamorgan he married Louisa, the youngest daughter of Vice Admiral Sir George Tyler, and they had four boys and two girls.

He served in the Indian Rebellion of 1857–1858, where he was present at the battle of Cawnpore and in the capture of Lucknow. For his service he received the Indian Mutiny Medal with *Lucknow* and *Central India* clasps.

In February 1884 he suffered an unfortunate fall from grace, as newspapers reported:

> A Degenerate Hero – It has been ascertained (says the *Balart Courier*) that the statement of George Robert [Richard] Browne, better known as Colonel Browne, is quite correct as to his service in the British Army. At his trial at the Assize Court on Monday, for false pretences, it was made known that he obtained his commission as ensign, by purchase, in the 88th Connaught Rangers on 17th June 1851. He was promoted to the position of lieutenant in 1854, and captain in April 1855. He served through the Crimean war of 1854–5, including the battles of Alma and Inkerman and the siege of Sebastopol, where he was dangerously wounded. He lost his right arm at the first attack on the Redan in 1855. He served in the Indian Mutiny, 1857–58, and was present at Cawnpore and the capture of Lucknow. He was promoted to the rank of major, for distinguished conduct in the Field, in 1868. He holds the Crimean Medal, with clasps for Alma, Inkerman, and Sebastopol, and the Turkish Crimea Medal. He has been admitted to the Order of the Legion of Honour, and the Indian Mutiny Medal, with clasps for Central India and Lucknow. He was appointed assistant adjutant-general in Canada in 1865, and was subsequently appointed lieutenant-colonel. He is well connected, having several titled relatives. His case was, therefore, a very painful one.
>
> He states that he has a banking account in Sydney. The jury found him guilty, and he was remanded for sentence. The prisoner on being called up for sentence on Wednesday, said that he wished simply to make a few remarks about his humiliating position he did not wish to occupy any time. He did his utmost in pleading guilty at the police court, as he was led to believe his case would be dealt with there. Under the circumstances he had since employed counsel, who had done his part ably. He had no excuse for his fault, but he would call attention to the fact that he had paid everyone he owed money to, so he had done everything in his power. He was sentenced to four months' imprisonment.

Browne died in 1901, in his 67th year.

90th (Perthshire) Light Infantry
Private John Alexander VC
John Alexander was born at Mullingar in County Westmeath, Ireland, and entered the 90th (Perthshire) Light Infantry as 2932 Private Alexander. He had married prior to receiving orders for active service in the East.

The award of the Victoria Cross to Private Alexander was announced in the *London Gazette* of 24 February 1857. He was also entitled to receive the Crimea Medal with *Alma*, *Inkerman* and *Sebastopol* clasps, the French Military Medal, the Turkish Crimea Medal and the Bentinck Medal. The latter was normally presented only to men of the Guards Brigade, but Alexander received it for helping to save the life of a Scots Guards officer on 6 September 1855. On the same day as the first investiture in Hyde Park, a letter was sent out authorising him to be presented with his medal at an investiture in Hong Kong. However, the 90th were diverted from the China station to India, where the mutiny among local forces had broken out in May 1857.

On 24 September 1857, during the British Expeditionary Force's advance towards the relief of the Lucknow garrison, he was at the Alum Bagh on the outskirts of the city and in rear of the main force with an escort of the 90th Light Infantry, which was protecting the baggage being transported to the front, when it was treacherously attacked by rebel cavalry. The officer in command was hacked to pieces, three other soldiers were killed and many more wounded before the enemy were driven away. Private Alexander was killed during the fight. His remains are believed to have been buried where he fell. For his service he received the Indian Mutiny Medal with *Relief of Lucknow* clasp.

His medals were sent by registered post to his widow, and they are now displayed at the National War Museum of Scotland housed in Edinburgh Castle.

2nd Rifle Brigade (Prince Consort's Own)
Captain Edward William Blackett
Edward William Blackett was born on 22 March 1831 in Napoli, one of four sons and two daughters (possibly four) born to Sir Edward Blackett, 6th Bt (1805–1885) and his wife Julia (formerly Monk). The family home was Matfen Hall in Northumberland, which is now a luxury hotel. All his three brothers entered the army. Edward was educated at Eton College.

For his service in the Crimea he was awarded the French Legion of Honour. He was promoted to major by purchase while serving in India in 1862, lieutenant colonel in 1870 and colonel in 1878. He gained the rank of honorary major general in 1881.

On 23 November 1871 at St Marylebone Church in London he married the Hon. Julia Frances, the daughter of Admiral Kenelm Somerville RN, 17th Lord Somerville. They had three sons and a daughter, including Sir Hugh Douglas, who became the 8th Baronet Blackett.

Captain Blackett held the office of aide-de-camp to Queen Victoria in 1878, being appointed Companion, Order of the Bath (CB). He succeeded to the title of 7th Baronet Blackett of Newcastle-on-Tyne, on 23 November 1885, and he held the office of High Sheriff of Northumberland in 1889.

Major General Blackett died at St George, Hanover Square, in London, on 13 September 1909, aged 78.

Captain Edward Rowland Forman
Edward Rowland Forman was born in 1822 at Merthyr Tydfil in South Wales, the son of William Forman of Penydarren House in Merthyr. William was an ordnance agent at the headquarters of the government arsenal housed in the Tower of London. Apparently he was known as 'Billy Ready Money' because of his wealth and readiness to finance speculative ventures, including becoming a part-owner of the Tredegar Ironworks.

Edward was educated at Eton College and entered the 88th Regiment before transferring to the Rifle Brigade, and served as a staff officer in the West Indies.

On 23 November 1853 at Newton Purcell near Oxford he married Louisa Mary Ann, eldest daughter of John Harrison Slater-Harrison of Shelswell House in Oxfordshire. After Forman's death, Louisa remarried but died in childbirth in 1865.

On the day after the battle on the 18th, a two-hour truce was agreed by both armies so that they could collect their dead. *The Times* correspondent stated: 'Poor Forman's body was one of the first found. It was far in advance of where he came out of the trench with his company of the Rifle Brigade, and it was terribly torn with shot.'

Captain Forman was buried in the 1st Brigade, Light Division cemetery: 'Sacred to the memory of Capt. E.R. Forman. 2nd Battn Rifle Brigade who was killed at the assault on the Redan on the 18th June 1855 aged 33 years. This stone is erected by his brother officers.'

His name appears on the Royal Garrison Church memorial in Portsmouth, which is dedicated to Old Etonians who were killed in the Crimean War.

The *Bicester Herald* for 30 June 1855 reported:

Captain Edward Rowland Forman of the Rifle Brigade, whose marriage to Miss Harrison, eldest daughter of John Harrison Slater-Harrison of Shelswell House, took place but about twelve months since, fell in the Crimea on the 18th. The disconsolate widow received the melancholy intelligence at Shelswell on Monday last. Captain Forman was in the 88th for some years, and served on the staff in the West Indies. Sad to relate, that on the day that the death of the gallant Captain reached Shelswell, intimation also arrived at the mansion of the death of Lady Caroline Scott, sister of Lady Louisa Harrison, and eldest daughter of the late Earl of Clonmel.

Lieutenant Charles Augustus Penrhyn Boileau

Charles Augustus Penrhyn Boileau was born on 9 August 1835 at Ketteringham Hall near Norwich in Norfolk, the fourth and youngest son in the family of nine children, born between 1826 and 1840, of Sir John Peter Boileau FRS JP DL (1794–1869), 1st Bt of Ketteringham in Norfolk, and his wife Lady Catherine Sarah (1798–1862), daughter of Gilbert Elliot-Murray-Kynynmound, 1st Earl of Minto. Sir John became a well-known archaeologist and on 24 July 1838 he was created 1st Baron Boileau of Tacolneston Hall, Norfolk.

Charles was educated at Eton and it would seem that he spent his time and inheritance on wine, women and song, incurring large debts, and at the age of only 19 he ran away to join the Rifle Brigade.

He died in the Bighi Naval Hospital in Malta and was buried in the nearby cemetery. The inscription on his grave reads: 'Charles Augustus Penrhyn Boileau, Died 3 August 1855. Lieutenant, Rifle Brigade. Buried in the Royal Naval Hospital Cemetery. He was wounded on 18 June at the assault of the Malakoff in the Crimea. Born 9 August 1835, son of Sir John Peter Boileau, 1st Bt, of Tacolneston Hall, and Lady Catherine Sarah Elliot.'

There is a somewhat harshly worded brass memorial dedicated to him in the family vault at St Peter's Church in Ketteringham, which states: 'Charles Augustus Penryn Boileau. Something of a rake. He went to the Crimean War as a way of escaping his debts, and died in Malta on his way home as a result of injuries suffered at the 1855 siege of Sebastopol.'

The Royal Garrison Church in Portsmouth has a memorial dedicated to Old Etonians who were killed in the Crimean War, which states: 'Charles Augustus Penrhyn Boileau, Lieutenant, Rifle Brigade, died at Malta in 1855, of wounds received before Sebastopol. This officer is also recorded as an Old Rugbeian, where it is noted that his gallantry had been especially commended by Lord Raglan. His date of death is recorded as 1 August.'

Lieutenant Fitzroy William Freemantle

Fitzroy William Fremantle was born on 15 December 1836 in London, the middle son of three in the family of four children, born between 1835 and 1843, of Major General John William Freemantle CB, a distinguished Peninsular veteran and formerly aide-de-camp to the Duke of Wellington, and his wife Agnes (formerly Lyon, 1803–1864). His elder brother was General Sir Arthur James Lyon Freemantle GCMG CB (1835–1901), who spent some time in the United States during the Civil War and was a witness at the Battle of Gettysburg.

Fitzroy William was commissioned into the 2nd Battalion, Rifle Brigade, on 14 July 1854 and was promoted lieutenant on 22 December 1854. He served in the Crimea from December 1854 until July 1855, including the siege of Sebastopol, and commanded 163 men at the last sortie of the Russians against the Quarries on 8 June 1855. Lieutenant Fremantle received the Crimea Medal with *Sebastopol* clasp and the Turkish Crimea Medal. He was rewarded with the Italian silver medal for Military Bravery, the citation stating: 'Joined in the Crimea on the 1st December, 1854, and did duty in the trenches from that date until the 18th of June, 1855.'

Promoted to captain on 24 November 1857, Captain Fremantle also served in the Indian Mutiny with the 2nd Battalion, including at the siege and capture of Lucknow, the Trans-Gogra campaign and the expedition into Nepal, for which he was mentioned in despatches (*London Gazette*, 2 September 1859). His exploits in the Indian Mutiny warranted several mentions in Sir William Cope's *History of the Rifle Brigade*, particularly for his part in the clearing of the Yellow Bungalow during the capture of Lucknow in March 1858, in the operations around Mejidia in December 1858 and in the expeditions near the Raptee in April 1859. For his service he received the Indian Mutiny Medal with *Lucknow* clasp.

He married Julia Elizabeth Henrietta (1840–1910), the daughter of Guy Campbell (1786–1849) and his wife Pamela (formerly Fitzgerald, 1795–1869).

Captain Fremantle exchanged into the Coldstream Guards on 17 July 1860 and was promoted major on 1 July 1881 and colonel on 29 September 1881. He was placed on half-pay on 8 December 1884 and appointed to the command of No. 11 Regimental District (Devon) at Exeter on 7 March 1885. He was gazetted CB in the *London Gazette* of 21 June 1887, on the occasion of the celebration of the fiftieth year of Queen Victoria's reign. Placed back on half-pay on 7 May 1890, he was promoted to major general on 7 August 1892.

General Freemantle died at The Chuffs in Holyport near Maidenhead on 12 February 1894, aged 57. His medals were sold at auction in 2002 and resold in 2003.

Lieutenant John Simpson Knox VC
John Simpson Knox was born on 30 September 1828 at King Street in Calton, Glasgow, of a yeomanry family. He was the son of John Knox, late of

the 90th (Perthshire) Light Infantry, and his second wife. He was big for his age at 14, and on 15 May 1843 he apparently ran away from an unhappy home and enlisted at Glasgow into the 3rd Battalion, Scots (Fusilier) Guards.

John kept a scrapbook into which he pasted letters, cuttings and pictures, which were kept by his family. He took to the army well, being promoted corporal on 11 June 1846, sergeant on 9 July 1851 and acting sergeant major and drill sergeant on 7 July 1853, thus becoming one of the youngest senior NCOs in the army. He was described as a man of magnificent physique, 'a formidable and conspicuous figure', and the numerous recommendations he received from high-ranking officers made him well-known throughout the army and beyond.

The gallantry of the three battalions of Foot Guards during the Battle of Inkerman had so impressed Prince Albert that he placed a commission at the disposal of General Lord Rokeby in the Rifle Brigade. Sergeant Knox had transferred to the 2nd Battalion, Rifle Brigade, and his selection for this honour gave widespread satisfaction among his colleagues. As a consequence he was appointed ensign in March 1855 and lieutenant on 11 May 1855. The Russian canister ball that struck him during the first attack on the Redan, causing the loss of his arm, was picked up by another soldier and given to him.

His award of the Victoria Cross was announced in the *London Gazette* on 24 February 1857 and he received the medal at the first investiture. He was one of three men whom Queen Victoria mentioned in her diary when she wrote it that night. He also received the Crimea Medal with *Alma*, *Balaclava*, *Inkerman* and *Sebastopol* clasps, the French Legion of Honour and the Turkish Crimea Medal.

He was promoted to brevet major, but the loss of his arm curtailed his army career and he retired from service on 8 June 1872. He became the Governor of Cardiff Goal from 1872 to 1876, before moving to Kirkdale Prison in Liverpool from September 1886 until January 1892. He had received an appointment as Governor of Hull Prison in October 1891 but he could not take it up because of ill-health, and was forced to retire. He was noted to be a stern disciplinarian, and he maintained perfect order, but 'at the same time showed the utmost kindness to the prisoners'. Soon after his wife died he left Kirkdale for Cheltenham on 25 April 1892.

In a letter home he had stated: 'The enemy endeavoured to drive us back, however, we stuck to them until we were masters.' However, in later life he seemed to scorn the various reunions that took place, and on learning of 'another' Crimean Dinner in 1894, he wrote to an old comrade: 'My presence would make some of our own friends uncomfortable; you must have spotted many of them, as I did, skulking under the banks of the Alma.'

John died on 8 January 1897, aged 70, at his home at 6 Oriel Terrace in Cheltenham and was buried in Cheltenham Cemetery; his headstone was refurbished in 2002 after being found badly damaged. His name appears on the Rifle Brigade Memorial at Winchester Cathedral, and on the ledger headstone of his wife Harriet Louisa at Anfield Cemetery in Liverpool. His Victoria Cross and other memorabilia, including the canister ball mounted on a marble plinth, were sold in 2010 and the Victoria Cross is now displayed on rotation at the Lord Ashcroft Gallery as part of the 'Extraordinary Heroes' exhibition at the Imperial War Museum in London.

Appendix I

Crimean War VCs by Units

Royal Navy (24)

Mate Charles Davis Lucas, 21 June 1854, at Bomarsund in the Baltic Sea.

Lieutenant John Bythesea, 8–12 August 1854, at Wardo Island in the Baltic Sea.

Stoker William Johnstone, 8–12 August 1854, at Wardo Island in the Baltic Sea.

Captain William Peel, 18 October 1854, at Sebastopol (*also on 5 November 1854 at the Battle of Inkerman, and on 18 June 1855 at the first assault on the Great Redan at Sebastopol*).

Midshipman Edward St John Daniel, 18 October 1854, at Sebastopol (*also on 5 November 1854 at the Battle of Inkerman, and on 18 June 1855 at the first assault on the Great Redan at Sebastopol*).

Acting Mate William Nathan Wright Hewett, 26 October 1854, Little Inkerman, Sebastopol (*also on 5 November 1854 at the Battle of Inkerman, as a lieutenant*).

Seaman James Gorman, 5 November 1854, at the Battle of Inkerman.

Seaman Thomas Reeves, 5 November 1854, at the Battle of Inkerman.

Seaman Mark Scholefield, 5 November 1854, at the Battle of Inkerman.

Botswain's Mate John Sullivan, 29 March 1855, at Sebastopol.

Lieutenant Cecil William Buckley, 29 May 1855, Genitchi in the Sea of Azov (*also on 3 June 1855 at Taganrog on the Sea of Azov*).

Lieutenant Hugh Talbot Burgoyne, 29 May 1855, Genitchi in the Sea of Azov.

Gunner John Robarts, 29 May 1855, Genitchi in the Sea of Azov.

Botswain Henry Cooper, 3 June 1855, at Taganrog in the Sea of Azov.

Lieutenant Henry James Raby, 18 June 1855, the first assault on the Great Redan at Sebastopol.

Captain of the Forecastle John (T.N.) Taylor, 18 June 1855, the first assault on the Great Redan at Sebastopol.

Botswain's Mate Henry Curtis, 18 June 1855, the first assault on the Great Redan at Sebastopol

Seaman Joseph Trewavas, 3 July 1855, at the Straits of Genitchi in the Sea of Azov.
Captain of the Mast George Henry Ingouville, 13 July 1855, at the Fort of Svaeborg in the Gulf of Finland.
Botswain's Mate John Sheppard, 15 July 1855, at Careening Bay near Sebastopol Harbour.
Botswain Joseph Kellaway, 31 August 1855, at Marionpol in the Sea of Azov.
Lieutenant George Fiott Day, 17 September 1855, at the Straits of Genitchi in the Sea of Azov.
Commander John Edmund Commerell, 11 October 1855, at Sivash in the Sea of Azov.
Quartermaster William Thomas Rickard, 11 October 1855, at Sivash in the Sea of Azov.

Royal Marines (3)

Corporal John Prettyjohns, 5 November 1854, at the Battle of Inkerman.
Bombardier Thomas Wilkinson, 7 June 1855, at the Quarries, Sebastopol.
Lieutenant George Dare Dowell, 13 July 1855, at the Fort of Svaeborg in the Gulf of Finland.

2nd Dragoons (Royal Scots Greys) (2)

Sergeant Major John Grieve, 25 October 1854, the Charge of the Heavy Brigade at Balaclava.
Sergeant Henry Ramage, 25 October 1854, the Charge of the Heavy Brigade at Balaclava.

6th Dragoons (Inniskillings) (1)

Surgeon James Mouat, 25 October 1854, the Charge of the Light Brigade at Balaclava.

4th Queen's Own Light Dragoons (1)

Private Samuel Parkes, 25 October 1854, the Charge of the Light Brigade at Balaclava.

11th Hussars (Prince Albert's Own) (1)

Lieutenant Alexander Roberts Dunn, 25 October 1854, the Charge of the Light Brigade at Balaclava.

13th Light Dragoons (1)

Corporal Joseph Malone, 25 October 1854, the Charge of the Light Brigade at Balaclava.

Appendix I: Crimean War VCs by Units

17th Lancers (Duke of Cambridge's Own) (3)

Sergeant Major John Berryman, 25 October 1854, the Charge of the Light Brigade at Balaclava.

Sergeant Major Charles Wooden, 25 October 1854, the Charge of the Light Brigade at Balaclava.

Sergeant John Farrell, 25 October 1854, the Charge of the Light Brigade at Balaclava.

Royal Regiment of Artillery (9)

Lieutenant Colonel Collingwood Dickson, 17 October 1854, at Sebastopol.

Lieutenant Frederick Miller, 5 November 1854, at the Battle of Inkerman.

Sergeant Major Andrew Henry, 5 November 1854, at the Battle of Inkerman.

Captain Matthew Charles Dixon, 17 April 1855, at Sebastopol.

Sergeant George Symons, 6 June 1855, at the Quarries, Sebastopol.

Gunner Thomas Arthur, 7 June 1855, at the Quarries, Sebastopol (*also on 18 June 1855 at the first assault on the Great Redan*).

Captain Gronow Davis, 8 September 1855, at the second assault on the Great Redan at Sebastopol.

Bombardier Daniel Cambridge, 8 September 1855, at the second assault on the Great Redan at Sebastopol.

Lieutenant Christopher Charles Teesdale, 29 September 1855, at the siege of Kars.

Corps of Royal Engineers (8)

Lieutenant Wilbraham Oates Lennox, 20 November 1854, at the Rifle Pits, Sebastopol.

Corporal William James Lendrim, 14 February 1855, at Sebastopol (*also on 11 and 20 April 1855 at the Quarries, Sebastopol*).

Colour Sergeant Henry MacDonald, 19 April 1855, at the Quarries, Sebastopol.

Lieutenant Howard Craufurd Elphinstone, 18 June 1855, the first assault on the Great Redan at Sebastopol.

Lieutenant Gerald Graham, 18 June 1855, the first assault on the Great Redan at Sebastopol.

Colour-Sergeant Peter Leitch, 18 June 1855, the first assault on the Great Redan at Sebastopol.

Sapper John Perie, 18 June 1855, the first assault on the Great Redan at Sebastopol.

Corporal John Ross, 21 July 1855, at Sebastopol (*also on 23 August 1855 at Sebastopol and on 8 September 1855 at the second assault in the Great Redan*).

Grenadier Guards (4)

Colonel Henry Hugh Manvers Percy, 5 November 1854, at the Battle of Inkerman.
Captain Charles Russell, 5 November 1854, at the Battle of Inkerman.
Private Anthony Palmer, 5 November 1854, at the Battle of Inkerman.
Sergeant Alfred Ablett, 2 September 1855, at Sebastopol.

Coldstream Guards (3)

Private William Stanlake, 26 October 1854, at Little Inkerman, Sebastopol.
Brevet Major Gerald Littlehales Goodlake, 28 October 1854, at the Windmill Ravine, Sebastopol.
Private George Strong, September 1855, at Sebastopol.

Scots (Fusilier) Guards (5)

Captain Robert James Lindsay, 20 September 1854, at the Battle of the Alma (*also on 5 November 1854 at the Battle of Inkerman*).
Sergeant John Simpson Knox, 20 September 1854, at the Battle of the Alma (*also on 18 June 1855 at the first assault on the Great Redan at Sebastopol, with the Rifle Brigade*).
Sergeant James McKechnie, 20 September 1854, at the Battle of the Alma.
Private William Reynolds, 20 September 1854, at the Battle of the Alma.
Sergeant James Craig, 6 September 1855, at the Great Redan, Sebastopol.

1st Regiment (Royal Scots) (1)

Private John Prosser, 16 June 1855, at Sebastopol.

3rd East Kent Regiment (The Buffs) (2)

Lieutenant Colonel Frederick Francis Maude, 8 September 1855, the second assault on the Great Redan at Sebastopol.
Private John Connors, 8 September 1855, the second assault on the Great Redan at Sebastopol.

4th (King's Own) Regiment (1)

Private Thomas Grady, 18 October 1854, at Sebastopol (*also on 22 November 1854 at Sebastopol*).

Appendix I: Crimean War VCs by Units

7th Royal Fusiliers (5)

Private William Norman, 19 December 1854, at the White Horse Ravine, Sebastopol.

Captain Henry Mitchell Jones, 22 March 1855, at Sebastopol (*also on 7 June 1855 at the Quarries, Sebastopol*).

Private Matthew Hughes, 7 June 1855, at the Quarries, Sebastopol (*also on 18 June 1855 at the first assault on the Great Redan at Sebastopol*).

Lieutenant William Hope, 18 June 1855, the first assault on the Great Redan at Sebastopol.

Assistant Surgeon Thomas Egerton Hale, 8 September 1855, the second assault on the Great Redan at Sebastopol.

17th (Leicestershire) Regiment (1)

Corporal Felix Philip Smith, 18 June 1855, the first assault on the Great Redan at Sebastopol.

18th (Royal Irish) Regiment (1)

Captain Thomas Esmonde, 18 June 1855, the first assault on the Great Redan at Sebastopol (*also on 20 June 1855 at Sebastopol*).

19th (1st Yorkshire, North Riding) Regiment (2)

Private Samuel Evans, 13 April 1855, at Sebastopol.
Private John Lyons, 10 June 1855, at Sebastopol.

23rd (Royal Welsh) Fusiliers (4)

Captain Edward William Derrington Bell, 20 September 1854, at the Battle of the Alma.

Sergeant Luke O'Connor, 20 September 1854, at the Battle of the Alma (*also on 8 September 1855 at the second assault on the Great Redan at Sebastopol*).

Assistant Surgeon William Henry Thomas Sylvester, 8 September 1855, the second assault on the Great Redan at Sebastopol.

Corporal Robert Shields, 8 September 1855, the second assault on the Great Redan at Sebastopol.

30th (Cambridgeshire) Regiment (1)

Lieutenant Mark Walker, 5 November 1854, at the Battle of Inkerman.

34th (Cumberland) Regiment (2)

Private William Coffey, 29 March 1855, at Sebastopol (*also on 10 April 1855 at the Green Hill Battery, Sebastopol*).

Private John Joseph Sims, 18 June 1855, the first assault on the Great Redan at Sebastopol.

41st (Welch) Regiment (2)

Sergeant Ambrose Madden, 26 October 1854, at Little Inkerman, Sebastopol.
Captain Hugh Rowlands, 5 November 1854, at the Battle of Inkerman.

44th (East Essex) Regiment (1)

Sergeant William McWheeney, 20 October 1854, at Sebastopol (*also on 5 December 1854 at Sebastopol and on 18 June 1855 at the first assault on the Great Redan at Sebastopol*).

47th (Lancashire) Regiment (1)

Private John McDermond, 5 November 1854, at the Battle of Inkerman.

49th (Hertfordshire) Regiment (3)

Lieutenant John Augustus Connolly, 26 October 1854, at Little Inkerman, Sebastopol.
Corporal James Owens, 26 October 1854, at Little Inkerman, Sebastopol.
Sergeant George Walters, 5 November 1854, at the Battle of Inkerman.

55th (Westmoreland) Regiment (2)

Private Thomas Beech, 5 November 1854, at the Battle of Inkerman
Brevet Major Frederick Cockayne Elton, 22 March 1855, at Sebastopol (*also on 7 June 1855 at the Quarries, Sebastopol, and 4 August 1855 at Sebastopol*).

57th (West Middlesex) Regiment (2)

Colour Sergeant George Gardiner, 22 March 1855, at Sebastopol (*also on 18 June 1855 at the first assault on the Great Redan at Sebastopol*).
Private Charles McCorrie, 23 June 1855, at Sebastopol.

68th (Durham) Light Infantry (2)

Captain Thomas de Courcy Hamilton, 11 May 1855, at Sebastopol.
Private John Byrne, 11 May 1855, at Sebastopol.

Appendix I: Crimean War VCs by Units

77th (East Middlesex) Regiment (2)

Sergeant John Park, 20 September 1854, at the Battle of the Alma (*also on 5 November 1854 at the Battle of Inkerman, on 19 April 1855 at Sebastopol, and on 18 June and 8 September 1855 at both assaults on the Great Redan at Sebastopol*).

Private Alexander Wright, 22 March 1855, at Sebastopol.

90th (Perthshire Volunteers) Regiment (2)

Private John Alexander, 18 June 1855, the first assault on the Great Redan at Sebastopol (*also on 6 September 1855 at Sebastopol*).

Sergeant Andrew Moynihan, 8 September 1855, the second assault on the Great Redan at Sebastopol.

97th (Earl of Ulster's) Regiment (2)

Sergeant John Coleman, 30 August 1855, at Sebastopol.

Captain Charles Henry Lumley, 8 September 1855, the second assault on the Great Redan at Sebastopol.

Rifle Brigade (Prince Consort's Own) (7)

Private Francis Wheatley, 12 October 1854, at Sebastopol.

Lieutenant Henry Hugh Clifford, 5 November 1854, at the Battle of Inkerman.

Captain William James Montgomery Cunninghame, 20 November 1854, at the Rifle Pits, Sebastopol.

Captain Claude Thomas Bourchier, 20 November 1854, at the Rifle Pits, Sebastopol.

Private Joseph Bradshaw, 22 April 1855, at the Quarries, Sebastopol.

Private Robert Humpston, 22 April 1855, at the Quarries, Sebastopol.

Private Roderick McGregor, 22 April 1855, at the Quarries, Sebastopol.

Appendix II

Redan 60th Anniversary Commemoration

The Times for 18 June 1915 reported:

The King sent a letter of congratulation to the veteran officers of the Crimean War who met at luncheon in the United Services Club yesterday, the 60th anniversary of the assault on the Redan at Sebastopol.

General Sir John Dunne, the host on the occasion, wrote to Sir Frederick Ponsonby a letter in which he said that severe as were the hardships they had to endure in the Crimean War, they felt that their sons and other distant relatives now fighting in Flanders had to face trials unexampled in warfare, and, as old men themselves, all they could do was to wait and pray for the final success. The King's acknowledgement was as follows:

Dear General –   Buckingham Palace, 17th June, 1915
The King has read with much interest your letter of the 17th instant to Sir Frederick Ponsonby, as well as the list of names which accompanied it. His Majesty congratulates you on the historic gathering of so many distinguished officers to celebrate the 60th anniversary of the attack on the Redan. Though time and modern contrivances have considerably changed the aspect of warfare, the King is proud to think that the same indomitable spirit which inspired the army of 60 years ago is animating his soldiers of today, and that the sons and relatives of those present at this meeting are nobly upholding their family traditions.

Yours very truly – Clive Wigram

The officers present at the luncheon, in addition to General Sir John Dunne, were: General Sir George Higginson, General Sir Robert Biddulph, Lieutenant-General Sir Henry Geary, Lieutenant-General George Moncrieff, Major-General H.T. Arbuthnot, Major-General William Allan, Major-General C.H. Owen, Colonel Lord Sinclair, Colonel W. Henry Champion, Lieutenant-Colonel Sir Fitzroy Maclean, and Major Herbert Jary.

The other survivors of the campaign, who for the most part were prevented from attending by the infirmities of age, are: General Sir W.H. Seymour, General Sir Horace Montagu, Lieutenant Henry Kent; Lieutenant-General, the Hon. Bernard Ward, Lieutenant-General Sir Albert Williams, Lieutenant-General Sir Edwin Markham, Major-General Henry Fielden, Major-General C. Fitzgerald, Major-General Henry R. Browne, Major-General Robert Mackenzie, Major-General Sir Charles Knowles, Colonel P.E. Hill, Colonel F.C. Hill, Colonel Corban, and Colonel C. Nicholson.

Additional Information

General Sir John Hart Dunne KCB, 21st (Scots) Fusiliers.
Born 11 December 1835, died 20 April 1924. After transferring to the 99th Regiment he also saw active service during the Indian Rebellion of 1857–1858 and in the Second China (Opium) War of 1858–1860.

General Sir George Wentworth Alexander Higginson GCB GCVO DL, 1st Grenadier Guards.
Born 21 June 1826, died 1 February 1927. He was a centenarian on his death.

General Sir Robert Biddulph GCB GCMG, Royal Artillery.
Born 26 August 1835, died 18 November 1918. He also saw active service during the Indian Rebellion of 1857–1858 and in the Second China (Opium) War of 1858–1860.

Lieutenant General Sir Henry Le Guay Geary KCB, Royal Artillery.
Born 1837, died 1918. He also saw active service in the Indian Rebellion of 1857–1858, and the expedition to Abyssinia in 1868.

Lieutenant General George Hay Moncrieff, Scots Guards.
Born 1836, died 1918.

Major General Henry Thomas Arbuthnot, Royal Artillery.
Born 1834, died 1919. He also saw active service at the siege and capture of Lucknow, during the Indian Rebellion of 1857–1858.

Major General William Allan, 41st (Welch) Regiment.
Born 1832, died 1918.

Major General Charles Henry Owen, Royal Artillery.
Born 1830, died 1921.

Colonel Charles William, 15th Lord Sinclair, 57th (West Middlesex) Regiment.
Born 1831, died 1922. He was severely wounded in the attack on the Redan. He also saw active service during the Indian Rebellion of 1857–1858 and in the Maori Wars in New Zealand in 1861–1862.

Appendix II: Redan 60th Anniversary Commemoration

Colonel W. Henry Champion.
Lieutenant Colonel Sir Fitzroy Donald Maclean KCB DL, 10th Baron Morvern, 13th Light Dragoons.
Born 1835, died 1936. Illness prevented him from taking part in the charge of the Light Brigade.
Major Robert Herbert Heath Jary, 12th Royal Lancers.
Born 1830, died 1920.

* * *

General Sir William Henry Seymour KCB, 2nd Dragoon Guards (Queen's Bays).
Born 1829, died 1921. He also saw active service in the Indian Rebellion of 1857–1858.
General Sir Horace William Montagu KCB, Royal Engineers.
Born 1823, died 1916.
Major General Sir Charles Benjamin Knowles KCB, 77th (East Middlesex) Regiment.
Born 1835, died 1924. He also saw active service during the Second Afghan War of 1878–1880.
Lieutenant General Henry Kent, 77th (East Middlesex) Regiment.
Born 1825, died 1921.
Lieutenant General the Hon. Sir Bernard Matthew Ward CB, 47th (Lancashire) Regiment.
Born 1831, died 1918.
Lieutenant General Sir Albert Henry Wilmot Williams KCVO, Royal Horse Artillery.
Born 1832, died 1919. He also saw active service in the Indian Rebellion of 1857–1858.
Lieutenant General Sir Edwin Markham KCB, Royal Artillery.
Born 1833, died 1918. He was Lieutenant Governor of Jersey from 1892 to 1895 and Governor and Commandant of the Royal Military College at Sandhurst from 1898 to 1902.
Major General Henry Wemyss Feilden CB, 42nd (Black Watch) Regiment and Royal Artillery.
Born 1838, died 1921. He also saw active service in the Indian Mutiny of 1857–1858, the Second China (Opium) War of 1858–1860 and the American Civil War of 1861–1865.
Major General C. Fitzgerald.

Major General Henry Ralph Browne, 9th (Norfolk) Regiment.
 Born 1828, died 1917.
Major General Robert Mackenzie.
Colonel P.E. Hills, Royal Artillery.
 He commanded the Royal Artillery in Canada in 1884.
Colonel Francis C. Hills, 44th Essex Regiment.
 He became a colonel in the 44th Essex Regiment in October 1881. He may possibly have been a jockey.
Lieutenant Colonel W. Watts Corban, 49th (Hertfordshire) Regiment.
Colonel C. Nicholson.

Bibliography and Research Sources

Books and Articles

Abbott, P.E., *Recipients of the Distinguished Conduct Medal, 1855–1909* (1987).
Addington, The Hon. Mrs Hiley, 'The Crimean and Indian Mutiny Letters of the Hon. Charles John Addington, 38th Regiment', *Journal of the Society for Army Historical Research* (1968).
Bancroft, James W., *The Victoria Crosses of the Crimean War: The Men Behind the Medals* (2017).
Blishen, Harry, *Letters from the Crimea* (1863).
Boulger, D.C. (ed.), *General Gordon's Letters from the Crimea, the Danube and Armenia* (1854).
Bowen, Roger, *General Julius Goodwyn, Crimean Commander* (2017).
Brereton, J.M. and Savory, A.C.S., *History of the Duke of Wellington's Regiment (West Riding), 1702–1992* (1993).
Caldwell, George and Cooper, Robert, *Rifle Green in the Crimea: An Account of the Rifle Brigade in the Crimean War, 1854–56, with a Full Medal and Casualty Roll, and Details of Weapons, Clothes and Equipment Used in the Campaign* (1994).
Carter, Thomas, *The Historical Record of the Forty-Fourth, or the East Essex Regiment* (1887).
Conolly, Thomas W.J., *History of the Royal Sappers and Miners, from the Formation of the Corps in March 1772 to the Date When its Designation was Changed to that of Royal Engineers in October 1856 (vol. 2)* (1857).
Conolly, Thomas W.J., *Roll of Officers of the Corps of Royal Engineers, from 1660 to 1898* (1898).
Conway RA, Sgt Patrick, *Royal Magazine* (1905).
Cook, Frank, *Casualty Roll for the Crimea, 1854–56* (2011).
Cope, Sir William H., *The History of the Rifle Brigade (Prince Consort's Own) Formerly the 95th* (1877).
Daniell, David S., *Cap of Honour: The Story of the Gloucestershire Regiment (28th/61st Foot) 1694–1950* (1951).
Delavoye, A.M., *Records of the 90th Regiment (Perthshire Volunteers)* (1880).
Elphinstone VC, Sir Howard Crawfurd, and Jones, Sir Harry David, *The Siege of Sebastopol, 1854–55. Journal of the Operations Conducted by the Royal Engineers, Part 1: From the Invasion of the Crimea to the Close of the Winter Campaign, 1854–55* (1859).
Fanshawe, Capt. Thomas Basil, Alexander, Derek (ed.) and Marculescu, Deirdre, *Sebastopol to Dagenham: Crimean War Letters of Captain Thomas Basil Fanshawe, 33rd (Duke of Wellington's) Regiment* (2016).
Fenton, Roger, *Letters from the Crimea* (1855).

Fisher, George Battye, and Lt-Col. Fisher RE, *Personal Narrative of Three Years' Service in China* (1863).
Fitzherbert, Cuthbert (ed.), *Henry Clifford VC: His Letters and Sketches from the Crimea* (1956).
Fitzpatrick, William J., *History of the Dublin Catholic Cemeteries* (1900).
Gowing, 7th Royal Fusiliers, Sgt Maj. Timothy, *A Soldier's Experience, Or A Voice from the Ranks* (1884).
Grehan, John, and Mace, Martin, *British Battles of the Crimean War, 1854–1856: Dispatches from the Front* (2014).
Grehan, John, *The First VCs* (2016).
Gretton, Lt-Col. G.M., *The Campaigns and History of the Royal Irish Regiment, 1684–1902* (1911).
Hamley, Lt-Col. E.B., *The Story of the Campaigns of Sebastopol, Written in the Camp* (1855).
Hamley, Gen. Sir Edward B., *The War in the Crimea* (1891).
Hibbert, Christopher, *The Destruction of Lord Raglan. A Tragedy of the Crimean War, 1854–55* (1962).
Higginson, Gen. Sir George Wentworth Alexander, *Seventy-One Years of a Guardsman's Life* (1916).
Ingleton, Roy, *Kent VCs* (2011).
Jocelyn, Col. Julian R.J., *The History of the Royal Artillery (Crimean Period)* (1911).
Kelleher, J.P., *The Royal Fusiliers Recipients of the Victoria Cross* (2010).
Kelleher, J.P., *The 7th Royal Fusiliers in the Crimean War, with the Medal Roll, 1854–1856* (2013).
Kelly, Gen. Sir Richard David, *An Officer's Letters to His Wife during the Crimean War* (1902).
Kinglake, A.W., *The Invasion of the Crimea* (1887–88).
Knollys, Maj. William W., *The Victoria Cross in the Crimea.* Deeds of Daring Library (1877).
London, Jack, *The People of the Abyss* (1903).
Lowth CB, Col. John J., *A Short Memoir of the Life of Colonel John J. Lowth CB, of the 38th Regiment, ADC to the Queen* (1855).
Lysons, Sir Daniel, *The Crimea from First to Last* (1895).
McClintock, Mary Howard Elphinstone, *The Queen Thanks Sir Howard: The Life of Major-General Sir Howard Elphinstone, VC KCB CMG* (1945).
Malan, Charles H., *A Soldier's Experience of God's Love and of his Faithfulness to his Word* (1874).
Mawson, Michael H. (ed.), *Eyewitness in the Crimea. The Crimean War Letters (1854–56) of Lieutenant-Colonel George Frederick Dallas* (2001).
Monday, Alfred J., *History of the Family of Yea* (1885).
Muddock, James E.P., *For Valour, The VC* (1895).
Napier, Gerald, *The Sapper VCs* (1997).
Noakes, George, *A Historical Account of the Services of the 34th Regiment* (1875).
Nolan, Edward H., *The Illustrated History of the War against Russia* (1857).
O'Malley, Cpl James, *With the Bengal Tigers in the Crimea. Recollections of a Soldier of the 17th Leicestershire Regiment during the Victorian Age* (2012) [Originally published as *The Life of James O'Malley*, (1893)].

Bibliography and Research Sources

Palmer, Alan, *The Banner of Battle* (1987).
Quin, W.J., 'Heroes of the Crimea', *Melbourne Argus*, 20 June 1890.
Ranken, W. Bayne (ed.), *Canada to the Crimea or Sketches of a Soldier's Life: From the Journals and Correspondence of the Late Major Ranken RE* (1865).
Reid, Douglas A., *Memories of the Crimean War, January 1855 to June 1856* (1911).
Reilly CB, Capt. W.E.M., *Account of the Artillery Operations Conducted by the Royal Artillery and Royal Naval Brigade Before Sebastopol in 1854–55* (1856).
Ross, Graham, *Scotland's Forgotten Valour* (1995).
Russell, William H., *The British Expedition to the Crimea* (1858).
Russell, William H., *The Great War with Russia* (1895).
Sims, Anthony, *John J. Sims: Bloomsbury to Sebastopol* (2013).
Smith, Brandon, *Portsea Island and the Victoria Cross: Portsmouth Burials* (nd).
Smith, Cecil Woodham, *Florence Nightingale, 1820–1910* (1950).
Smith, Melvin C., *Awarded for Valour: A History of the Victoria Cross and the Evolution of British Heroism* (2008).
Springman, Michael, *Sharpshooters in the Crimea: The Letters of Captain Gerald Goodlake VC* (2005).
Steevens, Lt-Col. Nathaniel, *The Crimean Campaign with the Connaught Rangers, 1854–55–56* (1878).
Steward, W. Augustus, *From the Breasts of the Brave* (1915).
Steward, W. Augustus, *War Medals and Their History* (1915).
Tyrell, Henry, *The History of the War with Russia* (1857).
Verney RN, Lt Edmund Hope, *The Shannon's Brigade in India: Being Some Account of Sir William Peel's Naval Brigade in the Indian Campaign of 1857–58* (1862).
Vetch, Col. R.H. (ed.), *Life, Letters, and Diaries of Lieutenant-General Sir Gerald Graham* (1901).
Victoria, Queen, *The Letters of Queen Victoria* (three volumes) (1908).
Wain, Derek, *The Hurts of Derbyshire* (2002).
Walker, Gen. Sir C.P. Beauchamp Walker KCB, *Days of a Soldier's Life: Being Letters Written During Active Service on the Crimean, Chinese, Austro-Prussian (1866); and Franco-German (1870–71) Wars* (1894).
Wallace, Sir Christopher and Cassidy, Maj. Ron, *Focus on Courage: The 59 Victoria Crosses of the Royal Green Jackets* (2006).
Waller, G.H., Cannon, Richard, Groves, John P., *Historical Records of the 7th or Royal Regiment of Fusiliers; now known as the Royal Fusiliers (The City of London Regiment), 1685–1903* (1903).
Warre, Col. Henry J., *Sketches in the Crimea* (1856).
Warre, Col. Henry J., *Historical Records of the Fifty-Seventh or Middlesex Regiment of Foot, 1755–1878* (1878).
Webb, Lt-Col. Edward A.H., *A History of the Services of the 17th Leicestershire Regiment. Containing an Account of the Regiment in 1688, and of its subsequent services, revised and continued to 1910* (1911).
Willey, Harry, *Seaman James Gorman VC* (2008).
Williams, Capt. Godfrey T., *Historical Records of the Eleventh Hussars, Prince Albert's Own* (1908).
Winton John, *The Victoria Cross at Sea* (2016).

Wolseley, Garnet, *The Story of a Soldier's Life* (1904).
Wood VC, Sir Evelyn, *From Midshipman to Field Marshal, Vol. One* (1906).
Woollright, Henry H., *Records of the 77th (East Middlesex) Duke of Cambridge's Own Regiment of Foot* (1907).
Wrottesley, RE ADC, Capt. the Hon. G., *The Military Opinions of General Sir J.F. Burgoyne* (1859).
Wrottesley, RE, Lt-Col. the Hon. G., *The Life and Correspondence of Field-Marshal, Sir John Fox Burgoyne, Bart* (2 volumes) (1873).

Newspapers and Journals

Aberdeen Press and Journal, 18 January 1902
Armagh Guardian, 20 July 1855
Army and Navy Gazette, 27 June 1863, 20 November 1869, 9 April 1898
Bell's Weekly Messenger, 27 December 1862
Bicester Herald, 30 June 1855
Cambridge Chronicle, 9 December 1854
Cork Constitution, 12 July 1855
Derby Mercury, 27 June 1855
Dublin Evening Mail, 9 July 1855
Eastern Daily Press, 2 November 1903
Fermanagh Herald, 20 January 1906
Globe, 2 September 1893
Graphic, 2 March 1907
Hereford Times, 21 July 1855
Homeward Mail from India, China and the East, 28 November 1896
Illustrated London News, 7 July 1855, 28 July 1855, 25 February 1865
Inverness Courier, 14 July 1911
Kent and Sussex Courier, 14 August 1914
King's County Chronicle, 27 June 1855
Liverpool Daily Post (various)
London Evening Standard, 28 July 1855, 12 April 1898
London Gazette (various, including the Victoria Cross citations of 24 February 1857, 5 May 1857, 25 September 1857 and 2 June 1858)
Londonderry Standard, 19 July 1855
Manchester Guardian (various)
Morning Post, 15 August 1855
Naval and Military Gazette and Weekly Chronicle of the United Services, 27 June 1863
Norfolk Chronicle, 11 September 1858
Norfolk News and Norwich Gazette, 24 July 1858
Otago Daily Times, 22 January 1866, 19 February 1866
Portsmouth Evening News, 30 March 1925
Portsmouth Times and Naval Gazette, 11 August 1855
Quebec Mercury, 1 September 1856
Reynold's Newspaper, 30 September 1855
Scotsman, 9 December 1910
Strand Magazine, March 1891

Bibliography and Research Sources

The Times, 19 July 1855, 31 March 1913, 19 June 1915
War Correspondent (various), Journal of the Crimean War Research Society
Weston-super-Mare Gazette and General Advertiser, 29 December 1855, 12 April 1856
Worcester Journal, 30 June 1855, 15 December 1855

Miscellaneous Sources

Ancestry.co.uk
Blackett, Captain Christopher E., *Crimean War Letters* at the *Cambridge University Library Special Collections*, 1854–1855
British Newspaper Archive
Brompton Cemetery burial records
Burke's Peerage
Census Returns, 1841 to 1921
Crimean War Research Society
Crimean War Veterans in Western Australia
Daniels, Michael [danielvc.com], *The Life of Edward St John Daniel*
Dictionary of National Biography
Dictionary of Welsh Biography
Elton, Captain Frederick Cockayne, Fifty-two letters to members of his family during the Crimean War, 1854–56, held at the National Army Museum
FamilySearch
Findmypast.co.uk
Friends of Brompton Cemetery
Grace's Guide to British Industrial History
Hampshire Record Office
Hart's Army Lists
Institution of Civil Engineers Obituaries
Journal of the Victoria Cross Society (various), ed. Brian Best
JWB Historical Library
King William's College Register
Lummis Files: Held at the Imperial War Museum and the National Army Museum on behalf of the Military Historical Society
Marlow Local History Society
National Archives: Crimean War Records
National Army Museum Templer Study Centre
New Oxford Dictionary of National Biography, 2004
Portsmouth History Centre
Royal Collection Trust
Scottish War Memorials Project
Spinks Catalogue, 22 April 2010
Teesdale, Sir Christopher, Letters written to his father dated 30 September 1855 and November 1865
Usherwood, Charles, *Charles Usherwood's Service Journal*, 1852–56
Victoria Cross Society
Who Was Who, 1897–1915, 1916–1928, 1929–1940
WikiTree

Index

4th (King's Own) Regiment, 45, 109–10, 164

7th Royal Fusiliers, 14, 15, 16, 19, 22, 31, 40, 43, 51, 65, 110–16, 165

9th (East Norfolk) Regiment, 27, 29, 43, 116–18, 172

17th (Leicestershire) Regiment, 22, 45, 65, 118–19, 165

18th (Royal Irish) Regiment, 13, 27, 28, 29, 32, 44, 45, 65, 119–20, 165

20th (East Devonshire) Regiment, 46

21st (Royal North British) Fusiliers, 5, 7, 46

23rd (Welsh) Fusiliers, 19, 26, 43, 46, 51, 165

28th (1st Staffordshire) Regiment, 20, 27, 46

33rd (Duke of Wellington's) Regiment, 19, 22, 43, 46, 120–3

34th (Cumberland) Regiment, 19, 21, 22, 43, 46–7, 66, 123–8, 166

38th (1st Staffordshire) Regiment, 19, 27, 29, 30, 44, 47, 128–33

41st (Welch) Regiment, 47, 133–5, 166, 167

44th (East Essex) Regiment, 10, 20, 27, 28, 30, 44, 47, 66, 135–41, 166, 172

57th (West Middlesex) Regiment, 11, 15, 25, 40, 47–8, 66, 141–50, 166, 167

73rd (Perthshire) Regiment, 48, 151–2

77th (East Middlesex) Regiment, 11, 15, 67, 150–1, 167, 171

88th Regiment (Connaught Rangers), 48, 152–3

90th (Perthshire) Light Infantry, 22, 51, 153–4, 167

Rifle Brigade (Prince Consort's Own), 43, 48, 67, 154–9, 167

Royal Engineers, Corps of, 11, 13, 19, 21, 23, 26, 42, 44, 64–5, 89–109, 163, 171

Royal Navy (Naval Brigade), 9, 19, 23, 26, 31–2, 40, 44, 63–4, 71–88, 161–2

Royal Regiment of Artillery, 22–3, 34, 44, 50, 64, 88–9, 94, 163, 170

Addington, Captain Honourable Charles John, 132–3

Agar, Captain Charles Welbore Herbert, 27, 30, 44, 47, 138

Alexander VC, Private John, 22, 67, 153–4

Alma, Battle of the River, 4–5

Arthur VC, Gunner and Driver Thomas, 15, 22–3, 64, 88–9

Ashwin, Lieutenant James Collins, 25, 48, 147–9

Balaclava, Battle of, 6–9

Bennett, Lieutenant Valentine, 22, 43, 46, 123

Blackett, Captain Edward William, 154–5

Boileau, Lieutenant Charles Augustus Penrhyn, 48, 156

Bourchier, Brevet Major Eustace Fane, 44, 95–6

Bromhead, Ensign Edward, 109

Brompton Cemetery, London, 5, 78, 93, 95, 113, 115, 120, 137

Browne, Captain George Richard, 43, 48, 152–3

Browne, Captain Henry Ralph, 116–17

Browne, Captain James Frankfort Manners, 93–5

Browne-Clayton, Ensign Robert John, 47, 127

Campbell, Major General Sir John, 19, 25, 40, 47, 128–30
Caulfeild, Captain Francis William Thomas, 27, 44, 47, 138–9
Cave, Lieutenant John Halliday, 44, 77–8
Cobbe, Colonel Henry Clermont, 45, 109
Croker, Captain John Lacy, 45, 118
Curtis VC, Botswain Henry, 26, 64, 86–7

Dalyell, Lieutenant Osborne William, 44, 76–7
Daniel VC, Midshipman Edward St John, 9, 10, 11, 63, 80–4
Davies, Lieutenant Owen Gwyn Saunders, 47, 133

Earle, Captain Arthur Maxwell, 47, 146–7
Elphinstone VC, Captain Howard Crawfurd, 64, 96–101
Esmonde VC, Captain Thomas, 27–8, 39, 65, 119–20
Eyre, Colonel, Sir William, 19, 26–7, 30, 35, 48, 151–2

Fanshawe, Captain Thomas Basil, 22, 46, 121–2
Fenton, Roger, 31–2
Fenwick, Captain Bowes, 27, 30, 44, 47, 138
Fisher, Lieutenant Arthur A'Court, 21, 105
FitzClarence, Lieutenant, Viscount, the Hon. Edward, 43, 111–12
Forman, Captain Edward Rowland, 25, 34, 48, 155–6
Freemantle, Lieutenant Fitzroy William, 43, 48, 156–7

Gardiner VC, Colour Sergeant George, 15, 25, 66, 149–50
Goodwyn, Lieutenant Colonel Julius Edmund, 47, 133–4
Gowing, Sergeant Timothy, 14, 30–1
Graham VC, Lieutenant Gerald, 11, 23–4, 64, 102–5
Graves, Lieutenant Thomas Molyneux, 21, 44, 105–6
Gwilt, Major John, 43, 46, 125

Heyland, Lieutenant Langford Rowley, 43, 46, 123
Hope VC, Lieutenant William, 22, 65, 113–15
Hoskins, Lieutenant Bradford Smith, 47, 139–40
Hughes VC, Private Matthew, 16, 22, 65, 115–16
Hurt, Lieutenant Francis Richard, 22, 46, 125–6

Imperial War Museum, 73, 88
Inglis, Major William, 25, 145–6
Inkerman, Battle of, 10–11, 14, 67–70

Jesse, Captain William Howard, 21, 44, 101–2
Johnstone, Lieutenant Colonel John Douglas, 22, 43, 46, 120–1
Jones, Major General, Sir Harry David, 42, 44, 89–91

Kidd, Lieutenant Thomas Osborne, 26, 44, 79
Knox VC, Lieutenant John Simpson, 4, 25–6, 39, 43, 48, 67, 157–9

Leitch VC, Colour Sergeant Peter, 24, 64, 106–7
Letters from the Front, 5–7, 12
Light Brigade, Charge of the, 6–9
Lowth, Colonel John Jackson, 30, 44, 47, 130–2

McWheeney VC, Sergeant William, 10, 27, 66, 140–1
Malan, Lieutenant Charles Hawiton, 43, 112–13
Mansfield, Captain William Henry, 27, 44, 47, 138
Mundy, Lieutenant Colonel George Valentine Edward, 22, 43, 46, 120
Murray, Lieutenant James, 44, 106

Norman, Captain George Herman, 25, 47, 149

Index

Park VC, Sergeant John, 4, 11, 67, 150–1
Peel VC, Captain William, 9, 11, 19, 23, 40, 43, 44, 63, 73–6
Pirie VC, Sapper John, 23, 65, 107–9

Quayle, Captain John Edward Taubman, 22, 43, 46, 122–3

Raby VC, Commander Henry James, 26, 64, 71–3
Raglan, Lord, 3, 7, 9, 17, 20, 26, 34, 35, 39
Redan, Great, 1, 17–48
Robinson, Captain John, 43, 46, 123–4
Robinson, Lieutenant Napier Douglas, 113
Russell, William Howard, 13, 27–30, 32–5, 42–3

Shadforth, Lieutenant Colonel Thomas, 19, 25, 40, 47, 141–4
Shiffner, Captain John, 46, 124–5
Sims VC, Private John Joseph, 66, 128
Smith VC, Corporal (Felix) Philip, 65, 118–19

Smith, Captain Frederick, 116
Spencer, General, Sir Augustus Almeric, 47, 137
Staveley, General, Sir Charles William Dunbar, 135–7

Taylor VC, Captain of the Forecastle John, 26, 64, 84–5
Tylden, Colonel Richard, 24, 44, 91–3

Urmston, Lieutenant William Brabazon, 44, 79–80

Victoria, Queen, 3, 61
Victoria Cross and Actions, 10, 15, 20, 22, 23–4, 26, 51, 61–70, 85, 161–7

Warre, Colonel Henry James, 25, 43, 144–5
Wolseley, Field Marshal Garnet Joseph, 15
Wood VC, Field Marshal Henry Evelyn, 10

Yea, Colonel Lacy Walter Giles, 4–5, 13–14, 15–16, 19, 21, 32, 40, 42, 110–11